Interpretation and Dionysos

Religion and Reason 16

Method and Theory
in the Study and Interpretation of Religion

MOUTON PUBLISHERS · THE HAGUE · PARIS · NEW YORK

Interpretation and Dionysos
Method in the Study of a God

PARK McGINTY
Lehigh University, Bethlehem, Penns.

MOUTON PUBLISHERS · THE HAGUE · PARIS · NEW YORK

ISBN: 90-279-7844-1

Jacket design by Jurriaan Schrofer

© 1978, Mouton Publishers, The Hague, The Netherlands

Printed in Great Britain

Preface

In an age in which the control of information has become one of the crucial determinants of human culture, the process of interpretation has assumed an increasingly important role. The present monograph represents a case study of how the ruling theoretical presuppositions of different interpretive systems have influenced the analysis of Dionysiac religion and have, in effect, led to remarkably divergent explanations of a single phenomenon. The scholars who serve as the focus of this work have all operated out of deeply held philosophical and ethical positions; yet they disagree as to what in human culture is valuable and what destructive. As a result, their presentations of the meaning of Dionysiac religion have been designed to shape the modern understanding of what is authentically human as well as to elucidate an important facet of classical civilization. Inasmuch as there is considerable truth in the aphorism that he who controls the past controls the future, these scholars can be seen as having participated in the cultural struggles of their time, investing remarkable talent and industry in the service of truth as they perceived it. The fact that they could not agree on the contents of this truth should not obscure their integrity and dedication.

Although this preface cannot adequately reflect my intellectual and emotional indebtedness to those who have shaped my thoughts and attitudes, it is my pleasant task at this point to acknowledge the most important of these debts. First, I wish to thank the History of Religions department of the University of Chicago Divinity School, both faculty and student colleagues, for a remarkably rewarding graduate program. I owe especial thanks to Jonathan Z. Smith and Mircea Eliade, the advisors of my dissertation, which served as the basis for this monograph. In addition to giving me exceedingly meaningful help, both provided ideal role models as teachers and scholars. I would also like to thank Jacques Waardenburg, editor of the series *Religion and Reason* for his help in shepherding this work through the publication process. To Jeffrey Wellaish and Peggy Stinson I owe thanks for patient help in suggesting stylistic improvements. I also wish to thank the journal *History of Religions* for permission to use sections from 'Three Models of Interpretation: Genealogy, Translation, Rearticulation' (Feb., 1975) in the introduction to this work. Finally, it gives me most pleasure to express my gratitude to and affection for Carol Denis, who has been tremendously important in my life and whose love and support have helped me not only to enrich my mind but also to grow as a human being. It is to her that the present work is dedicated.

Contents

Introduction: Dionysos Redivivus

In the past one hundred years Dionysos has re-entered the Western consciousness with an intensity unparalleled since the Hellenistic era. For centuries a minor symbol of luxurious ease and hedonistic frivolity, he has resurfaced as a central focus in modern man's attempt to define his own authentic humanity. In a time when traditional Jewish and Christian world-views are either under siege or increasingly ignored, his image has provided an alternative mode of thought and life. For some, Dionysos represents the most legitimate paradigm for one's stance in the world; for others, a deep-seated tendency to prefer fantasy to reality. Yet all scholars, including those espousing compromise positions, have taken Dionysos seriously as a manifestation of some important truth about humanity.

The first major revalorization of Dionysos, and still the most fertile, was Friedrich Nietzsche's *The Birth of Tragedy*. Writing in 1872 for a culture which he felt was becoming increasingly routinized and pedestrian, Nietzsche tried to show that the ecstatic transcendence of the commonplace represented by Dionysiac religion had been as necessary for Hellenism as the more ordered Apolline cult. In later more explicitly anti-Christian works he portrayed Dionysos as the most effective symbol for man's creative hunger for change and becoming, as opposed to Christianity's meek self surrender and wheedling for security. As he described it, this Dionysian hunger leads the man who has mastered himself to deal joyously with the world, even though it may cause him anguish and even though he can expect no eternal peace as a recompense. Nietzsche's two conceptions of Dionysos—as the foil to the ordered calm of Apollo and as the worthy antagonist to the life-denying instincts of Christianity—have ever since been the basic models for interpreting Dionysos as a crucial symbol in the conflict of cultural patterns and life styles.

Measured by its impact on subsequent thought, *The Birth of Tragedy* was one of the most fruitful works of nineteenth century scholarship. Since its publication classicists have invoked the differences between Apollo and Dionysos as manifestations of an essential duality in Greek religion, whether this duality be labelled Apolline/Dionysian, Olympic/chthonic, Homeric/pre-Homeric, Indo-European/Mediterranean, or legalistic/mystical. In fields outside classicism, most notably in anthropology, scholars have utilized the Apolline/Dionysian dichotomy to talk about holistic differences between cultural and personal life styles. Here, outside the trammels of classical scholarship, Dionysos has assumed a Protean character reminiscent of myths in which he takes on different forms in order to elude his would-be captors.

The anthropologist Alfred Smith has detailed some of these different configurations which Dionysos has been taken to symbolize in his instructive article 'The Dionysian Innovation'.[1] As he notes, Ruth Benedict was the first to apply the Nietzschean dichotomy to anthropology in her *Patterns of Culture*. She interpreted the Dionysian as the urge to transcend the senses and to break through into another order of experience.[2] Focusing on other values in Dionysiac religion, E. A. Hoebel portrayed it in a radically different manner, claiming that the Dionysian 'emphasizes sensate experience'.[3] Applying Jungian categories, Melville Herskovits labelled the Dionysian as 'extraverted',[4] while Felix Keesing identified it as 'introverted'.[5] Mischa Titiev equated the Dionysian with Sheldon's category of the 'somatotonic'.[6] It has been identified with both group conventions and individual inspiration, release from inhibitions and pursuit of things which transcend the pleasure principle.[7]

All of these interpretations see aspects of Dionysiac religion as exemplifying specific cultural and psychological traits. Since the evidence about Dionysiac religion is quite rich and sometimes appears contradictory, scholars can, in fact, appeal to documented accounts about Dionysos to justify seemingly incompatible interpretations. As a result, 'the Dionysian' as a category has been most effective as an impressionistic orientation and, as Smith points out, has been used almost exclusively in works written for the general public rather than for professional anthropologists. Given the lack of agreement on the content of 'the Dionysian', it is easy to see why such a concept has played more of an illustrative than an analytical role in anthropology. Still, its widespread use by social scientists has contributed to Dionysos' increased visibility in the modern period.

On the less descriptive, more polemical side, scholars seeking new models for organizing human existence have often fastened on Dionysos as the most effective expression of a non-repressive life style which avoids the inhibitions imposed by previous cultures, whether they be otherworldly Christianity, a pleasure-hating Puritan ethos, or abstract Western science and technology. Nietzsche's proclamation of Dionysos as the model for a secular redemption from alienation has been taken up and advanced in diverse fields, such as literature with the work of Frank Wedekind[8] and psychology with the work of Norman O. Brown.[9]

Yet Dionysos is a controversial figure, who arouses as much execration as sympathetic interest. Another stream of interpretation sees the Dionysiac pattern as a neo-romantic betrayal of the hard-won advances begun by the Enlightenment and continued by the rational and scientific elite of the modern period. From this perspective the Dionysian willingness to abandon the mediations of thought and language as impoverishments of direct experience risks abetting a new obscurantism and fanaticism. The most effective spokesmen for this cautionary view have been classicists who have pointed out what they consider the regressive aspects of the original Dionysiac cult. In literature the ambiguous quality of the Dionysian ecstasy has been effectively captured in Thomas Mann's *Death in Venice* where the language describing Aschenbach's voluptuous dissolution is very largely borrowed from Nietzsche's portrayal of the Dionysian in *The Birth of Tragedy*.

It is not clear whether the contemporary era will sustain its interest in Dionysos as providing a model, either positive or negative, for human existence. It is clear, however, that if this interest continues, the richest source of information about the actual significance of 'the Dionysian' as an experienced reality will continue to be ancient Greek civilization. Thus, classical scholarship, as in the past, still has its lesson for the modern period. The question is, what is the content of that lesson?

*   *   *

It strikes us as completely different
when we examine the concept 'Greek'
which Winkelmann and Goethe developed and find it incompatible with
that element from which Dionysiac art
proceeds—the orgiastic element. I do
not doubt that Goethe had on principle
excluded such a thing from the possibilities of the Greek soul. As a result,
he did not understand the Greeks.

FRIEDRICH NIETZCHE[10]

Also it is true that there is a Dionysiac
spirit in the rapturous poems to which
Nietzsche subsequently rose. This is just
why he has always been not only alien
but hostile to the truly Hellenic.

ULRICH VON
WILAMOWITZ-MOELLENDORFF[11]

Classical scholars disagree over the most fundamental facts about
Dionysiac religion. Was Dionysos a necessary and integral part of
Greek civilization, as Nietzsche argued; or did he represent an alien
intrusion, as Wilamowitz suggested? Was belief in Dionysos the
product of stupidity, a creation of playful fantasy, a reification of
misunderstood natural reality, or the expression of a serious vision
of the world? Given the modern world-view and the strangeness of
much of Dionysiac religion, how can an interpreter organize and
explain the extant evidence concerning Dionysos? Such questions
transcend the issue of the Dionysian lifestyle and go to the deeper
question of why the Greeks believed in and worshipped Dionysos in
the first place. For although Nietzsche treated Apollo and Dionysos
as aesthetic rather than religious phenomena, the inescapable fact is
that both were deities. That is, they were symbolic entities with a
sufficiently forceful reality in the Hellenic consciousness to occasion considerable sacrifice on the part of the Greeks and to provide
intense religious fulfillment in return.

Historically, the driving force behind 'the Dionysian' as a manner
of orienting human action has been an ecstatic religious urge, and

anyone wishing to understand 'the Dionysian' in Hellenism must begin from that fact. It is, naturally, quite possible to demythologize the Dionysian so that it can be appropriated as a style without regard to religious considerations. Most contemporary thinkers see this as the only acceptable manner in which the Dionysian can become part of the twentieth century consciousness. However, it should be recognized that once 'the Dionysian' has been sec-ularized, it has been divorced from that which made the Greeks interested in Dionysos and can no longer be claimed as a historical precedent for the contemporary period. It may well be that Nietzsche's 'Dionysian' vision has much more to say to the twentieth century than what the Greeks thought and did with respect to Dionysos, but Nietzsche's vision was basically an individual aspira-tion rather than a long-term communally experienced social reality. For the explanation of what that publicly shared social reality signified for the ancient Greeks, one must turn to theories which interpret Greek religion as a historical phenomenon and Dionysos as a part of this wider religion.

THE ISSUE OF HERMENEUTICS

Once one has accepted historical understanding as the goal, one immediately confronts the problem of hermeneutics, the principles of interpretation. In classics, as in almost every area of the humanities and social sciences, there are different and competing *systems* of interpretation. These systems determine how the scholar will organize the multitude of data at his disposal into a meaningful whole. While certain questions which appear to be purely 'factual' (dates, provenance, audience, etc.) have been answered by classics and its related fields, questions of 'meaning' (the original form of a belief or practice, its purpose, the referents of terms like 'gods', etc.) have been treated according to canons of interpretation derived from non-classical fields such as anthropology, sociology, psychol-ogy, and comparative religion. The present work is an exploration of the impact of these interpretations on the study of Dionysos, since they, more than classical studies in the strict sense, have defined the significance of Dionysos as a cultural phenomenon. To be sure, the scholars considered in this work were or are professional classicists; but almost without exception as soon as they addressed the problem of what Dionysos meant to the Greeks and what the Greeks' allegiance to this god signifies about human existence, they relied on paradigms developed by the great theoreticians of the social sciences.

Dionysos is an extraordinarily rich subject for anyone interested in the conflict of interpretations. The extreme nature of the Dionysiac cult seems to call for some explanation. Compared to modern scientific or logical behavior, the behavior of the Dionysiac worshippers has struck many as barbaric or 'primitive' in the nineteenth century's pejorative use of the term. In his worship there were dramatic, often dangerous rites. His devotees roamed about the tops of mountains on winter nights, dancing with ecstatic abandon, nursing young wild animals, only to tear them apart with their bare hands and devour the still warm, raw flesh. They saw strange visions and heard strange sounds, and in their exaltation they stuck the earth and perceived it as bringing forth milk, honey, and wine. Legends tell of human sacrifice to Dionysos; in the rites his worshippers were pursued, often beaten, and sometimes killed. Dionysos himself has a multiplicity of forms, sometimes appearing as a child, sometimes as a youth, sometimes as a mature man. Sometimes he incarnated himself in animal and plant forms as well. Numerous other wild, non-rational associations and actions were also part of his cult.

Faced with such an emotional and non-rational religion, scholars have been very explicit in judging its meaning and value. Even scholars who have restricted themselves to description have stated their understanding of Dionysos in a sufficiently forceful manner to reveal their stance toward Greek religion and religion in general. As a result, interpretations of Dionysos reveal more about scholars' presuppositions than almost any other issue in classical studies.

As in the case of religious studies as a whole, presuppositions used in interpreting Dionysos operate at different levels of abstraction. On the most concrete and verifiable level are questions about the nature of the evidence, dates, provenance, authorship, audience, and the like. Having catalogued these facts, the scholar then arranges them so that he can point out meaningful relationships. He can situate individual facts in several different contexts: within the historical flow of events, within the total configuration of the culture at a particular moment, within the purely ideological realm of the culture, and so forth. Once he has related the specific fact to other phenomena, the scholar has at least partially demonstrated its significance.

For example, the issue of whether Dionysos was 'authentically Hellenic' or a foreign intrusion determined a great deal about his significance. Nietzsche and Walter F. Otto, the latter being one of the subjects of this study, saw Dionysos as an essential and authentic aspect of Hellenic culture. Accordingly, they assumed that the Greeks were making a meaningful statement about the nature of reality through Dionysiac religion and tried to explain this 'statement' in modern terms. Most other scholars have seen Dionysos as an alien intruder into Hellenism and have interpreted his presence in the Greek pantheon as the result of a religious invasion or epidemic rather than as the result of the Greeks' attempt to portray authentic reality. Therefore, the primary hermeneutical task for these scholars has been to explain how, once Dionysos had been forced into Greek culture, the Greeks modified the irrational Dionysiac religion to correspond more closely to their own highly rationalized religion. They focused more on the 'resistance' of Greek civilization to the Bacchic cult than on the content of the Dionysiac vision of the world.

If the 'place' of Dionysiac religion in Greek culture is important, its 'place' in the context of human history as a whole is even more crucial for interpretation. The meaning and value of all religious data is vigorously debated: is religion an error propagated by primitive man, or a flawed but partially appropriate manner of expressing man's humanity, or else the highest human activity and the goal of man's history? Answers to these basic questions determine more about a scholar's interpretation than do opinions about particular historical relationships within Hellenism.

There are many different ways of defining the nature and role of religion, and Dionysiac religion has been explained in terms of almost every possible method. Succeeding chapters will explore ·specific interpretations and show how each is a systematically organized unity. On the issue of hermeneutics as a whole, however, one can best orient oneself at a high level of abstraction where a limited number of systems of interpretation have guided classical scholars in their explanations. Once one sees the dynamics of these systems, then one can see what is gained or lost by adopting any of the basic interpretive paradigms.

All of the interpretations of Dionysos begin with a fundamental problem: *distance*. The interpreter confronts a document whose meaning is not obvious to him. The passage of time and the change of cultures have imposed a distance between the meaning the document had for the person who produced it and the culturally determined 'meanings' accepted by the interpreter. Or, if one assumes we no longer have access to the original meaning that the document held for its creator, this distance can be described as that between the surface appearance of the document and the intelligible, 'real' world of the interpreter. The interpreter is supposed to bridge this distance and reveal the document's meaning by relating it to some aspect of his own world whose meaning and authenticity are unproblematical. The already comprehended significance of the 'real' facts of the interpreter's world then gives meaning to the document.

Divergent systems of interpreting religion exist partly because scholars disagree as to how to relate religious data to 'self-evident' aspects of contemporary reality. For example, some scholars relate the religious expressions of other persons to their own religious lives. For them, the existence of God, or gods, or the Sacred, or a supernatural or non-empirical realm is either self-evident or plausible or else serves as a fundamental presupposition. These scholars can interpret religious phenomena in terms of 'the Sacred' or 'the supernatural' because such a category has not been invalidated by their conceptions of the real world and is, therefore, seen as a legitimate mode of understanding reality.

For others, the non-existence of 'the Sacred' or 'the supernatural' is 'self-evident'. Naturally, these scholars do not relate religious expressions to their own religious lives. And since, for them, conceptions of supernaturalism are problematic, they feel that interpretations using such conceptions only paraphrase the document and do not dispel its original strangeness. Interpretation must continue until the belief in such problematic notions has been explained in terms of elements that are relevant to the real world of the interpreter. Thus, the ontological assumptions which a scholar brings to any specific problem of interpretation influence the type of hermeneutic he will employ. Put simply, different ontologies produce different hermeneutics.

THREE MODELS OF INTERPRETATION: GENEALOGY, TRANSLATION, REARTICULATION

In the conflict of interpretation, scholars have explained religious phenomena through three basic hermeneutics, which I will call *genealogy, translation,* and *rearticulation.* Each presupposes a different 'distance' between religious behavior and meaningful present existence, and as a result each sees a different measure of legitimacy in religion. However, they all share the same strategy of relating the religious phenomenon to other cultural data and explaining it in terms of that relationship. It is the choice of the data to which the religious fact should be related that distinguishes them.

In genealogical interpretations, religious behavior is seen as an unintended parody of scientific technique dating back to the origins of human problem solving. According to this hermeneutic, science and technology, themselves obviously meaningful aspects of human existence, are the genuine means to achieve the results which religious man vainly hopes to attain through his own practices. In interpretation based on translation, religion is related to non-scientific natural concerns within the culture, such as social structure of psychological images. Here, the religious terminology of supernaturalism may be illegitimate, but concerns for social solidarity and psychological integration which lie at the base of religion are self-evidently fundamental and meaningful aspects of human life. Finally, in interpretations based on rearticulation, the specific datum is related to the entire religious system of that culture. The larger religious system is analyzed 'from within' to find the central stances it takes towards ultimate reality. When these central patterns have been discerned, the specific phenomenon can be understood as a manifestation of the larger ensemble and the mass of analyzed material can be re-articulated into a coherent pattern which has an 'obvious' meaning on its own terms.

There is a limited number of basic issues which have been at the center of religious studies for the past century. Since each of these three hermeneutical models is systematic, proponents of any one method tend to share basically the same stance across the board on these issues as against the stances assumed by proponents of other methods. The remainder of this chapter will present an overview of the ways in which general theoretical decisions made on five crucial issues have shaped classicists' interpretations of Dionysos. However, before considering these specific issues, one needs to understand how the basic directions of the three primary hermeneutical models have influenced interpretation in general.

(A) The genealogical method is appropriate, even necessary, when the distance between religious phenomena and the accepted reality of the modern investigator is unbridgeable. Such a situation arises with the judgment that religion fails at what it sets out to do, that is possesses no intrinsic meaning, and that its actual procedure corresponds to no authentic human enterprise. The classic proponent of this viewpoint in general religious studies is J. G. Frazer, author of the most celebrated genealogical treatment of religion, *The Golden Bough*, who portrayed religion as the confused and ineffective attempt to control the material world. As the by-product of magic, religion was a travesty of scientific technique rather than an authentic means of maintaining contact with reality. In the same vein, E. B. Tylor derived soul belief, in his view religion's original state, from a misguided attempt to clarify the cause of certain biological phenomena. Like Frazer, he analysed religion as a faulty conclusion based on an initial error. Indeed, this approach to interpretation characterizes all genealogical theories; they demonstrate that religion is based on a mistake and explain what led to the mistake. Usually the blame falls on the undeveloped intellect of primitive man as the creator of religion. The drive to control one's environment is authentically human, but the earliest human attempts at this control have been inept. This general interpretation led Jane Harrison in her early works and Martin Nilsson to explain Dionysos as the refinement of the magical world view and Erwin Rohde and E. R. Dodds to explain him as the erroneous explanation for highly emotional states of consciousness.

(B) When the distance between the investigator and the religious phenomenon is not assumed to be so great, translation becomes an interpretive option. In this case the interpreter sees religion as successful in fulfilling certain important human needs, although he rejects as ultimately illegitimate such conceptions as the 'Sacred', the 'Holy', the 'supernatural', or the 'transcendent'. Here the way to overcome hermeneutical distance is to show what the religious phenomenon 'really' means; that is, to translate the 'manifest' conceptions of supernatural reality into language appropriate to the 'latent' or actual significance of the phenomenon. The classic example of this approach is Durkheim's translation of the object of religion—the supernatural category 'god'—as the natural entity, 'society'. The objects of religious expression have also been translated into psychological categories. For example, Jung's interpretation of religious forms as manifestations of archetypal structures posits psychic contents embedded in man's unconscious stratum which express themselves not only in dreams but in religious phenomena as well. The French structuralist Claude Lévi-Strauss also examines religious data, primarily myths, to find a natural referent for the language of supernaturalism. Unlike Jung, he is uninterested in the contents of the psyche and instead sees myth as an expression of the mind's deep structure. Scholars using translation differ from genealogists in not trying to eradicate religion by exposing it as patent error. However, they agree with genealogists that one cannot adequately explain religion by referring to supernatural beings. Instead they try to identify those inescapable facets of human life which religion objectifies in a confused manner. Of the works treated in this study the clearest example is Jane Harrison's later work *Themis*, in which, having shifted from a Frazerian to a Durkheimian model, she explained Dionysos as the projection of the social solidarity of the primitive Greeks. To some extent Rohde and Dodds interpreted Dionysos as the projection of violent psychological states; although by stressing his role as a prescientific explanatory device over his role as the expression of authentic urges they tended to follow more of a genealogical approach than one of translation.

(C) When a scholar views religion as an authentic and comprehensible human enterprise and sees no necessary distance between religious behavior and legitimate contemporary behavior, he uses re-articulation. He relates each phenomenon to the culture's total religion so that its 'sense' in the hierarchy of the system becomes obvious. At least for the sake of analysis, if not for personal reasons, he presents the entire religious structure as a viable option for understanding and acting in the world. Like the scholar using translation, he organizes his material in order to bring out its intelligibility; but unlike the former, he retains the language of supernaturalism to explain the significance of religious behavior. In his view, man's attempt to structure his world in terms of ultimate, supernatural reality is an important activity; therefore, he treats concepts of transcendence as plausible presuppositions for human orientation. Instead of attempting to prove that religion is based on 'self-evident' error, he bypasses casual explanations in favor of understanding the religious structure from within. By treating the phenomenon in question as a partial expression of an intelligible system of dealing with the universe, he shows the religious fact to be an authentic human product. One can point to several examples of this type of analysis: Eliade's morphological approach, phenomenological studies of religion, the culture-morphology school begun by Frobenius and continued by Jensen, and numerous anthropological and historical analyses not explicitly associated with specific philosophically oriented methods but concerned to show how religious phenomena make sense to those 'inside' the system. All of these interpretations accept concepts of supernaturalism as 'givens' for their analysis and attempt to show how such concepts are integrated into an intelligible orientation within the ideological universe of the people being studied. In classical studies Walter F. Otto has been the most aggressive proponent of rearticulation, portraying the Dionysiac vision not only as a meaningful metaphysical orientation for the ancient Greeks but even as a more adequate expression of reality than contemporary scientific models. In a more neutral fashion, W. K. C. Guthrie has also interpreted Dionysiac religion as an expression of perennial metaphysical concerns.

All three of these basic methodological positions have their representatives today. In attempting to interpret or explain religious phenomena, each in its own way must resolve particular questions raised by the nature of religious data. However, in the case of certain fundamental questions which all three methods have addressed, serious disputes have arisen because the general logic of the different methods has forced them to take antithetical positions. The rest of this chapter will spell out the five issues which have been the main centers of debate, showing how each model of interpretation deals with these individual problems differently. Each hermeneutic's responses to these five issues provide a framework for a global interpretation of Dionysos. The order in which these issues will be treated is as follows: (1) the origin of religion; (2) the function of religion; (3) the human locus of religion; (4) the unity of each religion; and (5) the referent of religion.

1. *The origin of religion*

The search for the origin of religion was initiated by genealogists and has continued to be their main concern. At its inception this search was a powerful tool for discrediting religion. The geneaolgists attempted to demonstrate a continuity in thought patterns between primitives and modern religious people and a corresponding discontinuity between both of these and modern, scientifically enlightened freethinkers. Since the primitive intellect was assumed to be inferior, comparing religious thought to primitive mentality was supposed to have devastating implications for the status of religion. If the earliest men had been in a confused mental haze as they performed their religious activities, then religion had been generated out of primitive error and superstition. It survived because of cultural inertia, which itself was due to the intellectual sloth and ineptitude of the masses.

The status of gods in human history was a key issue throughout this discussion. Every culture seemed to have them. More importantly, these gods could be compared with the Judeo-Christian deity, which numerous scholars wished to unmask as a product of error or fantasy. One way to accomplish this unmasking was to show that gods were relative latecomers in the development of religion, originating only after some earlier, and therefore more essential, religious concept or practice. Since, given the intellectual progress of the modern period, these earliest concepts were destined to die out, the object of the theists' belief was vulnerable to attack on two sides: gods were eminently dispensable at the beginning of religion and outmoded at its demise.

In order to demonstrate the pre-theistic or pre-deistic origin of religion from primitive simplicity, genealogical scholars elaborated a standard method of evolutionary stratification. From various 'primitive' traditions they sorted out different 'levels' of complexity. Then on the basis of the assumption (rarely argued and nowhere proved) that this hierarchy of forms corresponded to man's temporal development, they drew up a history of early religion in which the simplest forms preceded the more complex. Accordingly, they asserted that all sorts of things preceded gods in the evolution of religion: ghosts, souls, magic, mana (supernatural power), totemism, and assorted conflations of these simple phenomena. Erwin Rohde, the earliest scholar examined here, derived gods from animistic belief in souls and spirits and interpreted Dionysos himself as a refinement of this logic. Jane Harrison postulated magic and, later, totemism as the origin of Dionysian religion, while Martin Nilsson attributed the earliest role to mana and magic.

This basic model of religion's origin defined the nature of the discussion for several decades and still receives its share of attention. Scholars using translation as a method of interpretation generally accepted the genealogists' account of the erroneous origin of concepts of supernaturalism, though they attributed a different function to the original religious behavior. For example, Harrison saw in the totemism which led to Dionysos a misconstrued expression of group solidarity rather than a simple mental flaw.

Even scholars who wished to assert early religion's authenticity at first accepted the way in which genealogists had defined the problem. Anti-evolutionist scholars such as Andrew Lang and Father Wilhelm Schmidt, like later scholars who used a hermeneutic of rearticulation, approached religion as a meaningful and intelligent human response to the world. However, they accepted the judgment of their era that much primitive religion was indefensible and accordingly were willing to dismiss a great deal of extant religion as a degeneration in order to salvage the legitimacy of an original kernel. Thus, in the fashion of the genealogists but with diametrically opposed intentions, they too looked for some original stage 'behind' existing religions rather than trying to make sense out of the data as they found it. Believing that 'primitive' man was as intellectually competent as modern man, they looked for and found evidence of religious genius—the high god concept—associated with the most 'primitive' (technologically backward) cultures. They argued that this high god belief had initially been relatively pure but had, over time, become adulterated with less exalted religious elements. Nevertheless, since the first stage of religion was comparable with sophisticated modern religious ideas for which intelligent and honest men still argued, interpretation did not require a causal explanation which traced religion back to primitive error.

Lacking sufficient evidence and with no sure means of controlling their data, scholars had arrived at contradictory results which were impossible to verify one way or the other. Other approaches followed which avoided this impasse. Functionalism refrained from evolutionary hypotheses and focused on the interrelationships between religion and social structures. It could thereby show how religion was a 'resource' for society, either by reinforcing existing social patterns (eufunction) or by disrupting them (dysfunction). Yet functionalism was more relevant to the analysis of society than of religion. More germane to interest in the nature of religion *per se* was the approach of rearticulation, which focused on the inter-relationships between specific religious facts and wider ideological contexts. Reversing the strategy of functionalism, it showed how social and cultural patterns were used as 'resources' for religion, especially for religious symbolism. Walter Otto interpreted virtually every aspect of the Dionysiac cult—the myths, the social groupings involved, the ritual paraphernalia, and the wider contexts with which Dionysos was associated—as expressions of a metaphysical truth. W. K. C. Guthrie also, though in a less partisan manner, attempted to elucidate how the Dionysian worshippers used their lived experience to express a deep truth about existence.

Neither functionalism nor rearticulation related religious facts to some 'original' state, but rather to the existing cultural and social configuration in which they operated. Both approaches tended to condemn the genealogical search for origins as purely speculative and to deal exclusively with the internal relations within extant materials. Sometimes, however, proponents of rearticulation seem to have felt themselves forced to postulate another 'origin' of religion which would serve as an alternative to that of the evolutionists. Otto, for example, followed Frobęnius' culture-morphological approach and agreed that a moment of profound insight or 'seizure' (*Ergriffenheit*) inaugurated religion. Nevertheless, while religion's hypothetical origin had a role in the hermeneutic of rearticulation, it did not play as important a part in defining the content of interpretation as it had in the evolutionists' account. When, as in the case of evolutionism, the origin was seen as infantile, one was excused from understanding the content of the religious vision and was responsible instead for accounting for the mistake. When, as in Otto's case, the origin was seen as a moment of creativity, one still had to rearticulate the religious vision involved to see what content it expressed. To define the origin of religion as insight was only to grant it a status commensurate with that of other products of creativity such as art, literature, etc. Afterwards one still had the task of explaining its meaning.

The issue of the origin of religion permeated the other questions of interpretation well into the twentieth century. Scholars tended to argue about religion's purpose, locus, and unity in terms of its origin and to decide to what religion referred in terms of their answers to these prior questions. Since all these issues were so closely related, a challenge to any part of the interpretive framework was a challenge to the entire hermeneutic. This situation led to some bitter exchanges in the early part of this century, but in recent decades the fervor over origins has cooled, allowing scholars to take more inclusive positions on the entire range of issues. Guthrie, for example, has attempted to follow a compromise approach, deriving some religious phenomena from primitive error and some from perennial metaphysical concerns.

2. *The purpose of religion*

Though scholars generally agreed that primitive peoples preserved the most primordial stages of religion, they disagreed over what purpose early man had for his religious behavior. Religious people, both primitive and modern, have offered many different reasons for why they have acted as they have, ranging from a desire to manipulate the natural world through occult means to a desire to celebrate the nature of the universe and its sacred dimension without any thought of gain. While the debate over the origin of religion was raging, it was crucial to be able to disentangle the mixed motives acknowledged for religious behavior and to find the primary and original motive, the 'real' reason that religious practices had been instituted. Then, on the basis of how effectively religious behavior fulfilled this original goal, religion could be evaluated as a product of error, transposition, or perspicacity.

There were two primary poles in this issue: *utility* and *expression*.

Was religion a utilitarian endeavor designed to produce certain beneficial effects? Or was it a means of making manifest and testifying to fundamental aspects of reality? There were of course, numerous intermediate positions between these two extremes, but the most vociferous and frequently the most instructive battles were fought by scholars near either end of the spectrum.

Genealogists saw religion as a misdirected attempt to gain certain things which were, in fact, accessible through scientific theory and practice but not through superstition or magical behavior. Frazer's portrayal of the origin of religion as magical technique to produce material advantage in the quest for food and sex was the most forceful exposition of this view and was applied to Dionysos by Harrison and Nilsson. Other genealogists discerned different problems which religion was supposed to address. In E. B. Tylor's animistic theory, cognitive needs were more relevant than palpably material needs. The earliest stage of religion, belief in spirits, resulted from curiosity about those biological states in which that part of man which produced conscious behavior seemed to be absent (sleep, trance, disease, and death) and in which immaterial forms were actually experienced (dreams and visions). Here the need met by religion was clearly more rarefied than that of Frazer's primitive man; but again science, in this case scientific explanation, was the only correct way to meet that need. Rohde and E. R. Dodds interpreted Dionysos as the refinement of an original animistic hypothesis designed to gain cognitive control over psychological states.

Arguing against the theory that religion is pseudo-scientific behavior, scholars using rearticulation asserted that religion had its own specific intention different from all instrumental activity. Viewed from within, religious behavior was not a means to some material or cognitive end but an end in itself—the disinterested expression of man's understanding of his relationship to the larger universe and to the Sacred which gives it form, sanctity, and meaning. This approach held that one of culture's essential roles was to provide shared means of expressing man's self-transcendence into something more ultimate. Each important feature of a culture (arts, language, social organization, religion, law, etc.) has incarnated an understanding of reality. Religion has played a crucial role since it has testified to how things have stood between man and the Sacred, *the* most fundamental reality. Struck by the holiness of some aspect of the world or of his experience, religious man turned away from his workaday relationship with things and gave objective manifestation to that which was divine for him by means of speech, gesture, action, and plastic creativity. Through this non-utilitarian behavior he found his true place in the world; and, although this act of self-orientation could not be said to be profitable in the ordinary sense, it was held to be what ultimately allowed him to claim his own humanity. In this vein, one of the most interesting interpretive maneuvers of Otto's *Dionysos, Myth and Cult* was the manner in which the frenzied and 'irrational' behavior in the Bacchic cult was explained not as a frantic attempt to gain some material advantage but as the only appropriate way to do justice to an insight which saw through the rationality of the world to a deeper, more primeval level and which allowed man to participate in this primordial reality.

When the adherents of the utilitarian and expressive approaches were not ignoring each other, they fought rather bitterly. The reason for this strife was tied to their conflicting presuppositions about man and culture. Each side identified different concerns as most essential to the human enterprise and interpreted religion accordingly. Each argued that people were religious because they thought religion would meet some specific concern, and each claimed that concerns other than the one he identified were secondary.

For example, genealogists portrayed early culture as the primitive's response to a basically hostile and difficult world in which man needed food, shelter, and other fundamentals of existence. Faced with these issues primitive man would have, quite understandably, spent his limited mental resources seeking solutions to practical problems and useful scientific knowledge. As portrayed by the evolutionists, primitive man would have had neither the desire nor the ability to indulge in metaphysical speculation. Unfortunately, in negotiating the world at hand, he occasionally misdirected his mental energies into the blind alleys of magical and occult explanations. Since the initial response to these problems of physical and mental life was flawed, later religious conceptions based on them (gods, spirits, Divinity, etc.) were indefensible. Religion failed to fulfill its purpose.

On the other side of the argument, some held that from the very beginning culture was primarily a way of expressing man's identity within a context of ultimacy. This position assumed that fundamental material needs were readily satisfied and that early man's desire for the amelioration of his condition was not the main driving force behind culture. Rather, only the profound confrontation with the deepest levels of reality could have called forth genuine cultural creativity. From this perspective, utilitarian goals for religious behavior signified a degeneration or misunderstanding of religion's original purpose. Originally religion was a complex endeavor in which all types of human behavior were used both to perceive and to articulate the ultimate, 'real' nature of the universe and man's place in it. Not only was religion not derived from utilitarian concerns; in some sense it was prior to them and was the mainspring for the entire culture. As a means of expressing man's spiritual and cosmic orientation, religion had a chance for success in a way it did not as a replacement for science and technology.

Between the utilitarian interpretation associated with genealogy and the expressive interpretation associated with rearticulation there was a compromise position usually taken by scholars using translation. This position acknowledged the expressive role of religion as more important than overt utilitarian concerns but denied that this acknowledgment necessitated interpreting religion as the disinterested expression of some supernatural dimension. Although those performing religious actions may not have known it, the actual function of religion was as expedient as that of the most rationalized technology. On a communal level religion strengthened social solidarity by giving members of the group a means of expressing shared values and traditions or even of expressing the very society itself as something which transcends the individual's own limited existence. Harrison's *Themis* represented the most thoroughgoing interpretation of Dionysos as the expression of social effervescence and unity. On an individual level, religion was seen as objectifying certain psychological drives and channeling them into socially approved outlets. E. R. Dodds followed this approach in treating the Dionysiac cult as an effective way for early man to express dangerous psychological urges which otherwise would have erupted with uncontrolled fury. In both varieties translation agreed with rearticulation that the purpose of religion was expressive but also agreed with genealogy that conceptions of the supernatural were due to inadequate modes of thought and were not suitable explanatory concepts. It was only by relating religious behavior to social and psychological forces operative within a particular culture that the scholar acquired observable phenomena which he could use for explanation. He could then interpret religion as having a purpose which it did in fact fulfill (as against genealogy), though it was not the purpose avowed by the actors involved (as against rearticulation).

In the latter nineteenth and early twentieth century scholars usually defended one of these three options to the exclusion of others. This mutual intolerance was largely due to the fact that the purpose of religion was a major issue in the dispute over the origin of religion. The validity of religion depended on how and why it had been produced. Once the scholar decided on the original stage, he could interpret other possible purposes as secondary. Depending on whether one used genealogy, translation, or rearticulation, the purpose alleged to be original by other interpretations would be treated as epiphenomena, rationalizations, or degenerations respectively.

This situation of mutual exclusion has changed significantly, largely because scholars no longer hypothesize about origins with the same fervor or certainty. There is now a growing appreciation for the multiplicity of purposes for religion; and since no one of these is seen as determining the rest, they can all be acknowledged without prejudicing the case for or against the validity of religion. Although his final position is not always clear, Guthrie has taken more types of purpose into account in explaining Dionysos than the other scholars considered here. He has interpreted some aspects of Dionysiac religion as pre-scientific attempts to influence reality, some as translations of historical realities, and some as meaningful metaphysical expression.

3. *The locus of religion*

Historically, most early modern interpretations located religion as originating and remaining centered in one of the three 'faculties': intellect, will, or emotion. This issue of the locus of religion within the human makeup was first posed in terms of the larger question of origins in such a way that religion's initial status would be understood as a product of error or of confusion or as a natural and valid response to the world. If religion emerged from a faculty which somehow was malfunctioning, then it was not legitimate. If it originated instead from the normal, healthy functioning of one or all of the faculties, then its legitimacy was not so easily dismissed.

With the exception of Max Müller's early 'emotionalist' interpretation, the first theories of religion were 'intellectualist'. That is, they portrayed religion as arising out of man's intellect and, more specifically, from primitive speculation and ratiocination concerning natural phenomena. As genealogical interpretations, these theories viewed religion as a misuse of the cognitive faculty. Trapped by his impoverished intellectual situation, primitive man had invoked occult forces to explain phenomena which are properly explained only in scientific terms. For example, according to Tylor and Spencer, primitive man had created a fantasy world of ghosts and spirits because he could not fathom the natural-scientific causes of waking and sleep, life and death, and so forth. According to Frazer, a different logic of explanation but the same ignorance of genuine cause and effect caused primitive man to invent magic and, following that, religion. All of these scholars assumed that early man operated with basically the same mental equipment as modern man but lacked sufficient experience and intellectual development. Rohde in *Psyche* and Harrison in her first major work, *Prolegomena to the Study of Greek Religion* both followed the intellectualist position, seeing Dionysos as a product of mental backwardness.

The anti-evolutionist school championed by Lang and Schmidt accepted the intellectualist position but challenged the early genealogists' assumption that religion resulted from intellectual malfunction. They denied that primitive man's earliest explanations would necessarily have been clumsy fabulations such as ghosts and spirits. Instead, they appealed to the existence of belief in a High God among peoples with extremely undeveloped technology as evidence that supposedly advanced notions (in this case, the conception of a moral, powerful, kindly, creative god in many respects similar to the Christian deity) can occur at the 'earliest' stage of man's cognitive life. Such a conception did not come from the mind's misadventure with verifiably explicable phenomena but was a natural and legitimate response of early man's desire to know the cause of the world. Through their powerful attack on the evolutionists' assumption that man's earliest intellectual maneuvers were flawed simply by virtue of their being early, the anti-evolutionists reduced the possibility of using the intellectualist stance as a way of demonstrating the inherent error of religion.

However, as the twentieth century began, the intellectualist approach was losing relevance for other reasons. As scholars paid increasing attention to non-intellectual factors such as psychological drives, economic forces, socially imposed patterns of behavior, and biological instincts, they attributed an increasingly smaller role to individual cognition, sometimes even reducing it to the status of rationalization or mask. Even as Schmidt was using the primitive's elevated concepts to neutralize the genealogists' use of the intellectualist approach, genealogists were turning to other faculties as the locus for religion.

When R. R. Marett identified the primitive emotion of awe as the wellspring of religion, he was the first of a wave of scholars to propound an emotionalist interpretation. Using this new approach, many scholars gave religion a more gentle hearing. For one thing, powerful emotions such as awe, reverence, and fascination were thought to be more permanent and even more legitimate than primitive man's spurious scientific hypotheses. For another, if religion originated in powerful currents of emotion, it was possible that some genuine human concern was being partially expressed through the confused facade of religious terminology. The shift to an emotionalist interpretation was, in fact, one of the chief factors in the emergence of the hermeneutics of translation. Religion may not have been what its adherents thought it was, but it was not an out-and-out mistake. It objectified authentic emotions or drives with at least partial success. Consequently, scholars could affirm these emotions and drives even as they disputed religion's explanation for them. With her shift to the Durkheimian position Jane Harrison was able to interpret Dionysian religion as the oblique expression of social emotions and evaluate it as considerably more legitimate than when she had judged it as a pseudo-rational attempt to manipulate the natural realm.

Despite the new possibilities for the hermeneutics of translation which resulted from the shift away from intellectualist interpretations, many scholars derived religion from emotions or will as part of a genealogical approach. They portrayed religion as arising when primitive man's emotions or desires overwhelmed his intellect. Religious cult was the immediate discharge of this emotional or volitional excess, and myth (or religious ideology in general) was the attempt to explain and/or express the excess. Religion was thus born under mentally debilitating tension. Though consistently drawn to a Frazerian interpretation of religion, Nilsson abandoned the intellectualist explanation of gods for the mana theory of R. R. Marett, thereby seeing awe and fear as the wellspring of religion.

Scholars using rearticulation generally accepted the role of emotions and desires in generating religion but denied that they had overpowered man into a mistaken enterprise. The culture morphologists, with Walter Otto as a prominent ally and spokesman, gave the most explicit retort to the genealogical approach. According to them, the creators of religion were neither poorly informed proto-technicians nor simple folk overwhelmed by their emotions and drives but persons of profound insight confronting the world with all of man's intellectual, emotional, and volitional richness. When he created religion, man had utilized *all* of his faculties to perceive the deepest reality of the world. The insight had a heavy intellectual component to be sure, but this component was neither the bumbling problem-solving cognition pictured by the evolutionists nor the dry excogitation on the first cause pictured by the rationalist anti-evolutionists. As a creative perception, the insight had involved man's fundamental existential concerns as well as his desire to know.

Such a total involvement on the part of the creator of religion necessitated a different interpretive strategy. Rather than explaining the peculiar religious interpretation or gloss which was supposed to create conceptions of the supernatural out of natural emotions and desires, that is, giving a causal explanation 'from without', the interpreter was supposed to understand religion 'from within', rearticulating the religious data into a coherent system that could clearly engage the totality of a person as his legitimate stance in the universe. Since the religious system represented the full commitment of a creative spirit operating at peak intensity, the interpreter's role was to *attain* this high level of total insight. Naturally, not all scholars using the method of rearticulation reached the degree of intersubjective participation urged by culture morphology, but they did tend to accept the fact of religion's engagement of emotions and desires in addition to thought as a reflection of religion's richness rather than of its illegitimacy.

4. *The unity of specific religions*

Once religious studies were broadened to include non-Western data, especially primitive religions, the number of phenomena which could be interpreted as 'religious' became immense. Since scholars had to organize these diverse materials into some kind of unified interpretation, they had to decide how all these facts cohered into the single phenomenon 'religion'. That is, in the lived historical experience of a culture, how did the multifarious religious phenomena relate to each other and how were they held together? Did religion start from a single simple nucleus and then grow as various elements were tacked on to this original point until finally the entire network of beliefs and practices was assembled and operating? Or was religion a formed structure from the very beginning, where individual elements were all articulated into a systematic unity in which each element's meaning was tied to its relations with the other interdependent elements and to its place in the general system?

To a great extent, such questions have more to do with method than with the intrinsic nature of the data. One can investigate religious phenomena diachronically, tracing changes to see how and why religious elements are added and deleted, or synchronically, describing its static structure and showing the interdependence between formal organization and individual elements. The Darwinian revolution was a tremendous impetus to the diachronic method which interpreted the present as a function of an evolving past. The discovery that the present complex hierarchy of biological life is not a static 'great chain of being' but is instead the result of a long process of incremental alterations suggested a more analytical way of viewing cultural phenomena such as religion. There were other, perhaps more important, scientific developments which provide the impetus to study evolution as the most effective way to understand religion.[12] In sciences as diverse as geology, paleontology, biology, prehistoric archaeology, and comparative philology, scholars could reconstruct bygone states by arranging phenomena presently observable into chronological stages and describing laws of development which accounted for the present situation. Given this powerful theoretical convergence, most nineteenth century scholars paid little attention to the inner logic and systematic functioning of religions and concentrated instead on diachronic investigations. For several decades that evolutionary approach was the dominant paradigm for the social sciences.

Finally a countercurrent began. In the late nineteenth and early twentieth century a number of things contributed to the interest in structure as over and against history. Well before the introduction of evolutionary thought, the German idealistic tradition as applied to history and social science had already viewed cultures as 'organisms' and had analysed them in terms of connections of meaning instead of historical relationships.[13] Culture morphology was but the latest expression of this stance. The emergence of functionalism was another factor which shifted interest from individual elements explained in terms of their antecedents to coherent structures which function interdependently.[14] On a more philosophical level, phenomenology has lent support to scholars dealing systematically with religious material on its own terms rather than in terms of its genesis. And more recently the interest in the synchronic dimension has been reinforced by Lévi-Strauss's structuralist anthropology. Each of these approaches makes available a means of grasping the holistic unity of culture at any specific point in time as over and against dealing only with historical change. Since both diachronic and synchronic approaches have theoretical justification, contemporary scholars tend to acknowledge that one may choose either, depending on what one wants to reveal.

Yet in the late nineteenth and early twentieth century this choice was not seen as a question of method left to the discretion of the scholar. Instead it was treated as though the material studied demanded the use of only one of these approaches; religion was seen as *by nature* either a jumbled conglomeration of ever changing elements or a meaningful organic structure functioning in its basic complexity from the start. Religion either began as a minor phenomenon which attracted supplements or as a structured whole; one had to choose. In early disputes the choice was not seen as one between methods which revealed different aspects of the same phenomenon but between the right approach and the wrong one. Evolutionists and their opponents presented the problem of the unity of religion as another variant of the question of origins and carried out their usual battles.

Evolutionists portrayed religion as originating in some simple phenomenon such as soul belief, ghost-worship, or magic. From this humble beginning, religion began acquiring additional elements. The increase of these elements, combined with certain refinements, produced religion's later stages which differed substantially from its origin. It was this difference between religion's later stages (that is, the present religious lives of primitive peoples) and its earliest stage (which was the key to understanding but which no longer existed in its pure form) that necessitated the evolutionist's attempts at historical reconstruction. Once this reconstruction was completed, the evolutionist could explain complex religious thought and behavior by means of its more simple antecedents, even though the material under study may have included simple and complex phenomena side by side. For example, according to Tylor's reconstruction, the first religious object was the human soul. When the animistic logic was extended to non-human aspects of the world, other imaginary beings were added to the panoply of primitive religious conceptions: animal souls, plant souls, object souls, 'upward to the rank of powerful deities'. The existing complex assemblage of religious forms resulted from a long process in which the simple origin of religion had been so overladen with additions and refinements as to lose its initial appearance. Frazer followed the same general interpretation: the simple logic and technique of magic had been expanded, refined, abandoned, and finally substituted for, so that the end product of these involved transformations diverged substantially from the initial stage. In all of these theories, notions of deity were offshoots of some original, non-theistic source of religion. Each of the evolutionists examined here, Rohde, Harrison, Nilsson, and to a lesser extent Dodds, has interpreted Dionysos as the result of a gradual growth from some more infantile or transparent stage.

As usual, the anti-evolutionists accepted the terms of the argument and made antithetical pronouncements. They also explained the present complexity of religions as due to the addition of secondary elements to an original core. However, for them this core was the rather elevated 'High God' belief with its simple and ethical cult practices rather than the 'superstition' associated with belief in magic, ghosts, demons, and the like. From an origin in many respects resembling contemporary monotheism, primitive religion had undergone additions and fragmentations until polytheism, ancestor worship, and other degenerative forms overshadowed the original pure belief in a High God. As had the evolutionists, the anti-evolutionists accounted for the difference between the observed complexity of primitive religion and the hypothetical simplicity of its origin by postulating that secondary elements had been added to the primary belief. The anti-evolutionists postulated a more sophisticated concept as the origin than had the evolutionists; but, for both approaches, primitive religion as it existed today was a conglomerate rather than an organic unity.

For the evolutionists, the newer additions had been improvements which had helped to mask the self-evident fallacies of the original state. For the anti-evolutionists, additions had been degenerations which had concealed the essential soundness of primitive man's first metaphysical explorations. Since, for both theories, the development of religion beclouded its actual significance, proper interpretation implied the analytical decomposition of the entire structure until the original nucleus had been isolated. And once scholars had shown these supposedly secondary elements to be, in fact, later accretions, they had also made an implicit judgment on the validity of contemporary religion. The genealogists had implicitly discredited gods as later stages and therefore inessential; the High God school discredited everything *but* gods. Neither was interested in discerning something which lay 'behind' the multitude of religious phenomena or in rearticulating the entire spectrum of religious phenomena into some coherent picture.

By and large, scholars using translation agreed with genealogists that the final state of religion resulted from a process of amelioration; but, rather than portraying the initial nucleus as originating in fantasy, they usually saw it as some facet of reality which had been misconstrued. The additions and refinements of religion were then seen as only disguising the original nucleus.

Scholars using rearticulation generally took a different stance on the unity of religion. They acknowledged the multiplicity of religious data within cultures; but instead of searching for some initial nucleus which had been supplemented, transformed, or debased, they viewed almost all elements of religion as expressions of a complex but organically unified insight and stance within the universe perceived as holy. Following this assumption, they portrayed religion as a structure of meanings, articulated in forms which could range from the sublime to the coarse. Consequently, they explained each religious practice or belief in terms of how it manifested or complemented the culture's basic insight rather than how it chanced to arrive and be tacked onto the original nucleus to which it was only accidentally related. Thus in analyzing the Bacchic cult, Otto argued that Dionysos had been present in Greek consciousness as a fully formed god from the start and that he was the center from which radiated the various levels of cult and belief. According to the general logic of rearticulation, since the fundamental insight of any culture was embodied in manifold ways, each specific belief and action contributed to the rich unfolding of this global insight. Therefore, complexity was not the result of *ad hoc* accretions or shifts in the logic of some early religious conception, but was a function of creativity. It demonstrated the pervasiveness of the culture's central insight and the profusion of its expressions. Otto's monograph on Dionysos is a sustained, at times almost desperate, attempt to relate everything in Dionysiac religion to such a fundamental insight.

In this type of interpretation the question of historical change has been subordinated to the question of a ruling system which justifies individual phenomena. Interpretation proceeds not by explaining the cause and effect chain that led to Dionysiac religion but by revealing an organization of meaningful interdependence. Even when it is necessary to analyse change, one should remember that change is not just the addition and subtraction of atomistic elements but the transformation of an entire system; that is, a passage between articulated and meaningful wholes.

Contemporary scholars tend to take a more moderate position on the issue of the unity of religion. They are generally sensitive to the systematic quality of religions, but at the same time most would not advocate the 'organism' metaphor for understanding cultures as vigorously as had the culture morphologists. A principle of organization which would allow them to bind together both change and structure into one unified methodological stance has not yet emerged, but they are attempting to overcome the tension between the two approaches. Of the scholars treated here, only Guthrie has both taken Dionysos seriously as reflecting a fully formed perception of the relation of man to the Divine and, at the same time, treated the historical changes Dionysiac religion underwent in its relationship to other religious currents in Greece. However, in his attempt to avoid the excesses of other approaches, he sometimes has taken ambiguous and, on occasion, methodologically inconsistent positions.

5. *The referent of religion*

If religion is illegitimate or illusory, then a concept like God or the Sacred has no referent. On the other hand, if religious conceptions and practices are not totally repudiated but cease to be seen on their own terms, one can point to some natural[15] datum or event and show that it is to this that religious language actually refers. Finally, if religion is still seen as a legitimate enterprise even with its conceptions of supernatural or sacred reality, one can try to present some approximation of what that divine reality might be, as refracted through the conceptions and experiences of the people under study. In the conflicts of interpretation no battles have been more intense than those fought over the question of to what religion refers—nothing, natural reality, or 'the Sacred'.

Genealogists have tended to see religion as referring to nothing at all real. The occult forces postulated by religious conceptions are the fabulations of a mistaken process of thought. Religion is intended to satisfy some quite empirical end, but the means invoked for these results (that is, supernatural entities) are fictitious. Thus, Frazer appreciated man's attempt to improve his situation; the problem was that, unlike scientific 'causal' connections, magical connections and gods neither exist nor work. Similarly, in Tylor's theory, the biological phenomena which led to animistic philosophy were real enough, but the entities invented to explain them were not. The result of the application of this general approach to Dionysos should be clear. For Rohde, Harrison in her *Prolegomena*, Nilsson, and Dodds, the god represented a conception which had no existence outside the imagination of those who worshipped him.

Scholars using translation have attempted to find a genuine referent of religion within the natural order—some material, psychological, or social object or process which man expressed through his religious life. For Marett, it was the awesome power reflected in various parts of the physical world; for Freud, the psychologically determinative drives and events of early childhood;

for Jung, the archetypal patterns of the unconscious; for Durkheim, the wider society; and for Lévi-Strauss, the deep structures of the brain. For all of these scholars, with the exception of Jung, religion referred to something which could be exhaustively explained within the canons of natural or social science. Thus, when in *Themis* Harrison changed to a Durkheimian interpretation seeing Dionysos as the projection of collective unity, she limited the reality of Dionysos to social reality and refused it any metaphysical transcendence.

Scholars using rearticulation have followed a different course. Not being theologians, they have had no duty to prove the objective existence of 'the Sacred'. But as historians they have felt themselves bound to acknowledge the existence of 'the Sacred' within various religious universes, that is, within what Eliade has called, in a phenomenological or value-free sense, '*l'univers imaginaire*' of specific cultures. Rather than explain such conceptions away as mistaken fantasy or translate them as hypostatized natural reality, they have tended to accept as an authentic part of the human condition the fact that men of all cultures have felt themselves in relationship with some dimension which transcends scientifically verifiable reality and yet is no empty fantasy but a foundation for their worlds as legitimate as the natural-scientific orientation is for the world of 'modern' man. To the extent that these scholars accept the plausibility of this transcendent dimension, they utilize the category of 'the Sacred' as an interpretive tool without feeling required to explain or prove it. Otto insisted not only that the Greeks used Dionysos to refer to that part of reality which transcends the scientific but that their vision provided ontological intimations which were valid for contemporary man. Guthrie has never advocated the contemporary validity of the Dionysiac vision, but he has interpreted Dionysiac religion as referring to metaphysical horizons over which debate is still possible.

The choice between no referent, natural referent, and supernatural referent often goes back to moral commitments made by each scholar. To speak of religious objects as transcending the natural world and being supernatural is to mark off some aspect of the world as having properties and actions which somehow, either in their ontological fullness or miraculous efficacy, go beyond what current natural and social sciences deem possible. For some scholars this supernatural quality of religious entities needs no explanation but is the hallmark of that legitimate human activity called religion. For others, the violation of the canons of science is a mental transgression rather than a legitimate transcendence, and it is precisely this transgression which calls for explanation. Depending on the distance between the scholar and religion as an ongoing behavior, the interpreter chooses his model so as (a) to demystify the credulous and free them from dissipating their lives in fantasy, so that they can enjoy the richness of the natural world (genealogy), (b) to reveal constitutive human needs which are to some extent satisfied by religion (though the language of religion beclouds their genuine nature) and to make more easily accessible a kind of self-transcendence which satisfies more than primordial animal needs while at the same time remaining within the natural world (translation), or (c) to display for appreciation or appropriation a stance in the world that both relates man meaningfully to a dimension of the universe which transcends scientifically understood reality and contributes to the fulfillment of the human spirit (rearticulation). Successive chapters will more fully discuss the ethical commitments of each scholar as reflected through his methodology.

Partially as a consequence of these different commitments, the three interpretive stances use the various issues just considered [(1) origin, (2) purpose, (3) locus, (4) unity and (5) referent of religion] to present different explanations of the essential nature and function of religion. According to those employing genealogy, religion (1) originates from the mental blunders of early man who (2) attempts to control various aspects of the natural world. The means used for this control are inefficient because (3) the primitive's intellect is extremely undeveloped and prone to error or is overwhelmed by pressing emotions or desires that are too strong for his dimunitive rationality. Religion (4) progresses through a process of increasing additions and refinements from this initial cognitive error to the complex composite which still exists in higher societies; but (5) no matter what ameliorations are made, religion remains a behavior which refers only to fictitious causal forces and obstructs man's attainment of true knowledge and control of his world. Rohde, the early Harrison, Nilsson, and to some extent Dodds analyzed Dionysos in this fashion; however, they structured their interpretations differently according to the latest developments in the genealogical paradigm.

According to those using translation as a mode of interpretation, religion (1) originates when certain deeply rooted human needs, which are poorly understood or even completely misconstrued, generate their own oblique expression (2) which itself partially satisfies these needs by giving them some concrete, social objectification. However, this expression is overladen with illegitimate supernaturalism because of (3) the primitive's inability to comprehend rationally forces which themselves are nonrational but which obtrude heavily on the primitive consciousness. Religion (4) is refined through a process of incremental changes; but (5) from the first simple stage to the most complicated secondary development, the only authentic portion of religion is that which refers to these original *natural* aspects of human existence. As will be seen, Jane Harrison's later analysis enabled her to celebrate Dionysos as a healthy expression of social urges while continuing to press her attack against theology and supernaturalism. Because of his awareness of the ineluctable nature of psychological pressures, E. R. Dodds also used aspects of the hermeneutic of translation.

Finally, according to those employing the hermeneutic of rearticulation, religion (1) originates out of some deep perception of or insight into the deepest levels of reality in which man feels himself addressed by Being, which reveals itself as holy and calls for a response. In this response (2) man claims his authentic humanity by expressing in manifold forms his relation to the Sacred discovered through this insight (3) which is itself brought about by the creative and accurate involvement of the totality of man's powers. Religion (4) possesses a systematic integrity from the beginning, an inner *logos* which objectifies itself in different ways during the life of a culture, but which (5) always refers to some deeply perceived level of reality that transcends the categories of the natural and calls man to a meaningful relationship with itself. One can use this hermeneutic to argue for the truth of a particular religious vision, as we will see Otto doing, or one can explore the metaphysical vision of an archaic culture, as we will see Guthrie doing. Both scholars, however, find it satisfactory to explain the Dionysiac vision in terms of its inner content instead of in terms of antecedent conditions or non-religious reality.

The preceding remarks have necessarily been rather programmatic. Naturally, scholars add their own individual touches to their explanations after accepting basic hermeneutical paradigms. Successive chapters will detail specific analyses of Dionysos, allowing the systematic quality of each method to emerge and showing interpretation at work from the most abstract presuppositions to the final judgments about a single phenomenon.

2

Erwin Rohde and the Study of Dionysos

Erwin Rhode[1] is still revered by many modern classicists as the giant on whose shoulders we stand for our present view of Hellenism.[2] His great work *Psyche* (1894) contained the first modern treatment of Dionysos which still commands attention from professional classicists. Indeed, *Psyche* can be said to have inaugurated the modern scientific study of Greek religion as a whole. Although Christian August Lobeck's *Aglaophamus* (1829) was modern in its sober criticism and analysis, *Psyche* was the first philologically sophisticated work which used the modern tools of archaeology and anthropology to break new ground in the interpretation of Greek religion. Naturally, archaeology and anthropology have evolved since Rohde's time and present rather different faces today, and many contemporary classicists restrict their roles to ancillary positions. Nevertheless, these fields continue to be necessary for modern interpretation, largely because of Rohde's influence. By combining brilliant philology with the most prestigious anthropological theories of his day, Rohde demonstrated the relevance of the social sciences for classical religious studies and more than any other scholar of his century shaped their direction for the modern period.

Rohde produced *Psyche*, a masterpiece of evolutionary scholarship, only after a major intellectual shift. He is instructive as a watershed figure because he chose to reject an earlier, Romantic interpretive paradigm in favor of the newer evolutionism. This shift reflects a great deal about the changing evaluation of religion in the late nineteenth century. If we understand something about the late Romantic perspective from which Rohde emerged, we can see much more clearly what he lost and what he gained by adopting a more positivist orientation.

THE ROMANTIC BACKGROUND OF ROHDE'S EARLY THOUGHT

As is well known, Romanticism arose largely as a protest against the Enlightenment's attempt to substitute reason for tradition and to establish a universally valid science of human action. The Romantics valued the diversity of human thought patterns and of behavior as more important than the hypothetical commonalities which Enlightenment scholars had abstracted from human history. To use more modern jargon, they conceived the human sciences to be ideographic rather than nomothetic; that is, they felt that it was more important to understand the specificity of human expressions than to trace causal regularities. As a result, many scholars, especially in Germany, tried to portray specific cultures as unique 'organisms', each with its own *Geist* or spirit. They approached each different form of human expression, such as mythical thought or art, as a specific embodiment of this *Geist* with a 'logic' peculiar to itself. In this manner they viewed traditional aspects of civilization as parts of the legitimate identity of a culture. Consequently, they could interpret religion as one meaningful way for each culture to deal with external reality rather than as a superstitious bastardization of reason.

The value of this approach to the human sciences was ambivalent. On the one hand, it took into account more data as causes of human action and from one perspective was therefore more 'empirical' in its explanation of human behavior. The Romantic conception of man was richer but, at the same time, less precise than that of the Enlightenment. The Romantics envisaged man as having a multi-layered interaction with his world from the basic biological to the most rarefied metaphysical level. His experience was described as 'thicker' than that of man as pictured by the Enlightenment; every action was an act of communication with a wider environment which somehow 'answered' him. Since they saw religion as an intelligible communion with a culturally defined universe, Romantic scholars devoted sympathetic attention to clarifying the internal logic of specific religious systems as important and legitimate determinants of human behavior.

Seen negatively however, this claim that man's religious orientation to the universe fundamentally shaped his behavior threatened to inundate the developing social sciences with an unmanageable number of causal forces, each asserted to be primary. By taking almost all human action and expression as significant in determining the nature of man, the Romantic perspective made it more or less impossible to arrange human behavior in a hierarchy of importance that would reveal which factors shaped the others, that is, which variables were independent and which, dependent. The positivist, evolutionary approach which followed would try to reestablish the hierarchy of action on much the same plan as begun by the Enlightenment. Late in his career, Rohde would agree that the evolutionists' causal explanation of human action was the proper mode for interpretation and would use the theories of the English positivists to explain why Hellenic civilization had practiced Dionysian religion.

However, at the beginning of his career Rohde was heir to the final phases of German Romanticism. In his last years as a student and his first years as a professional classicist Rohde was the best friend of Friedrich Nietzsche, initially a classicist himself, though subsequently one of the most revolutionary of modern philosophers. In their youth both Rohde and Nietzsche revered Arthur Schopenhauer as the model of an authentic philosopher. Later, Rohde abandoned his allegiance to Schopenhauer, and the friendship with Nietzsche cooled as Rohde became more established in the academic world and settled into family life; but his first understanding of the Greeks was conditioned by the perspectives of these two men, and he never fully abandoned certain of their insights.

To be sure, Rohde's early association with Schopenhauer and Nietzsche does not mark him as a typical son of the Romantic era. Whereas most of the main figures of the early Romantic movement, notably Herder and Schelling, used their intellectual perspectives to support theistic belief, Rohde, Nietzsche, and Schopenhauer consistently supported atheism. Nevertheless, they differed from the emerging positivist stance: with the rest of the German Romantics they shared an abiding interest in metaphysics, in man's constant tendency to want to see into the most fundamental and primordial secrets of the universe. Schopenhauer's philosophy, though largely based on the Kantian 'Copernican revolution' in epistemology which had rendered metaphysics problematic, itself had this quality of revealing the ultimate nature of the world. It was a profound, pessimistic reflection on the nature of existence and had a greater existential impact on its readers than did most nineteenth century philosophical systems. In their youths Rohde and Nietzsche cherished the tragic grandeur of Schopenhauer's vision and hoped that it would lead men to return to heroism and tragic greatness as the proper response to the human situation. Consequently, even though atheists, they acknowledged man's metaphysical thirst and were much more willing than the evolutionists to interpret religious phenomena, especially myth, as authentic expressions of a natural human drive for a world view. Following Schopenhauer, Rohde understood the basis of human action in a very different way than he was to do once he had accepted the tenets of evolutionary positivism.

As in W. H. Auden's fine apostrophe to Yeats, '. . . mad Ireland hurt you into poetry', so in Schopenhauer's theory it had been death and the misery of life which had hurt man into metaphysics.[3] Confronted with these two inevitable evils, man had to have some way of understanding the ultimate nature and meaning of the world. For most men religion filled this need. Speaking through the persona of Demopheles in his 'Religion. A Dialogue', Schopenhauer characterized religion as an authentic though somewhat rudimentary reponse to a genuine problem:

> Religion is the metaphysics of the masses . . . Just as they must have popular poetry, and the popular wisdom of proverbs, so they must have popular metaphysics too: for mankind absolutely needs an interpretation of life; and this, again, must be suited to popular comprehension.[4]

Schopenhauer and the majority of the positivist thinkers could agree on their atheism and on their belief that in certain realms man had increased his knowledge and his understanding of the universe. What distinguished Schopenhauer (and both Nietzsche and Rohde in their early years) from the evolutionists was an insistence on the human need for some metaphysical orientation. For the majority of the positivists, with whom Rohde would later ally himself, the metaphysical stage of human evolution was epiphenomenal, produced only as an offshoot of more basic concerns and destined to die out with the advance of science. From their perspective is was a mistake to credit all men with this supposed thirst for cosmic orientation when much more practical problems had fueled human action. Schopenhauer, for his part, by insisting on metaphysics as a basic factor in human action, implied that man, *qua* human being, had to deal with issues which transcend the verifiable truths of science. In the words of a later social scientist, man had to adopt some 'orientation to the nonempirical aspects of the universe, of his life and experience'.[5] As Schopenhauer expressed this need, again through the mouth of Demopheles, he suggested that without such an orientation men would be beset by a kind of cosmic agoraphobia: '. . . the metaphysical needs of mankind absolutely require satisfaction, because the horizon of man's thoughts must have a background and not remain unbounded'.[6] Schopenhauer shared enough of the Romantic and idealist legacy to hold that language about the ultimate horizon of reality transcends scientific truth. For the majority of mankind, he argued, religious language (myth and allegory) had been the most comprehensible and effective mode of expressing this ultimate horizon.[7]

In his early years Rohde agreed that a distinctive world view was indispensable for men and nations. It need not be religious in the sense that it contained some positive sacred dimension, but he thought that it should provide man with a total vision of his universe which would call forth his creativity. Thus, when Rohde reviewed Nietzsche's *The Birth of Tragedy* in the *Norddeutsche allgemeine Zeitung*,[8] his concern was to draw the readers' attention to the possibilities the work offered for a creative renewal of German culture and to its challenge to the optimistic world-view of the times. Unlike most of his contemporaries, he applauded Nietzsche's ontological pronouncements. Later, Rohde would cease to see classical scholarship as the proper place for direct discussions of contemporary philosophical problems, partly because he had become more 'established', but also because he seems to have increasingly lost his taste for world views on the grand scale.

At the same time that he acknowledged man's metaphysical needs, Rohde was aware that religious language used to construct a world view had its own specific properties. From reflections recorded in his notebook ('Cogitata') it is clear that instead of seeing myth as a faulty approximation of scientific statement, Rohde saw it as having its own truth.[9] In his view, mysteries and myths were not simple concepts but operated at the deeper, more inchoate preconceptual level. Rohde identified the truths of myths as *Ahnungen*,[10] 'surmises', 'presentiments', an important intuitive mode of knowing which Romantic thinkers felt the Enlightenment has ignored in its insistence on clarity. To be sure, in its place clarity was legitimate, even indispensable; but in religious matters it was not sufficient. Given the fact that religion integrated deep reflection with global value judgments relative to man's total horizon, the intuitive nature of myth was entirely appropriate.

Unfortunately, the young Rohde did not produce any independent work on Greek religion, and we are unable to see in any detail how he would have applied his early theoretical perspective to Dionysos. However, we do know that at the time of its publication he agreed enthusiastically with Nietzsche's presentation of Dionysos in *The Birth of Tragedy* and that his thoughts before publication of this work paralleled those of Nietzsche. If used carefully, Nietzsche's ideas and Rohde's response to them provide considerable information about Rohde's early understanding of Dionysos.

Nietzsche's *The Birth of Tragedy*, though rejected by his contemporaries among professional classicists, did to a large extent establish the direction of later investigations of Dionysos. After Nietzsche, the history of Greek religion was most often seen as the result of a powerful dialectic of contrasting forces. Later scholars have consistently analyzed and explained Dionysos in terms of opposition to the other, more ordered pole of Greek religion, variously described as 'Apollinian', 'Homeric', or 'Olympian'. Not surprisingly, in light of deep friendship, Rohde was the first to be influenced by this dichotomy. Even in his mature work, he continued to apply it, to the point that he has been criticized for its overuse.[11]

The Birth of Tragedy was Nietzsche's daring treatment of Hellenic civilization through the perspective of its art. He used the two Greek deities of art, Apollo and Dionysos, as natural foci for his thesis, claiming that they expressed a fundamental duality in Greek culture.[12] Apollo, the patron of form and limit, often opposed the chaotic creative and destructive drives associated with Dionysos. The result of this tension was positive: the Greeks synthesized these conflicting forces to make Attic tragedy, one of the highest forms of world art.[13]

For Nietzsche, Apollo was best represented by the dream, man's most effective producer of images. He was the deity of light, but he also ruled 'the beautiful appearance of the inner world of fantasy'.[14] His task was to give form and limit to this world. By imposing boundaries on the dream images, he preserved them from being pathological and maintained the order which was his characteristic: 'that measured limitation, that freedom from the wilder emotions, that wise calm of the god of images'.[15] In turn, Apolline order and emotional restraint guaranteed the integrity of man's individuality in the midst of life's chaos and terror. Apollo was, in fact, the divine image of the *principium individuationis*, the principle of individuation.[16]

German classicists had never underestimated the importance of Apollo for Hellenism. Prior to the publication of *The Birth of Tragedy* they had stressed the sober ordering of Greek culture; its 'noble simplicity, calm grandeur'[17] which Apollo represented. They had, however, neglected Dionysos. Nietzsche tried to overcome this neglect by showing that Dionysos had been as important as Apollo in the development of Greek culture.

In its natural state the Dionysian impulse was revealed in the terror and ecstasy occasioned by the breakdown of the principle of individuation. Its closest analogy was intoxication.[18] In this state the barriers between men and between men and nature were eliminated, and the world took on the aspect of primordial oneness:

Now all the rigid, hostile barriers which need, caprice or 'insolent fashion' have fixed between men are smashed. Now, with the gospel of the world harmony, everyone feels not only united, reconciled, merged with his neighbor, but one with him, as though the veil of Maya had been torn and only fluttered in tatters before the mysterious primordial One.[19]

Produced by this return to the primordial ground of existence, the Dionysian intoxication transcended all limits and negated separate individualities. Those swept up into this mystic rapture, though losing their separate identities, were redeemed by a mystical feeling of oneness with the larger whole.[20]

Nietzsche thought that the Apolline/Dionysian duality operated in nature herself. Artists of various cultures had chosen to imitate one of these natural powers in their art, either the Apolline order which supported individual existence or the Dionysian transcendence of all boundaries. Each culture then modified the basic principles as suited its genius. Because the Greeks could support the tension generated by the equal presence of both, their art had gone beyond that of other nations. At the same time, the Dionysian rites of Greece, because they were tempered with Apolline restraint, escaped the cruelty, licentiousness, and sensuality which characterized the Dionysian urge in other civilizations.

Apollo had restrained Dionysos. As the Dionysian impulse grew stronger, Apollo could no longer simply oppose it directly. Finally Apollo was reconciled with Dionysos, accepting his presence while being satisfied 'to take the destructive weapons out of his hands'.[21] For Nietzsche, this reconciliation was one of the most important moments in Greek culture. Though the distinctions between the two gods remained, the Dionysian rites were elevated from animalism to genuine art. By integrating these two conflicting urges the Greeks had attained a vision of the world which did justice to its horror and yet allowed them to affirm existence. The world of the eternally cheerful, clearly individualized Olympian gods, epitomized by Apollo, was erected on that of the eternally suffering, creative and destructive primordial unity, represented by Dionysos. The horror of existence awakened the Greek to nausea, yet he was not without metaphysical comfort. Believing that his deities participated in the pathos of existence themselves, the Greek was able to accept the world as worthwhile. He realized that existence was a dream based on cruelty and terror; but, fortified by the aesthetic world-view expressed through his religious forms and Attic tragedy, he had the strength to say to himself and to the world, 'I will dream on'. Dionysian religion and art thus embodied a powerful tragic perception of the nature of reality.

Nietzsche was not, in *The Birth of Tragedy*, trying to substitute the Greek gods for the Christian Trinity as actual ontological principles, though his preference was clearly with the former. Paganism taken literally would alienate man from his freedom as much as Christianity, though in a healthier direction. What Nietzsche wanted to do was to define the manner in which man might still satisfy the metaphysical urge apart from traditional religion. He wanted to mark out a world-view which would not invoke a false moralism for the universe. In his view those too weak to take existence 'straight', as it really was, used morality to impose on themselves and others a more comforting illusion. They tried to show that the world could be justified ethically 'in the long run', most often by holding out the promise of some post-mortem redress of grievances. Nietzsche rejected all such moralisms as mendacious. He insisted that the only legitimate way to conceive reality was to have the heroism to perceive it in all its amorality and meaninglessness and yet to celebrate it positively, even though it was but mere appearance. Thus he rejected traditional, ethically based metaphysics in favor of art as the appropriate way to situate oneself in the universe;[22] in his powerful and chilling words, 'Only as an aesthetic phenomenon is the existence of the world justified'.[23]

Clearly Nietzsche presented a radically new way of conducting the metaphysical enterprise. He had shifted metaphysics from the status of ultimate truth about changeless reality to the status of cultural product. Congruent with an emerging radical historicism and anticipating twentieth century cultural relativism, Nietzsche presented world views as part of the game of human cultures. He was obviously not trying to resuscitate older religious visions; in fact, his later philosophical works used his perspectival approach to truth to relativize away the old views. But in our context what is important is Nietzsche's portrayal of man as perpetually beset by questions of cosmic meaning. Nietzsche then interpreted Dionysos as the Hellenic embodiment of man's need for a profound perception of reality. Though his total philosophy was largely given over to the dissection of the hidden uses and dissemblings of ideology, *The Birth of Tragedy* was one of his most powerful acknowledgements of the power of ideology over the development of culture.

The Birth of Tragedy was icily received by classicists.[24] Rohde alone supported the work. However, direct evidence confirms that his support was not merely a reflex of loyalty but came from his agreement with Nietzsche's position.[25] In a letter to Nietzsche of April 22, 1871, *before* the publication of *The Birth of Tragedy*, Rohde enunciated several themes found in Nietzsche's work. Annoyed by Lobeck's lack of sympathy for the Dionysiac phenomenon, he complained,

How I despise this annoying Göttingen wisdom about the 'serenity of genuine Hellenism'. Dionysos had just as deep an influence as the 'Göttingen-enlightened' Apollo. Between Homer and Aeschylus there is a period of the deepest mystical excitement and a growing inner profundity of which the superficial clarity of the Alexandrian epoch has left very little. The serious natures of this unique populace never stooped to the superficiality of the modern, optimistic view of the obviousness (*Selbstverständlichkeit*) of the world and of the destiny of man.[26]

Within this statement there are three central points which show how Rohde's understanding of Greek culture paralleled Nietzsche's. First, Rohde rejected the concept of 'serenity' as insufficient for understanding Hellenic culture. This rejection implied that some deeper tension gave Greek civilization its strength. Second, having asserted that Dionysos was as important as Apollo, Rohde linked Dionysiac religion to the inner profundity of Greek ontology. Like Nietzsche, Rohde saw the Dionysiac mystical impulse as the ground for the creative tension of Hellenism, enriching its 'serenity' beyond superficiality. This positive evaluation of mysticism contrasts strongly with Rohde's later analysis of Bacchic mysticism in *Psyche* which treated it as a regression. Third, Rohde evaluated the clarity of the Alexandrian and modern periods as superficial compared to the vision attained by those whose world view acknowledged the Dionysian reality. Rohde judged the rational, scientific world view in which things become transparent to man's gaze as a symptom of intellectual poverty rather than as a deeper perception of reality.[27] At this stage in his career, Dionysiac religion represented a powerful metaphysical vision with its own abiding claim to truth, largely because it dared to look into the abyss without blinking. By the time he wrote *Psyche* Rohde's evaluation had changed.

As Rohde matured, he became increasingly critical of Schopenhauerian philosophy. It may well have been a heroic perception of reality, but its net effect was to paralyze a person into inaction. Even with a profound world view such as that of Schopenhauer, one was still left with the rest of one's life to spend. Also, there were genuine problems that needed to be addressed. One could acknowledge the chronic and seemingly incurable pain of the world and live in the shadow of this vision or one could choose to focus on the kinds of issues which could be improved. The older Rohde became, the more oppressive the first alternative became, until finally he opted for the second.[28]

Rohde was not only moving away from his youthful Romantic position; he was moving toward a new stance. His biographer Crusius states that early in the 1870's he discovered the English positivists, especially J. S. Mill and E. B. Tylor.[29] These men presented perspectives that allowed scholars like Rohde to see a different thread running through history than that presented by philosophers like Schopenhauer. Instead of centering on the inevitable defeat attached to the human condition, they focussed on the changes that the evolution of ideas and institutions had wrought. To be sure, one could point to problems which still existed and one might even be pessimistic about the future; but if one had eyes to see, it was clear enough that man had made substantial progress and could make more. It was more helpful to chronicle these advances and to indicate changes that needed to be made than to remain mired in a pessimistic world view. Ultimately, the clarity and logical rigor of the positivist evolutionist was preferable, even with its potential superficiality, to the obscure and unhappy profundities of the metaphysician.[30]

In Rohde's *Psyche* the influence of the positivists was stronger than that of Nietzsche or Schopenhauer. Once Rohde accepted the evolutionary position, his analysis of the nature of Greek religion changed accordingly. As we have seen, while he was under the influence of Schopenhauer and Nietzsche, he saw man's confrontation with the universe and the problem of meaning or the lack of it as a determining force in man's cultural creativity. Accordingly, he interpreted religion as the understandable response to metaphysical problems. The myths, rituals, and symbols constellating around Dionysos were the powerful, preconceptual embodiments of a dark but grandiose vision of existence. Under the influence of the evolutionists, Rohde would view man's voyage toward rationality, control of himself and his environment, and freedom from destructive natural and social constraints as the most legitimate human concerns. From this perspective, religion obstructed man's progress. Since human action should be directed towards rational ends, religion must have sprung from primitive man's insufficient attempts to achieve rationality.

THE EVOLUTIONARY POSITIVIST BACKGROUND OF ROHDE'S *Psyche*

Rohde apparently was never religious, in spite of the appreciation he showed for classical religion. Much like the young Nietzsche, he seems to have been attracted to Greek religion from aesthetic considerations. As he matured, even his aesthetic regard for religion paled before a growing interest in historical (and ultimately, causal) succession and the genesis of ideas and institutions.[31] This shift corresponded to a general transition in the social sciences and is best understood in terms of the emergence of evolutionary positivism as an interpretive paradigm.

Behind all the separate issues that the positivists addressed and behind all the arguments that divided positivists into factions stood one basic endeavor: the creation and elaboration of a science of man. The evolutionists continued the Enlightenment faith that man was part of the natural world and that, in principle at least, he could be analysed as part of that world. Therefore, rather than seeking the ways in which man appropriated what another perspective would call his freedom, they set about trying to chart scientifically the ways in which man had been shaped. The evolution of human cultures could, they argued, be studied in the same way as other phenomena. Conceiving of the human sciences as analogous to the natural sciences, they hoped to explain human cultures causally. This scientific, 'empirical' approach differed vastly from that which Rohde had been used to from German philosophy with its emphasis on philosophical introspection and *Verstehen*, empathic understanding from within.[32] The conceptual power of such an enterprise, if successful, is obviously enormous. Man might be understood in the same way as the shaping of the earth's crust or the formation of biological species. Once understood causally, the human world might be shaped in more humane directions.

The critical investigation of man was not merely an act of observation. By its very nature it also shaped the development of man as it attempted to explain this development. Looking at man as caused meant looking at his ideas and institutions as also caused. This would ultimately lead to the problem of wholesale relativism, but nineteenth century evolutionists saw the explanation of man as relativizing only the irrational and undesirable aspects of social life. As J. W. Burrow has pointed out, evolutionary social science was both relativist and non-relativist; it satisfied the late-nineteenth century's need to acknowledge the almost complete diversity of social patterns while still affirming the absolute validity of their own.[33] With considerable relish the evolutionists proposed to describe and explain the genealogy of traditions like religion which were not acceptable in the modern world; or at Tylor put it with mock sorrow, 'to expose the remains of crude old culture which have passed into harmful superstition, and to mark these out for destruction'.[34] What would remain would be a culture that truly served rather than oppressed man. Along the way, one of the chief things to go would be religion and the hurtful things—the fears, false hopes, the tyranny, and the irrational waste—imposed on men by the claims of 'revelation'.

Burrow has described the striking convergence of factors in the latter part of the nineteenth century which gave evolutionary anthropology and religious studies their prestige. In the realm of science a confluence of methods in several different disciplines gave evolutionism the status of a universal paradigm. Not only evolutionary biology but geology, paleontology, prehistoric archaeology, and comparative philology all effectively reconstructed bygone states by classifying remaining phenomena into stages and elaborating laws which governed each stage's succession by another.[35] Here was a model with which the scientist could explain man. Evolutionism provided the covering laws; the stages of development represented by the different cultures of which we have knowledge provided the antecedent conditions on which these laws operated. With the laws of development one could read backward through the evolutionary sequence until one arrived at the absolute origin of an idea or institution. Once one saw how a phenomenon originated (the ultimate antecedent condition) and what laws operated on it after its inception, one had achieved a total causal explanation.

Evolutionism not only presented a new and powerful paradigm for the understanding of social life; it also satisfied critical non-scientific needs of late nineteenth-century intellectuals. As mentioned earlier, it provided a stance with which Westerners could partially acknowledge the relativism of cultures while still having confidence in the validity of their own.[36] In a similar vein, it allowed scientists to reformulate the theory of the essential unity of mankind while taking into account the diversity of cultures. Differences could be acknowledged, but as merely different stages of a single process.[37] In this manner scientists could continue to believe in the possibility of a unified explanation of man. On a more existential level, it was not accidental that evolutionism prospered as traditional religious beliefs and classical utilitarian assumptions about the basic rationality of man were losing their credibility for growing numbers of people. Even as evolutionism contributed to undermining these old faiths, it also served as a replacement for them by reassuring men that prospects for the human situation were favorable, especially over the long haul.[38]

Finally, evolutionism presented men with the hope, in default of supernatural guidance, of a scientific basis for ethical and political views. Ever since the Enlightenment, the study of other cultural patterns had been used as a relativizing force to help free man from the yoke of the dominant Judeo-Christian world-view; but once this freedom had been attained, intellectuals were faced with the threat of total anarchy in the realm of values. A defensible hierarchy of cultural patterns would identify the highest form of ethical and political life and would thereby specify norms that were not arbitrary.[39] As Burrow points out, part of what lay behind the evolutionists' arrogant ethnocentrism was a genuine humanitarian zeal for improving the lot of man.[40] The evolutionists saw it as self-evident that innumerable social practices (and, it should be mentioned, not always those of other cultures) hurt people and were morally unacceptable. In retrospect it is, of course, clear that the norms for this value judgment came largely from unconscious allegiance to Christian ethics minus its theological justifications. Nevertheless, the point is that evolutionists wanted to provide some blueprint to bring all men closer to what they held to be a better life. Of course, evolutionism also appealed to darker strains of nineteenth century thought, justifying the exploitation of 'retrograde' cultures at the height of Western imperialism. Yet it is a mistake to view it as merely an ideology for exploitation. To a great extent it sprang from a kind of naive compassion on the part of Western theorists for people handicapped by a 'lower' form of culture. Needless to say, at the same time the West was elevating other cultures to its own level, it would also be getting the not inconsiderable satisfaction of having its own values justified.

It is against this background that evolutionary treatments of religion should be understood. E. B. Tylor's treatment of religion illustrates this trend quite helpfully, since his views had a predominant influence on Rohde's attempts to explain early religion. (There are, however, significant differences in the two men's views which demonstrate the ways in which Rohde maintained his independence from the evolutionary mode and remained in touch with his earlier understanding of religion.) For Tylor, the portrayal of the genealogy of religion was a major part of anthropology's role as a 'reformer's science'.[41] Religion was one of the superstitions whose destruction was marked out by the discoveries of anthropology. Rather than refuting it logically, one could destroy it simply by showing how religious beliefs originated in error.

The manner in which Tylor went about constructing this genealogy is revealing in its differences from the late Romantic approach just considered. At the basis of Tylor's analysis was the unproved assumption that in social evolution simple forms always preceded complex forms. (In retrospect, it is clear that the evolutionists' argument was circular on this point. Stages could be arranged that progressed from simple to complex; but lacking a verifiable history of development outside of the sphere of technology, evolutionists could only *assert* that these logical sequences corresponded to chronological succession.) As important, however, for Tylor's analysis as the hypothetical simple-to-complex schema were his assumptions about the nature of man and of human motivation.

Basically, Tylor continued the utilitarian model of man as one who acted out of self-interest in as rational a manner as was possible. He said little or nothing about man's susceptibility to the problem of meaning, of deep seated feelings, or of non-rational value judgments as a constitutive part of any society. For Tylor, man was a practical, thinking organism. Therefore, when a custom seemed to make no sense, the proper approach was to reconstruct the utility which its creators thought that it had. As Tylor said in his article 'The Religion of Savages', 'It is, I think, a principle to be held fast in studying the early history of our race, that we ought always to look for practical and intelligible motives for the habits and opinions we find existing in the world'.[42] This twofold nature of man—his practicality and his basic intelligibility—was the guide to understanding human action. As Tylor would say in *Religion in Primitive Culture*, the doctrines and rites of primitives were 'results of point-blank natural evidence [man as rational] and acts of straightforward practical purpose [man as practical]'.[43]

The combination of the assumption that man was basically a puzzler over natural data and a practical problem solver with the assumption that the simplest forms of these activities had been the earliest pre-disposed Tylor to view the creator of religion in a very different way than had the German Romantics. Unlike the latter, Tylor assumed that metaphysical activity was neither intelligible nor practical enough to have played a role in the origins of institutions, and he therefore read it out of the earliest stages of religion. In identifying the original stage of religion as animism, or the belief in spiritual beings, Tylor explained this belief as the result of primitive man's attempt to solve rationally a biological mystery. The mystery was real enough:

> In the first place, what is it that makes the difference between a living body and a dead one; what causes waking, sleep, trance, disease, death? In the second place, what are those human shapes which appear in dreams and visions?[44]

And the solution was also, at the primitive level of development, rational enough: 'the obvious inference that every man had two things belonging to him, namely a life and a phantom'.[45] The problem was not that man had been wasting his time in cosmic irrelevancies or that man had not been thinking as rationally as his condition permitted; the problem was that his fund of scientific experience had been too limited to allow a genuine solution to this genuine problem. Primitive man gave an occult explanation when a natural one was proper. At the time, though, he could not have known better. Later, his extrapolation from his fancied spirits and ghosts to grander but equally fancied deities was a result of a mental improvement, the growth of his ability to abstract. Thus the animistic philosophy which produced religion was a necessary stage in the intellectual evolution of man. It became problematic only when authentic science had advanced enough to render it superfluous and yet it refused to cede its ground and remained embedded in culture as a 'survival'.

Tylor is significant for our exposition because he, better than any other evolutionist, illustrates the positivist background on which the mature Rohde would come to draw in order to explain Dionysos. Like Tylor, Rohde would use the notion of 'survivals' both to uncover primitive levels of thought in the midst of more advanced cultures and to demonstrate the ultimate falsity of religion.[46] Rohde's appreciation of what religion meant for practitioners was richer than Tylor's, but he used the latter's interpretation to show how the entire process began from an error.

ROHDE'S MATURE INTERPRETATION OF DIONYSOS

Rohde's masterful treatment of Dionysos in the context of Greek religion came in his *Psyche. The Cult of Souls and Belief in Immortality among the Greeks.*[47] *Psyche*, as is obvious from its subtitle, analyzed Greek beliefs and practices concerning post-mortem existence.[48] Yet, although organized around a central theme, the book treated virtually every important issue in the area of Greek religion and may be taken as Rohde's final word on the subject.

The work was both a history and a scientific explanation. It was a history in the sense that Rohde took a bewildering number of facts and arranged them into a remarkably lucid account of the development of Greek religion while still managing to convey a sense of the individual integrity of specific movements. Also it was a history in the sense that Rohde used the facts of Hellenism itself to account for the changes in Greek religious beliefs rather than hypothetical sequences of development drawn from other disciplines.[49] Finally it was a history in the sense that it was an attempt to show what the interior, subjective reality of Greek religion had been like for those practicing it. On the other hand, *Psyche* was a scientific explanation in the sense that in a very unobtrusive fashion Rohde went beyond or, perhaps more accurately, behind Greek phenomena to anthropology in order to explain their origin.[50] It was a scientific explanation also in the sense that it took the hypothesis of a discipline (evolutionary anthropology) which had elaborated laws of human behavior and used that hypothesis to explain human action without attempting to justify that explanation in terms of what the actors thought they were doing.

In the academic context of its day *Psyche* was satisfying both as history and as scientific explanation. Rohde had mastered the facts and developments of Hellenic religion and presented them with a sensitivity that few scholars have ever matched. At the same time, he was extremely judicious in his use of the scientific paradigm supplied by evolutionary anthropology to explain the meaning of those religious facts. He selected the most reasonable and best established verdicts of evolutionary positivism; in applying them to Greek religion he never let them get in the way of his historical account. Unlike several classicists who became enamored with anthropology as a key to classical culture, Rohde used primitive parallels only to *explain* Greek facts, never to reconstruct their sequence. This restraint has lent the work a 'safe', seemingly unbiased quality; in reading *Psyche* classical scholars have not felt beset by implausible theories.

Yet it is impossible to read *Psyche* attentively and to miss the presence of a sophisticated frame of reference which Rohde used to make sense out of Greek religion. Because Rohde's primary concern was not to present a genealogy of religion as a total phenomenon, this presence was a quiet one; but ultimately it formed the structure of explanation for the entire work and for the analysis of Dionysos in particular.

Rohde's subject was Hellenic beliefs and practices relating to the *psyche*, what we may call 'the soul' if by that we are careful not to impose Christian values on this notion. Obviously a study of Greek beliefs about the soul has its own intrinsic interest. For a nineteenth century intellectual like Rohde such a study also offered the possibility to consider a more relevant question: how was it that certain ideologies concerning the nature of man and reality allowed people to value their existence in this world as the fundamental locus of enjoyment and meaning while others caused people to look on their lives with disregard, even contempt, and to long for another world? Religion was the chief cause of this disregard for present existence, though as Rohde showed with sophistication, different forms of religion evoked differing levels of world-negation. In terms of this question, the central focus of *Psyche* was the emergence of the belief in the immortality of the soul which opposed previous affirmative Hellenic views of reality and epitomized the world-denying direction of thought. Dionysos was the source for this hatred of life, though he was much more as well. In the main, Rohde would treat him as the furthest extension of certain primitive currents of thought related to pathological states of consciousness that resulted in the devaluation of ordinary, natural reality. The evolutionary framework would make possible not only the exposition of the origin of this fateful impulse but its exposure as based on a rather simple mistake as well.

Psyche is extraordinarily rich, however, and cannot be restricted to a genealogy of Greek religious beliefs. Rohde's brilliance lay in his ability to interweave several different types of analysis into the same narrative while maintaining firm control over his material.

This multi-layered quality of the work is both the envy and the despair of the expositor. The only way to convey intelligibly the richness of Rohde's interpretation is to break it down into four separate movements. Although this will sacrifice the unity of the original, it will facilitate systematic analysis of Rohde's hermeneutics. First, Rohde's basic identification of Dionysos as a problem in the Hellenic context will be presented. This will be followed by Rohde's description of how the worshippers of Dionysos understood the god. Rohde's explanation of Dionysiac religion from the perspective of modern science will be the third facet of this analysis, followed by his account of the modification of the extremes of Dionysian religion by the basically stable Greeks.

Dionysos was crucial in Rohde's history of Greek religion because he was a kind of storm center in Hellenic civilization. For Rohde, Dionysos was the great subverter of classicism. The true genius of Hellenic religion had come about through the Homeric revolution. The authors of the *Iliad* and the *Odyssey* had forgotten, ignored, or suppressed common primitive anxieties about the continued existence and power of the dead. Thereby they had successfully presented a new world-view in which man's allegiance was totally to the world of the living, its pleasures and glories. True existence depended on the combination of the body and the soul; once death occurred, the soul was essentially valueless. This judgment, while pessimistic about life after death, to a great extent freed Homeric man from the fears and hopes of some other existence and directed his attention to the perceptible world. This heroic vision had Rohde's obvious assent as an enlightened mode of religious thought. Yet the level of courage and intelligence had been too demanding for the entire Greek culture to sustain, and more superstitious elements began to work their way back into Hellenism.

As time passed, the influence of Homer slowly waned. People paid increasing attention to post-mortem possibilities and became more pious as a result. Still, throughout this development one aspect of the Homeric view was maintained: the distinction between god and man. To aspire to godhood was the worst sin in the Hellenic world. The great injunction 'Know thyself' meant 'Know that you are a mortal; content yourself with mortal pursuits'. The existence of an absolute boundary between divine and human meant that the Greeks lived in this world, not in the hope of another.

The introduction of Dionysos into Greece worked to change all this. As will be detailed later, Dionysiac religion resulted in the breakdown of the divine/human separation. The Dionysiac worshipper, once having experienced the possibility of transcending human limitations, could no longer remain satisfied with his incarnate life. The Dionysian vision presented a powerful opposition to the 'this-worldliness' of the original Hellenic religion by insinuating its own 'other-worldly' hopes into the Greek consciousness.

Rohde structured his analysis to show the opposition between Dionysiac religion and the original 'Hellenic' religion, of which Homer was the chief representative. There is little reason to suppose that he was merely elaborating the Nietzschean dichotomy between Dionysos and Apollo and that this opposition did not reflect his independent judgment. Nevertheless, one should note the interesting similarities between the two men's approaches to the basic opposition. Just as Nietzsche had presented Apollinian religion as the guarantor of limits and as the embodiment of the principle of individuation, so Rohde presented the original Hellenic pole of Greek religion as one which also watched over boundaries, in this case between the human sphere and the divine. Through its teachings man recognized that he was mortal and therefore identified his real self with his present individual embodiment. On the other side of the spectrum, just as Nietzsche had presented Dionysian religion as the breaker of boundaries and the force which dissolved individual forms into the primordial One, so Rohde presented Dionysian religion as the destroyer of the distinction between the human soul and divinity and the force which promised man unification with god in an eternal ecstasy.

The similarities of the two analyses are interesting; the differences are even more instructive. According to *The Birth of Tragedy*, Dionysos had been as necessary for Greek civilization as Apollo. It was the tension between these two aesthetic and philosophical principles that gave Hellenic culture its profundity. In Nietzsche's view, whatever the origin of Dionysos,[51] the Dionysiac spirit contributed to the ongoing creation and maintenance of authentic Hellenic culture. In *Psyche*, on the other hand, Rohde presented Dionysiac religion not as an integral component of Greek culture and religion but as a force which threatened to destroy an already formed Hellenism.

Nietzsche had presented only the way in which Dionysos shaped the Greek's conception of earthly existence and had not discussed Dionysos' role in thoughts about life after death. By so limiting himself, he was able in *The Birth of Tragedy* to present Dionysos as the source of tragic profundity in Greek art and thought and, in his later philosophical works to present the god as the source of the Greek's heroic 'yea-saying' to existence.[52] Yet, as Rohde was only too aware, Dionysos did more than simply awaken man to the tragic contradictions of earthly existence. He also had an immense role in creating notions of another existence where these contradictions would be abolished, and it would be an inadmissible restriction not to treat his connection with the belief in immortality. Dionysos may have been for some a stimulus for tragic heroism; for most he had been, at least as Rohde understood his original form, a stimulus for world-denial.

Yet, as far as the Greeks who worshipped him were concerned, Dionysos had not caused a flight *from* reality, but had made possible man's elevation *into* reality in its ultimate state. Rohde was aware of how much Dionysiac religion meant to those who had experienced the raptures of the cult. Accordingly, *Psyche* was, in part, a sensitive description of how the followers of Dionysos understood their god and their religion. Rohde was especially forceful in spelling out the inner logic of this religion that led its participants to believe in the immortality of the soul. Though it did not form the main body of his treatment, this presentation of the structure of the worshippers' subjective experience of Dionysos was a highly effective, if brief, use of interpretation by rearticulation and has earned Rohde classicists' enduring respect for his deep insight into the religion.

The distinctive feature of Dionysiac religion was, as Rohde pointed out, the elevation of the worshipper from everyday reality to a state of exaltation so intense that it was called a divine madness (mania), even by those sympathetic to it. In this state the self-conscious spirit of the votary was overwhelmed and possessed by the being of the god. Ordinary reality was momentarily suspended.[53] Understandably, we are limited in our knowledge of this fundamentally ineffable state to descriptions of what went on in the rites and to the testimony of the worshippers, but even these indirect documents evoke a sense of the power of this exaltation.

The externals of the cult itself were completely different from the

sober Homeric worship and entirely suited to dissolving the boundaries which restricted man to a knowledge of mere ordinary life.
Thoroughly unrestrained, orgiastic in character, the cult led the
participants to the extreme limits of their ordinary experience and
beyond. Rohde's description of the original Dionysian cult of
Thrace is unsurpassed:

> The festival was held on the mountain tops in the darkness of
> night amid the flickering and uncertain light of torches. The loud
> and troubled sound of music was heard; the clash of bronze
> cymbals; the dull thunderous roar of kettledrums; and through
> them all penetrated the 'maddening unison' of the deep-toned
> flute, whose soul Phrygian *aulêtai* had first waked to life. Excited
> by this wild music, the chorus of worshippers dance with shrill
> crying and jubilation. We hear nothing about singing: the violence
> of the dance left no breath for regular songs. These dances were
> something very different from the measured movement of the
> dance-step in which Homer's Greek advanced and turned about
> in the *Paian*. It was in frantic, whirling, headlong eddies and
> dance-circles that these inspired companies danced over the
> mountain slopes. They were mostly women who whirled round in
> these circular dances till the point of exhaustion was reached; they
> were strangely dressed; they wore *bassarai*, long flowing gar-
> ments, as it seems, stitched together out of fox-skins; over these
> were doeskins, and they even had horns fixed to their heads. Their
> hair was allowed to float in the wind; they carried snakes sacred to
> Sabazios in their hands and brandished daggers or else thyrsos-
> wands, the spear-points of which were concealed in ivy-leaves. In
> this fashion they raged wildly until every sense was wrought to the
> highest pitch of excitement, and in the 'sacred frenzy' they fell
> upon the beast selected as their victim and tore their captured
> prey limb from limb. Then with their teeth they seized the
> bleeding flesh and devoured it raw.[54]

Through this 'festival of fanatic enthusiasm' the participant underwent a tumultuous excitement unknown in his ordinary experience
and felt the presence of the god. In fact, he felt possessed by
Dionysos. Ultimately the ecstasy elevated him to a feeling of having
participated in the life of the god himself.

The religious impulse operating here was, Rohde believed, a
world-wide phenomenon which occurred at all levels of cultural

development. Dionysos was the god of mysticism among the Greeks and, before them, the Thracians. Throughout the world, mysticism was one of the most fundamental religious techniques to bring the soul into contact with divinity. The yearning to break down barriers and to unite one's being with god was found among certain types of people in all cultures. The mystical state satisfied this yearning. In it, where the conditions of normal life were abolished, the soul was considered to be moving independent of the body in the divine realm. The soul was in *ekstasis*, 'standing outside' the body; the person was filled with a god within, in *enthousiasmos*.[55]

Such was the emotional import of the Dionysiac experience. This mysticism, however, was not limited to emotions. An important set of beliefs grew logically out of the mystical experience wherever the latter was understood as an actual breakthrough to another level of existence. Throughout the world, where men experienced ecstatic raptures as a result of their religious rites, they believed that the soul was that part of their being which had been lifted up in the momentary transport. And when they believed this, they almost always believed that the soul has an independent life and power after it leaves the body. Rohde argued that mysticism and belief in the immortality of the soul occurred together again and again in widely divergent religions,[56] and that the case had been no different in Greece.

In the Hellenic view immortality was the paramount character of the gods and was reserved for them alone. One could even say that to be immortal and to be a god were one and the same thing, according to the Greeks. In the mainline popular religion this equivalence was but one further proof of the absolute barrier between mortal men and the immortal gods. Yet the Dionysiac religion represented a crack in this barrier. The worshipper of Dionysos experienced an ecstasy which convinced him that he or, rather, his soul had taken part in the joys and terrors of the divine existence and had been one with the god. Since the worshipper had experienced his soul as divine, the conclusion was obvious that it too must be immortal. The implications of this belief were profound. The Dionysian ecstasy made everyday existence seem drab by comparison. And when the mystic realized that, but for the body, the soul would be experiencing this ecstasy without interruption or end, he came to despise earthly life as a prison keeping him from a richer, truer reality. Quite naturally, he longed for release from this world.[57]

Such was Rohde's treatment of Dionysiac religion as it would have been perceived by a sympathetic Greek. He described both what happened externally and how the participants in the rites understood their own actions. Yet in his view one could not merely chronicle the Greeks' religious actions and their rationales. Interpretation required more. He felt that, as modern men, we needed to know *why* the Greeks believed what they did. Dionysiac religion, in Rohde's view, was not compatible with intelligible, legitimate human action. Therefore genuine understanding went beyond just identifying its presuppositions and perceiving its internal logic. Rohde, reflecting the high demands nineteenth century scientists were placing on themselves, sought a more complete explanation. What made the Greek think in this way? Why did he organize his world in such a manner? If there were some possibility that beliefs in another existence after death corresponded to reality, then the Dionysiac devaluation of this life might have been defensible. Yet in Rohde's view, there was no such possibility, and the world-denial had been indefensible. Faced with behavior which was incommensurate with modern conceptions of reality, Rohde felt the responsibility to explain it genealogically.

Evolutionary anthropology supplied the means to uncover the causes of this religious behavior which was so foreign to the modern view.[58] Greek civilization had obviously grown out of a more primitive matrix, and the origins of its religious beliefs and practices were to be sought there. Although not enough material existed from Greek prehistory to indicate the direct lines of development, anthropological accounts of contemporary primitive cultures presented parallels to the various stages of succession which must have taken place in prehistoric Greece. More importantly, evolutionary anthropology revealed the primitive logic which lay at the base of all religion. Dionysiac religion was to be understood as the working out of this primitive logic. Dionysos represented the most violent form of primitive fantasy, but the mental processes which produced him were operative already in generating even simpler forms.

Psyche presented an explicit genealogy of soul-beliefs but not of belief in Dionysos or the other Greek gods. For the latter we have to go to Rohde's short programmatic work, *Die Religion der Griechen.*

Here Rohde took three of the leading evolutionary hypotheses about the origin of religion and combined them as reflecting the earliest Greek religion. Surviving even into historical times, these primitive phenomena were (1) fetishism, (2) the belief in the mythological spirits of field, wood, river, and mountain, and (3) the cult of souls.[59] It seems to be only with further evolution that religion developed full-blown deities such as Dionysos. Even so, the logic that led the primitive to believe in gods was still rudimentary and deficient. As Rohde explained it, wherever the primitive confronted manifestations of independent inner life and movement in the natural world, he suspected the workings of invisible powers which he imagined as persons with souls and conscious wills much like his own.[60] Though Rohde never said so directly, it is clear from the direction of his argument that he understood Dionysos either as a later development of early soul belief or as a parallel elaboration of the animistic logic.

Thus it was Rohde's genetic account of how primitive man came to believe in the soul that held the key to the genealogy of Dionysos. Here Rohde's explanation conformed closely to that of E. B. Tylor and Herbert Spencer, who had concurrently developed similar animistic theories. The Greek's belief in the *Psyche* originally came from the primitive's perplexity at certain human states: death,[61] dreaming, swoons, and ecstasy.[62] Through what Spencer had called a 'fantastic logic', primitive man imagined that the moving force in these states was a second self with the same characteristics as a living person.[63] This logic was, of course, perceived as unnecessary and misleading by positivistic scientists, who understood themselves as offering demonstrably correct explanations for such biological and psychological states. They saw it as natural that in an age lacking such correct explanations, the Greeks were forced to rely on the idea of the *psyche* as 'the oldest primitive hypothesis'[64] for explaining these states.

This is a stock evolutionary positivist explanation. Confronted with peculiar empirical phenomena, the primitive felt compelled to explain them and fit them into his known world. He created this religious belief in order to attain cognitive control over his environment. Since the only way he, with his undeveloped science and intellect, could understand phenomena which seemed to act or move by themselves was by projecting his own nature onto them, he constructed an imaginary double of himself behind the natural world. Religion was, therefore, the product of ratiocination by a confused intellect. It temporarily served its purpose of satisfying man's curiosity, but it did this at the price of obscuring the true nature of reality and directing man's interest away from the empirical world to occult matters.

The specific belief in Dionysos also originated out of early man's attempt to understand a heightened emotional state. In carrying out the rites associated with this religion, the worshipper felt himself lifted up out of his ordinary self and merged with a larger power. According to the primitive hypothesis, whenever such psychological states seem beyond the control of the individual and he feels himself in the grip of an alien power, this power must be a divinity. Dionysos was the name the Greeks gave to this infusing power, just as Sabazios was its name in Thrace.

If primitive logic and its anthropomorphizing impulse caused early worshippers to believe in Dionysos in the first place, his existence was continually verified by experiences produced by his cult. In fact, one could even say that he was continually created by the cult. Unlike most of the other deities who were by nature distant from man and in a real sense owed their existence to man's extrapolation from natural events, Dionysos was a god who, in the ritual, descended upon his worshippers and lifted them to a higher yet palpable reality. Thus, Rohde, with fine psychological and ethnological acumen, looked to the nature of the Bacchic rites themselves for part of his explanation of Dionysos.

As he developed his account of how the actions of the cult produced the mystical effects, Rohde clearly stood in the materialist tradition. According to this perspective, increasingly important since the Enlightenment, man is a unitary being, not a duality of body and 'soul'.[65] Human consciousness (the mind) is inextricably related to and dependent on its organic base. Therefore, if the organism is put under certain extreme conditions, disruptions of the usual modes of perception can be expected to occur. This is exactly what had occurred in the Dionysiac cult. The ritual was organized so that the worshipper's exertions would culminate in mystical raptures associated with the presence of god. Rohde even asserted that the worshipper undertook these 'strange proceedings' expecting and intending that they should result in the ecstasy.[66] Thus the delirious whirl of the dance, the jerking of the head by the worshipper, the strange, disturbing music, the darkness, and the other circumstances of this frenetic worship, including, perhaps, intoxicants and narcotics, all stimulated the senses beyond the point where they could function properly. This excessive stimulation led suitably disposed people to visionary states in which they saw reality according to their fancies and imaginations.[67]

The Dionysian ecstasy was, thus, basically pathological, a state of hallucination and *alienatio mentis.*[68] For Rohde, Dionysos himself was, at least in part, the object of a hallucination. The beliefs about him have emerged from a state of temporary derangement which itself has resulted from violent ritual action. Implicit in Rohde's analysis is a causal hierarchy: physical activity produced emotional states which, in turn, produced ideology. This is the point of his comment that if we want to know why Dionysiac religion was attended by belief in immortality, we must look at the nature of the Bacchic cult rather than to what the Greeks believed about the nature of Dionysos. The ideology of immortality was produced by the cult and its attendant emotional exaltation, not by other religious beliefs.[69]

Rohde's sensitive treatment of Dionysiac religion has earned considerable acclaim; yet throughout *Psyche* there was a note of distaste for Dionysos.[70] The rantings of the cult, the conscious self-hypnosis of the votaries, all the excessive trappings of this religion—'strange and barbaric, attractive only through man's fascination with the shocking'[71]—these were realities too drenched in mystification and obscurantism for him to regard with disinterest. Yet unlike many of his contemporaries, Rohde consistently maintained an appreciation for the profound inner fulfillment which such a religious movement could bring its devotees. In his view the purpose of Dionysiac religion lay in the spiritual satisfaction which it produced.

Other scholars argued differently. According to the theory of animism, which Rohde himself used to explain why men believed in souls and gods, religion was primarily a way to account for otherwise inexplicable phenomena. Its appeal lay in its ability to help man structure empirical data more intelligibly. Rohde was also familiar with theories which explained cultic activity as designed to help nature in her fertility, yet he dismissed these explanations as unsatisfactory. In his view it was unnecessary to invoke any goal for the rites other than the pure exultation experienced in the mystical states themselves. Such ecstasies were their own reward, and religion fulfilled the expectations set for it by producing them.

Here Rohde was much more complex than most of his positivist colleagues. He basically agreed with them that religion originated out of fundamental needs; in this case a need for, let us call it, 'cognitive consonance'. Yet implicit in his analysis was an acknowledgment of the dialectical character of religious development. Whatever its origin, religion became 'functionally autonomous' at a certain point. Once religion had been set in motion with all its usual paraphernalia (gods, souls, etc.), it produced its own needs and offered its own satisfactions. The worshipper really did want to be with his god and took part in the cult for this reason. He may have been weak on epistemology, but he knew what he wanted and how to get it. On this point Rohde's analysis was richer than that of most theorists of his day. His approach allowed him to acknowledge the patent satisfactions of the religion while still withholding his assent.

Thus far we have discussed Rohde's interpretation of the Dionysiac phenomenon in general. The specific interaction between Dionysos and Greek culture formed a separate portion of his analysis. Essentially the significance of this interaction followed from the disparity between Hellenism and its surrounding cultures. One was not surprised at the presence of mystical currents in primitive societies at low levels of critical and scientific development. One expected something else from the Greeks. On this assumption Rohde devoted significant effort to explaining how Dionysos was able to gain entrance into Hellenic culture.

Here again the contrast with Nietzsche's analysis is illuminating. We have already noted how, for Nietzsche, Dionysos was a necessity for Greek civilization, whereas, for Rohde, he was a threat to it. Nietzsche had treated the opposition between Dionysos and the more rational side of Greek religion as an aesthetic and philosophical tension running through Hellenism. One of Rohde's most forceful strategies for demonstrating the threat Dionysos posed to Hellenism was to convert this opposition into an historical one. He argued that indeed there was an antagonism between the Hellenic 'firmly bound and regulated equilibrium of disposition and behavior' and the Dionysian 'extravagance of agitation'. However, this opposition was due not to the ongoing tension between equally strong competing urges but due to the fact that the second impulse had invaded the territory of the first. Dionysos had entered as something alien and had been integrated into Greek culture only after considerable resistance.[72] Accordingly, Rohde devoted a considerable portion of his analysis to proving that Dionysos came originally from Thrace. It is significant that the only chapter in *Psyche* to deal with a *non-Greek* phenomenon is Rohde's account of Dionysiac religion in its purest form ('Der *thrakische* Dionysosdienst').[73] This indicates how important it was to his interpretation to prove that Dionysos represented a foreign incursion. Dionysos was also the only deity to rate two chapters, and this too was not accidental. We have already seen the interpretation Rohde advanced in the chapter on the Thracian Dionysos. In a brief fashion he had attempted to portray the inner logic of Dionysiac worship by presenting the beliefs and practices of the religion and showing how they were interrelated and how they contributed to the belief in immortality. At the same time he had analyzed Dionysiac religion genetically, tracing the causes that allowed people to think and act as the Dionysiac votaries had. What was left for the chapter on 'Dionysiac religion in Greece' was to show how the Greeks *resisted* the alien incursion, how they *modified* it once it gained a foothold, and what *after-effects* its presence had on the original Hellenic religion.

Rohde's chapter on Dionysiac religion in Thrace advanced imposing evidence that Thrace had been the original home of the cult. He pointed out that the Greeks frequently testified to this origin of Dionysos themselves. Yet the question remained; why had the Greeks admitted Dionysos into their religious world? There were innumerable beliefs and customs from a multitude of surrounding cultures which never gained access to Greece. Why Dionysos? In Rohde's view, given modern knowledge of the Greeks' notion of balance and of human mortality, one would have expected them to have resisted such an unbounded and fanatical phenomenon. In fact, he argued, there appeared to be evidence of such a resistance. Certain myths telling of conflicts between Dionysos and mortals who refused to worship him and were punished for their impiety seemed to record an historical opposition to the incoming cult.[74]

Yet despite resistance, Dionysos swept into Hellenic culture. This leads us to the third facet of Rohde's genealogy of Dionysos. It will be remembered that Rohde derived the initial belief in deities from primitive logic. Constrained by this logic the primitive saw everything in terms of human parallels and therefore conceived of natural events as moved by occult but powerful wills similar to man's. In the case of Dionysos, this initial miscalculation was reinforced by a second-level origin: the existence of Dionysos was repeatedly confirmed by individual pathological states—hallucination and *alienatio mentis*. In addition to language of primitive mentality and psychological derangement Rohde used a third vocabulary to account for the spread of Dionysos, a primitive phenomenon, into a non-primitive culture. He explained this spread in the language of epidemiology: 'contagion', 'infection', 'epidemic', 'morbid susceptibility', 'constitutional weakness'. In *Die Religion der Griechen* he even spoke in terms of a transfusion of bad blood.[75]

The spread of the frenzied Bacchic religion had been due to a religious epidemic such as have occurred in modern times. As in the dance madness of the late Middle Ages, the epidemic had been carried by contagion.[76] Rohde wished to point to some historical condition that would have contributed to such a collective illness. Just as the medieval dance sickness followed the mental and physical shocks of the 'Black Death', so perhaps the spread of Dionysian religion had followed the disruption of spiritual equilibrium caused by the Doric migrations.[77]

Since Dionysos had won Greece by means of epidemic, the interpretation of his meaning for Hellenism was a special problem. In one way Dionysos was not alone in Greek history. There were other cultural forms which also came into Hellenism from the outside. Wherever the Greeks borrowed these cultural forms from other societies, one should ordinarily ask about the reason the Greeks would have wanted to borrow such conceptions from another people.[78] However, since Dionysos had been forced onto the Greeks like a disease on a people of weakened resistance, one would not discover his meaning for Hellenism by asking why the Greeks had willfully taken him into their religion. The real question was once he had been forced onto the Greeks, what did they do to *modify* the excesses of his worship? Hellenic religion showed its essential nature by moderating Dionysiac religion, not by accepting it.

Between the time Dionysos had first brought his frenzy to Greece and the time he was finally accepted as part of the Olympian pantheon, the Greeks changed him. 'His nature became hellenized and humanized'.[79] Cities and states celebrated yearly festivals for him as a calmer, more beneficent god: the giver of wine, the daimonic protector and promoter of all growth and prosperity in the plant world and in all of nature, the godly incarnation of the whole extent and richness of the natural fullness of life, the model of the heightened joy of life. His cult even gave stimulus to art, the highest flower of fortitude and life's high spirits.[80]

In Rohde's view this humanized and hellenized Dionysos demonstrated the molding power of Greek civilization. For the more rudely developed Thracians the god had fostered the impulse to transcend earthly life. Dionysos promised to help them get away from the sorrows of this worldly existence into the ecstasies of a divine life won after the separation of the soul from its sorry body. The fact that the Greeks could modify Dionysos from such a world-denying religious form into the incarnation of the fullness and joy of life shows what healthy instincts and power the original Hellenic culture had. Unlike the emotional longing for union with a world-denying religious form into the incarnation of the fullness and *this* world characterized the spirit of Greece and helped shape the newly arrived Dionysos into a more urbane deity. Yet other than noting this transformation of Dionysos, Rohde did not deal with the affirmative side of the Dionysiac cult. Naturally, given his interest in the belief in immortality, he did not have much time for this side of Dionysos, which in any case had not been original but taken over from the Greeks.

Notwithstanding the modification of Dionysos' nature, there still remained survivals of the old, more savage worship in Greece. His festivals in Athens may have been cheerfully celebrated in the daylight, but there were celebrations for Dionysos in the dark too, with mountaintop ragings, with the god in his primitive form as Lord of Spirits and souls, with human sacrifice and the frenzied devouring of animals raw—such traits as are preserved for us by Euripides' *Bacchae*.[81]

Because of the epidemic of Dionysiac religion which had flamed through Greece and still broke out in nocturnal festivals, there remained in the Greek nature, Rohde believed, a morbid predisposition, a tendency to temporary disturbances of the normal ability of

observations and perception. This explained the Greeks' susceptibility to the orgiastic worship of Kybele and to the continuing
enthusiastic worship of Dionysos. Yet the Greeks regulated the
Bacchic cult, and this fact set them apart from other cultures. In the
fully formed Greek cult the dark frenzy of the god was balanced by a
calming aspect; the soul was awakened to ecstasy under the touch of
Dionysos in his manifestation as the frenzied 'Bakcheus', but was
also stilled and made gentle by other manifestations of Dionysos—
as 'Lysios' (the 'Releaser') or 'Meilichios' (the 'Gentle One'). It had
taken conscious reform on the part of the Greeks to calm Dionysiac
religion in this way. Otherwise, it would have continued to rage
through Greece unchecked and destructive. It was only through the
exercise of the authentic Hellenic instincts as represented in Apollo
that Dionysos had been made more palatable to Greek taste.[82]

Rohde believed that it was through a reconciliation with Apollo
that Dionysos was tamed. The two gods seem to have entered into
an alliance at Delphi, where both deities received worship and
became increasingly alike. The fact that the Delphic cult to
Dionysos was milder and more well-mannered than the Thracian
rites also suggested that Dionysos was tranquilized at Delphi.[83]

Though Apolline religion, true to the more rational Hellenic
spirit, moderated the excesses of the Bacchic cult, Dionysos left his
mark on Greek religion and on Apollo himself. Eventually, the
Apolline cult took on a rather ecstatic, frenzied air. In particular,
Rohde argued, Apollo took over inspired prophecy from Dionysos.
Before, the Apolline seers had been trained to interpret external
signs as omens according to a developed, self-conscious technique.
Later, the prophets got their information directly from the god
through a state of ecstasy. Since this process was the form of
Dionysiac prophecy in Thrace, Rohde inferred that at Delphi
Dionysos must have given over this technique to Apollo.[84]

Rohde associated other non-rational phenomena with Dionysos.
Individual figures who in exalted states were lifted to the presence of
the god and could then speak as the deity's intermediaries are
preserved for us in the legendary forms of the Bakids and Sibyls.[85]
Superstitious cathartic purifications,[86] the irrational, cruel, and
gloomy worship of Hekate.[87] and 'divine' men such as Abaris,
Aristeas, Hermotimos, Epimenides, Pythagoras, and Pherekydes
who taught the separation of the soul from the body and ascetic

practices[88] all continued the dark, irrational, basically world-denying impulse initiated by the intrusion of Dionysos. By grouping these often divergent phenomena with Dionysos, Rohde had an effective way to explain their presence in Greek religion and to bolster his interpretation of Dionysos as the subverter of Greek civilization. By implication they also were alien intrusions, either direct offshoots of the Bacchic cult or similar to it in their unbridled irrationality and distance from genuine Hellenic order.

In the succeeding chapter Rohde turned to a phenomenon with indisputable ties to Dionysos: Orphism. Here we find the same richness of interpretation as encountered in his treatment of the initial Bacchic cult. Rohde presented Orphism in unusually lucid form, showing how beliefs about the nature of god, man, and existence grew directly and logically out of the myths told about Dionysos. This analysis is the most effective example of the interpretation by rearticulation in *Psyche*. Even if scholars have modified Rohde's interpretation because important critics have challenged our ability, given our spotty sources, to know anything really substantive about Orphism, the type of restructuring of the material to make sense out of its inner logic which Rohde offered at the end of the nineteenth century will always remain an effective model. However, just as in the case of the outdoor cults of Dionysos, Rohde, in analyzing Orphism, did not restrict himself to rearticulation. Here too he showed how the incoming impulse had to be modified to suit the more rational Greek temper.

Orphism represented the closest thing to a philosophical justification of world-denial that Dionysiac religion ever developed, although it was closer really to theosophy than to genuine philosophy. Taking the mythical accounts of Dionysos and his tragic murder, the Orphics constructed an anthropology and a scheme of salvation which revealed existence to be radically different than conceived by the 'common-sense view'. The material world was not what it seemed—the ambiguous, at worst, neutral arena of creation and human action. Rather, the world was a vast trap for the spirit. Human life as ordinarily experienced was the result of a tragedy which was at the same time a crime. It should be escaped.

The chief source for the mythology of Dionysos in the Orphic context was found in the Orphic 'Theogonies', poetic accounts of the early history of the gods. According to the basic form of the myth, after an initial succession of world-rulers, Zeus gave over the control of the world to Dionysos in his child form (usually called Zagreus in these myths). Evil Titans, the primordial antagonists of the gods, attacked the child Dionysos, who tried to escape by transforming himself into various creatures. His attempts to escape were in vain, and in the form of a bull he was torn apart by the Titans and eaten. His heart was rescued by Athena, and from it a new Dionysos was created. Enraged, Zeus slew the Titans with his lightning and created the race of men from their ashes. Thus, since the Titans were evil but had ingested part of the god Dionysos before being destroyed, the Ophics saw man as a creature predominantly evil (Titanic) but with a spark of the god buried within. If he purified himself of the Titanic nature through the sacred mysteries and by leading an ascetic 'Orphic life', then he could escape the painful wheel of birth and return to the god.[84]

Orphism was, for Rohde, the culmination of Dionysian world-denial. It also represented a new incursion of Dionysiac religion into Greece, unrelated to the earliest invasion. As such its presence in Greek religion had to be justified in much the same manner as the original cult. As Rohde explained it, the new wave of Bacchic interest may have been an ironic result of the humanizing and hellenizing transformation which Greek culture had worked on the original Dionysos. What the Hellenes would have viewed as reform, the Thracians would have judged as an emasculation of the real character of the cult, and they may have started a new private cult to rejuvenate the old religion. However, once again Greek modes of thought must have exercised a restraining hand and adapted the new impulse to Hellenic patterns. At that time mythological and primitive modes of thought were being converted into theosophy in preparation for the final transformation into authentic philosophy. This new Dionysiac impulse was swept along in this reformation but only attained the level of theosophy.[90] Orphism was one of the most impressive mystical movements in antiquity, but it was still grounded in a misapprehension of reality.

Clearly Rohde thought of Dionysos as a regression to primitive life and hence as a threat to the rationalistic, humanistic basis of Hellenism. Even the structure of *Psyche* suggested this regressive character of Dionysos. In Rohde's account, Greek culture knew two peaks of rationality and high civilization: the Homeric age and the era of emerging natural science and philosophy. Between these two peaks there emerged movements which were basically superstitious and world-denying and which reached their culmination in Dionysiac religion and its final product, Orphism. The philosophers and lay authors, who followed these mass movements based on superstition, reasserted concepts which did not rely so heavily on occult principles. The last section, dealing with the popular belief and its return to superstition, gave *Psyche* an interesting symmetry: two periods of humanism and rationality each followed by a period of regression.

Yet even though Rohde dealt with Dionysos as a primitive cultural form, his analysis was too rich to be labelled pure genealogy. In spite of the fact that he agreed with the evolutionary positivists in not attributing fundamental metaphysical concerns to primitive man, in dealing with Greek forms of Dionysiac religion he was sensitive to the metaphysical freight this religion had picked up in its passage through time. This allowed him to see the intrinsic rewards of mysticism and to bypass explaining Dionysiac religion as utilitarian activity designed to procure something objective.[91] Consequently *Psyche* presented a considerably more sophisticated picture of the mystical value of Dionysos than did many later expositions. Again, it is evident that it was the tension between the old hermeneutic supplied by late German Romanticism, with its interest in mysticism, world views, myths, and the like, and the newer evolutionary positivistic hermeneutic, with its emphasis on rational, utilitarian activity, which provided Rohde with his remarkable ability to deal with both the internal logic and the historical causation of Greek religion.

On balance though, Rohde's rearticulation of Dionysiac religion was secondary compared to his attempt to explain its origin causally. For the Greeks of the archaic and classical periods, Dionysos may have been an objective reality shaping the world in a certain direction through his strangely electrifying power. For the nineteenth-century classicist sensitive to metaphysical currents like the young Rohde, he may have been the cultural form used to express a certain perception of the world. Yet for the later Rohde, the author of *Psyche*, Dionysos was the figment of a primitive fantast trying to understand the world with inadequate means. As a figment of the imagination, Dionysos still had the subjective existence enjoyed by widely spread beliefs. His social reality was given further thickness when certain states of temporary madness were inter- preted as signs of his presence. Thus Dionysos was essentially a delusion produced by primitive logic and psychological derange- ment. In the Hellenic context, Dionysiac religion represented the intersection of these undeveloped and pathological thought forms with a civilization which would have been beyond such behavior except for an unfortunate susceptibility for culture-wide sickness.

This analysis was congruent with the main lines of evolutionary interpretation. Yet though Rohde shared common points with other evolutionists, he still maintained his own distinctive interpretation. To jump ahead for a moment, a brief comparison between Rohde and Jane Harrison, the subject of the next chapter, may suggest the commonalities and the differences.

Rohde and Harrison both recognized a certain provisory intelligi- bility in the Dionysiac cult, at least from the perspective of the Greeks themselves; yet the logic of their analyses led clearly to the conclusion that the beliefs associated with Dionysiac religion were false, as were those of all other religions. Both shared the same disparaging view of primitive mentality and its ability to deal with the real world. The predominant sentiment in the analyses of both was that religion had been the progressively additive and self- transforming conglomeration of imaginary fancies and attendant actions designed initially by man to help himself improve his position in the world. For both, the original referent of religion had been purely imaginary.

On the other hand, Rohde and Harrison differed entirely on what were the worthwhile features of Hellenic religion. Whereas the mature Rohde remained true to the prevailing German vision of Greece as a civilization of moderation, nobility, and rationality and therefore regarded Dionysos as a bane on Hellenism. Jane Harrison preferred the woolier, more lively aspects of Greek religion and accordingly always looked on Dionysos as her favorite deity. Whereas Rohde saw the goal of Bacchic religion as 'spiritual' satisfaction, Harrison saw it in terms of, first, material and, later, social benefits. There were other differences as well, as the following chapter will make clear.

The point to be stressed here is that although Rohde and other scholars to be treated in this study worked out of the same evolutionary hermeneutic, this does not mean that their interpretations were all copies of one another. The evolutionary model has been criticized for several things; disguising a priori assumptions as established fact, flattening out the image of man, and so on. One thing it should not be accused of is lack of creativity in advancing alternative interpretations within the same general paradigm. The example of Jane Harrison will show how exuberantly new anthropological theories continued to be welcomed among classicists well into the twentieth century.

3

Jane Ellen Harrison and the Study of Dionysos

Jane Harrison[1] was one of the most extraordinary figures in the history of classicism, a field that has had more than its share of extraordinary figures. A person of remarkable contrasts, she was or at least publicly claimed to be an atheist, yet at the same time saw herself as 'deeply, perhaps almost insanely religious'.[2] She claimed to be disgusted by the 'beastly devices of the heathen',[3] yet visited upon her readers primitive comparisons to classical phenomena in such loving detail and with such ill-disguised enthusiasm as to belie that claim. She acknowledged the superiority of advanced stages of evolution over simpler forms, yet clearly envied the 'protoplasmic fullness' of primitive culture. (She stated that the latter guarded an important and legitimate truth about life, though it was a truth which was falsified as soon as one tried to express it discursively.) Like all of the scholars examined here, she saw the study of Greek civilization as a morally engaged task which could aid man to achieve his humanity, but she surpassed all the others by far in her overt enthusiasm for classicism as a key to the understanding of man and for preliterate culture as a key to classicism. No other scholar ever sustained such a mood of rapt discovery in each of his scholarly works throughout an entire career.

Clearly prompted by a sense of mission, she spent her efforts and considerable abilities trying to get rid of belief in God while salvaging the worthwhile part of religion from both the false verbiage of the theologians and from the essentially correct but sometimes too rational criticism of evolutionists. In this mission her analysis of Dionysos served two functions. By showing the origin of religious beliefs in primitive mentality, it helped demonstrate why the language of theology should not be taken seriously. On the other hand, it preserved the legitimate dimension of religion by demonstrating that even when a genealogy of religion has exposed religious beliefs as false, there was still something that religion expresses about reality that helped man live more effectively. Like Rohde before her, Harrison was moved by a tension between two not easily reconciled allegiances.

Rohde's problem had not been a religious one. Whether as a romantic or as a positivist, he was convinced that religion was not an unambiguously authentic mode of being human. The major transformation which took place in his career involved the shift from a negative world-view to a stance toward existence which was no more religious but which allowed participation in and enjoyment of the world. Through his pessimistic world-view the young Rohde had achieved a vision of the ultimate scope of reality and acknowledged the pain at the heart of things. Two consequences followed from this stance. First, since this world-view was so important to Rohde himself, he recognized the importance of some sort of metaphysical position toward existence for all men. Even though Rohde's own universe was devoid of a sacred dimension, he still could understand what was at stake when a person took a religious stance toward reality. Accordingly, in his youth Rohde carried out interpretation primarily through rearticulation so that the internal logic of the religious position would be manifest. In this view, religion was an autonomous way of structuring reality so that the holiness at the horizon of existence made sense out of life as experienced. Religion was not pseudo-science or deluded utilitarian behavior.

The second consequence of Rohde's immersion in the pessimistic world-view was the one which caused problems and led him to modify his position. Recognition of the horror of existence made it difficult to think of the doings of men with any hope or confidence. From the perspective of religious nihilism, human progress was at best an anodyne rather than a cure. It was almost as if Rohde had to choose between the sweeping vision of cosmic misery and meaninglessness and the more narrow view of incremental improvement within a very strictly defined time span.

As we have seen, Rohde chose the latter. Turning from the total vision of existence to the history of human development meant an essential change in his hermeneutic. The origin of religion became the key to explain why religion existed in the modern world, and this origin was interpreted as part of the history of the incremental improvement of human life. In this case, religion was an attempt for

improvement which was inappropriate and which failed. Rearticulation became secondary for the mature Rohde; genealogy was the
fundamental explanation. By applying it, Rohde could show how
man had made false steps in his attempt to know and control his
environment. At the same time, by exposing the false basis of
certain contemporary beliefs and practices, which obscured the
nature of reality from man and bound him to non-rational behavior,
he could assist this process of knowledge and control in the modern
situation.

Jane Harrison was, at least on the overt level, even more ethically
committed than Rohde to using classicism to help man attain his
own humanity. Rohde's thought was so balanced and complex that
one has to read between the lines to see what moved him and how
his work was an ethical response to the nineteenth century situation.
With Harrison, it is totally otherwise. If anything, we suffer from an
embarras de richesse: tendentious pronouncements, programmatic
generalizations, heartfelt exhortations, and autobiographical claims
and confessions dot her writings and indicate quite explicitly her
hopes for a non-supernaturalistic religion. Perhaps because the
religious question meant more to her than to Rohde, she explained
much more fully what her scholarship implied for the contemporary
religious scene.

The mission which emerged with increasing clarity as Harrison
progressed was the twofold one of exposing theology as false while
preserving the authentic core of religion. As Harrison conceived it,
her first duty was to use evolutionary anthropology to unmask the
error which lay behind the concepts of religion. The need for this
unmasking came from the fact that people still believed the old
myths and were caught up in the old fears[4] in a time when such
thoughts were intellectually indefensible. Spelling out a long held
conviction in a late work, she contrasted *Dike* (in her presentation,
'Natural Order', the way things really are) with *Themis* ('Social
Order', the way man would like things to be, the way he tried to
regulate reality). Like Nietzsche before her, she proclaimed the
complete disregard of the Natural Order for the moral standards
embodied in human societies and puzzled over the question 'Why
does man make this strange confusion between moral right and
natural law'?[5]

The idea, the 'pathetic conviction'[6] that if man were morally good, he could affect the workings of nature for his own benefit was 'from the outset preposterous'.[7] The mystery for interpretation was why people believed such a doctrine? It was not only the insolubility of the problem of evil which caused Harrison to want to expose the erroneous foundation of theology. It was also the epistemological impossibility of knowing anything about the unknowable which mandated the unmasking of God and theology: 'God and reason are contradictory terms. . . . Theology is dying'.[8]

Harrison saw her own work as hastening that death.[9] It was her sense of the moral rightness of this intellectual euthanasia combined with her absolute confidence in the evolutionary perspective that led her to genealogy as the appropriate hermeneutic. If man's contemporary awareness of his epistemological limits meant that he could not know of the supernatural through his reason or his senses, then some sort of supernatural revelation was the only basis of a knowledge of God. Western religions claimed to possess such a revelation in their scriptures and extra-canonical tradition. But if these could be shown to be derived from mistakes, then man was free from theology and from God. Harrison spelled out the implications of evolutionary theory for the study of religion in an article in the Darwin memorial volume, and her statement summed up the presuppositions of the entire era.

> Psychology was henceforth to be based on 'the necessary acquirement of each mental capacity by gradation'. With these memorable words the door closes on the old and opens on a new horizon. The mental focus henceforth is not on the maintaining or refuting of an orthodoxy but on the genesis and evolution of a capacity, not on perfection but on process. Continuous evolution leaves no gap for revelation sudden and complete. We have henceforth to ask, not when was religion revealed or what was the revelation, but how did religious phenomena arise and develop. For an answer to this we turn with new and reverent eyes to study 'the heathen in his blindness' and the child 'born in sin'.[10]

As Harrison unfolded her argument, it was not because of their innocence or simplicity that savages and children served as the models for the original creators of religion but because of their affinity for delusion: 'The outcome of our examination of *origines* seems to be that religious phenomena result from two delusive processes—a delusion of the non-critical intellect, a delusion of the over-confident will'.[11] Here very explicitly one could see genealogy in the service of the god-killer.

Yet if the gods had to die, this did not mean that religion itself had to be totally eradicated. In fact, Harrison was explicit in saying that getting rid of theology and all its discursive attempts to define a supernatural power was an essential step for the contemporary religious person. As she said in an essay defining the relationship of religion and theology, 'if we are to keep our hold on religion, theology must go'.[12]

At this point one might ask, why retain religion at all? If it has lost its ability to pierce the veil of the unknown and bring back the truth about some supernatural dimension which will redeem the world's hurt, what good comes of preserving its external apparatus? Or, once one has shown that the creator of religion had been deluded, why pay him further attention? Harrison's arguments for maintaining religion after gutting theology were seldom clearly expressed or consistent, but basically they ran along the following lines: reason is not and can not be everything.[13] Even the genealogy of religion leaves some residue of authentic human behavior behind, and we need to understand this residue which transcends the causal explanation. Though theology inevitably spoils it, there is an aspect of religion which points to something real and greater than the individual. It is the source of our values and of our fulfilment as humans. It is other than science or reason and as such it cannot really be explained. Yet it can be pointed to as part of that which moves man in his rituals and other forms of religious behavior. For Harrison it was Dionysos more than any other god who embodied this truly religious dimension in Hellenism.

In her first major work, *Prolegomena to the Study of Greek Religion*, Harrison really had no way to integrate into her total analysis her conviction that religion expressed something genuinely important though not supernatural. *Prolegomena* was grounded in a thoroughgoing genealogy, and all those remarks which went beyond her demonstration that religion had begun in error essentially did no more than contradict the rest of the work. It was only when she became familiar with Bergson's notion of *durée* and Durkheim's understanding of religion as an expression of social forces that she acquired a method which logically entailed treating religion as encapsulating some obscurely felt but misformulated truth.[14] In

Themis her interpretation changed from genealogy to translation as she excavated the truth which stood behind religion. Shifting from Tylorian and Frazerian explanations based on the primitive's deficient mentality to an explanation which looked for those parts of life and human experience which called for expression in religion,[15] led her to recast her analysis of Greek as a whole and, in a very striking manner, of Dionysos in particular.

DIONYSOS IN HARRISON'S *Prolegomena*

Dionysos was the last major deity Harrison discussed in *Prolegomena to the Study of Greek Religion*. By the time she got to him, she had already presented the development of Greek religion from primitive antecedents and explained religion's general significance. However, Dionysos transcended her earlier explanation. Although he stood in the same current as the rest of religious forms, he, almost alone among all of the Greek deities, preserved something she considered to be *truly* religious. Therefore, in order to understand what Dionysos meant to Harrison in *Prolegomena*, one must do two things: first, analyse him in terms of the general development of the gods and, second, show how he retained a religious element which the other Greek deities lost. The first of these procedures involves explicitly applying the genealogy Harrison used on divinities in general to Dionysos.[16]

Whereas Rohde had singled out Dionysos' mystical rites and his connection with post-mortem conceptions, in *Prolegomena* Harrison focused on his connections with intoxicating drinks and the life of nature.[17] This shift in the subject matter was related to her choice of a new model of explanation. Ideological components of religion such as doctrines of immortality were not her primary interest, largely because she took religion itself to be basically concerned with securing more favorable physical conditions in this life. She therefore organized her analysis to show how Dionysos was thought to ameliorate these conditions.

Harrison based her reconstruction of religion on the model that James George Frazer had begun to elaborate in the first two editions of *The Golden Bough*.[18] Frazer's influence led Harrison to interpret Dionysos as a mythical being who had originated out of magical thought and who was worshipped in the hope that he would improve man's material condition. Based on this evolutionistic blueprint, Harrison's interpretation then involved digging back behind the evolution of Greek religion until she reached its initial stage. This stage would demonstrate what the original creators of magic and religion thought they were doing and why. Even more fully than Rohde, Harrison utilized primitive logic to clarify the essential strangeness of original magico-religious thought.

Much of the first part of Harrison's treatment of Dionysos, like that of Rohde, was concerned to show that Dionysos was a foreign deity derived from Thrace.[19] The question then arose as to why the Greeks had accepted him into their pantheon. Here Harrison differed strongly from Rohde who had explained the god's victory as an epidemic. In Harrison's view, the Greeks had accepted Dionysos into their culture because of his associations with wine.[20] In Greece, as in all traditional cultures, a new, incoming plant was always attached to some mythological figure.[21] Dionysos had been the patron of the grape and therefore won a place in Greek civilization.[22] Yet Dionysos was more than the alleged mythical patron of the grape. He also was the spirit which invaded the consciousness of the intoxicated. Harrison argued that primitive man inevitably interpreted inebriation as possession by some outside force, by some god. 'All intense sorrow or joy is to him obsession, possession'.[23] Due to the primitive's inability to conceptualize strong emotions in a naturalistic way, he explained them as supernatural.[24]

As important as intoxication was to Dionysos, it was not his only association. 'There go to his making not only this distinctive element of intoxication but certain other primitive factors common to the gods of other peoples'.[25] These other factors involved Dionysos' character as a god of the impulse of life within nature. Two aspects of the worship of Dionysos showed this connection most clearly: his worship as a tree god and his worship as a bull.[26]

If the belief that intoxication is produced by divine possession came from primitive logic, conceptions of Dionysos as a tree-god were more primitive still. As a tree (Dendrites), Dionysos 'is but a step back from the familiar canonical Vine-god'.[27] Primitive mentality needed a way to account for the life in growing things and Dionysos supplied a seemingly viable explanation. He was first related to all growing things, but eventually the realm of his vegetative associations became more circumscribed, and he was connected exclusively with trees and the vine.[28] He was also associated with animal life and was even thought of as a bull, an identification which Harrison felt was even more primitive than his connection with plant life.[29]

In the case of Dionysos as tree and as bull, interpretation involved understanding primitive logic. As will be explained in more detail later, Harrison held that savage logic led the primitive to make his spirits and deities in his own image. Dionysos in the form of a tree or a bull only seemed to contradict this law. In seeing Dionysos as tree and as bull, the early worshippers were indeed portraying him in their own image of themselves. The reason the god was not seen as human, Harrison argued, was that early man still had not realized that he was different from plants and non-human animals. 'Man when he worships a bull or tree has not, even to himself, consciously emerged as human. He is still to his own thinking brother of plants and animals'.[30] In this primal confusion the primitive Greek worshipper supplicated Dionysos for material blessings.

Primitive logic also explained the ritual of the omophagia, the raw flesh feast in which the worshippers slew and ate a bull. The worshippers thought that by performing the omophagia they would gain the bull's fertile powers. Harrison based her interpretation on Robertson Smith's explanation of 'St. Nilus' camel':[31] 'The idea that by eating an animal you absorb its qualities is too obvious a piece of savage logic to need detailed illustration ... the educated and even priestly Greek had not advanced beyond this stage of sympathetic magic'.[32] The original intent of the rite, therefore, was magical and utilitarian. Later it was spiritualized into a means for entering into mystical communion with the deity.

For Harrison the only way to understand the meaning of Dionysos as wine, tree, or bull god was to see the *process* which led the Greeks to project supernatural spirits onto the canopy of natural events. In her analysis this process, the evolution of religion, had a kaleidoscopic quality. Conceptions sprang up out of primitive thought, were refined, transmuted, outgrown, and abandoned. Each stage was followed by a successor, which also went through the same development. In this maelstrom of change, any particular phenomenon found its meaning in terms of its relation to preceding and succeeding stages. It is this 'dynamic' quality of Harrison's treatment which accounts for the peculiarity of her treatment of Dionysos and of Greek religion in *Prolegomena*.

Prolegomena is peculiar in that it diverged radically from the usual conception of classical scholarship. In it evolutionism took over completely as the guiding thread. Whereas Rohde had used evolutionary anthropology to explain ostensibly unintelligible beliefs and practices that clustered around Dionysos, his reconstruction of the progression of Greek soul-beliefs followed long-established historical methods. With Jane Harrison it was otherwise. She used primitive parallels not only to provide a context by which otherwise incomprehensible phenomena might be understood but also to reconstruct the development of Greek religion as it had occurred *in the prehistoric period*.[33] For her the truth of the evolutionary paradigm was an established fact; all that was left was to apply the findings of evolutionary anthropologists to classical culture. She believed that the necessary laws of development hypothesized for primitive religion held good for higher civilizations as well, and on the basis of these necessary laws, she presented Greek religion as passing through each major stage of evolution. This hypothetical development then became virtually the whole of her explanation. Dionysos (and every other fact of Greek religion) was to be understood in terms of his place in this evolution.

Harrison depended so heavily on evolutionism that, the general theory of the evolution of primitive religion having been overturned, her analysis has lost most if not all of its cogency. Thus, Harrison's works today are much more dated than, for example, Rohde's. Harrison may have sensed this herself, for she seized passionately on each new development in the human sciences relevant for the study of religion and pressed it into service. The age in which she wrote was one of great ferment for religious studies, and in her productive lifetime she discovered and adopted in succession the theories of Max Müller, E. B. Tylor, J. G. Frazer, Emile Durkheim, and Sigmund Freud.[34] As a result, to read her oeuvre in chronological order is almost like reading a multivolume history of the discipline of comparative religion disguised as a series of histories of Greek religion.[35]

Within this series, *Prolegomena* represents Harrison's 'Frazer phase'. Frazer's theory of magic as the basis of religion provided her with the leitmotif for her first massive treatment of the evolution of

Greek religion. She used this theory to argue that the beliefs and practices of archaic and classical times existed because of the material advantages they were supposed to secure. She could now make sense out of the entire structure of Greek religion by showing how early man's practical desire to improve his lot had led to an erroneous stance toward the world and how this stance had been modified and 'improved' to a point of high aesthetic if not philosophical sophistication.

Once again the comparison is useful between Harrison and Rohde, this time in connection with the evolutionary models which they used. Although they were alike in attributing the origin of religion to the mistakes of primitive mentality, the model of man which each presupposed was different. Rohde portrayed primitive man as extrapolating from his own subjective experience and thereby postulating a second world behind the natural world, a world in which souls and spirits and gods all operated with conscious wills to help shape the course of events. Primitive man thus thought of himself as imbedded in a community of consciousnesses ranging from sub-human to the super-human levels. Although these spiritual figures were later supposed to be useful to man in his daily life, at their origin they had been hypothesized in order to account for seemingly mysterious states and events rather than for any practical reason.

Using the Frazerian model, Harrison saw man as from the start more practical and in many ways more scientific. In Frazer's account the magical stage of thought operated with a basically naturalistic theory:

> It assumes that in nature one event follows another necessarily and invariably without the intervention of any spiritual or personal agency. Thus its fundamental conception is identical with that of modern science; underlying the whole system is faith, implicit but real and firm, in the order and uniformity of nature.[36]

In accordance with this theory the earliest magico-religious action had been a direct manipulation of nature to compel her to deliver man's wants. Primitive man had not appealed reverently to a god, nor, in fact, to a soul or spirit. He had seen himself as alone in the universe with a traditional technology (magic) which he confidently believed would bring him what he wanted.

In Frazer's theory magic resulted from a basic error: the misapplication of the association of ideas. Primitive man, associating things which were similar, identified as literally the same those things which, in fact, only resembled one another. Thinking they were the same and that like produced like, he attempted to produce the desired effect simply by imitating it; for example, harming the image of an enemy in order to harm the enemy himself ('imitative' or 'homoeopathic' magic). Through another error, associating things which have been in contact with one another, the primitive thought that the two things once in contact would continue to act on each other even despite physical distance; for example, the destruction of a person's hair or nail clippings in order to harm the person himself ('contagious' magic).[37] These errors were rudimentary but corresponded to the primitive level of mental development. As man became more knowledgeable, he discovered that magical associations were only subjective and that magic did not work. In despair, but knowing that something must control the world, he invented supernatural beings who were thought to have wills like his own and to rule nature. Hoping to please these imaginary forces in order to gain his desires, he supplicated them in reverent worship, and created traditional religion. Eventually, he recognized that religion was just as inefficient as magic and turned his energies to science.

According to this view, man is motivated by fundamental needs (basically food and sex), and in primitive times all human actions were oriented toward their satisfaction. Operating with this anthropological model, Harrison saw no need to interpret religious phenomena as primitive substitutes for poetry or philosophy; she could explain them quite adequately as the results of man's search for a fuller, richer material life. At the beginning man had no need to communicate with a wider being or to explain to himself impressive natural or biological phenomena; he had more essential things to do. He might invent gods later to help him attain his goals, but he had no need for them as long as magic seemed satisfactory. Consequently, Dionysos was a later development in religion and could be understood only as a transition product of primitive thought. The beliefs and rituals which centered around Dionysos emerged only as early man developed intellectually.

Harrison called Dionysos a *daimōn*. A *daimōn*, as she used the term, was a mythical being who had evolved out of impersonal, pre-deistic forces and had acquired the rudiments of a personality but who had not crystallized into a full-blown god. As a mental product, a *daimōn* represented a significant advance over magical thought and the turbid, fearful emotions engendered by this thought. It was, however, still allied with magic, since the primitive thinker looked to it to provide a supernatural solution for his problems.

Harrison organized the entire first half of *Prolegomena* so as to demonstrate that the earliest Greek religion had been magical and that *daimones* and gods were only later accretions.[38] Noting the difference between chthonic gods (gods of the earth of which Dionysos was a prominent example) and Olympic gods (heavenly deities), she attempted to demonstrate that the former cult chronologically preceded the latter[39] and that originally it consisted entirely of magical practices designed to drive away evil.[40] In her reconstruction, the earliest Greeks believed that they lived in a world filled primarily with evil and destructive forces[41] and that the only way to deal with these forces was to compel them through magic to go away. To a lesser extent they thought that they could activate helpful forces and constrain the earth to be fertile through sympathetic magic, but predominantly they used rites of purification and expulsion (apotropaic rites) to get rid of the evil. These rites concerned no deities or even *daimones* but were pure magic— 'ceremonies of *aversion* based on ignorance and fear'.[42] Parallel to the impersonal evils to be averted were ghosts which needed to be placated, and rituals to eliminate them were also based on ignorance and fear.

As the Greeks progressed, they began to personify the physical evils and to create rudimentary mythical (supernatural) beings.[43] In the same process, they came to focus more and more on the beneficent side of existence, and this eventually led them to practice reverent worship of kindly beings as much as magical placation and expulsion of destructive forces. As Harrison summed up this development, 'To mark the transition from rites of compulsion to rites of supplication and consequent thanksgiving is to read the whole religious history of primitive man'.[44] As the Greeks grew in the ability to think abstractly, to personify, and to classify, the mythical beings passed from sprites to *daimones* to gods. This shift—apotropaic magic to worship and service of the gods—took centuries to accomplish,[45] and ironically it carried within it the seeds of religion's destruction. As the major deities became increasingly glorious and urbane, they seemed to be unapproachable by man and accordingly lost all religious importance. Eventually they became merely the 'lovely dreams' of the Greek, 'playthings of his happy childhood'.[46]

Harrison's genealogy of religion out of magic served to expose Greek religion as false. She had argued that religion began in error and that belief in gods was merely the refinement of this error rather than a legitimate conception. Throughout the evolution of religion, man had tried to gain practical benefit from these imagined powers, changing his religious conceptions whenever newer beliefs seemed to answer his needs more efficiently.[47] *Daimones*, gods, and the entire panoply of mythical beings had been but later additions to an original core, itself based on mistaken logic.

Dionysos was to be understood in the same manner. His associations with trees, vines, and animals were not important as symbolic expressions of his nature but as indications of the primitive's inability to classify properly and to distinguish between essentially incommensurable categories. Most of the conceptions and practices centered around Dionysos were basically magical in intent and designed to help man attain health and wealth.

Other conceptions and practices, rather than being reflections of the original magical stage, represented later stages in the evolution of religion. For example, the conception of the Maenads as nurses tending Dionysos as a baby in his cradle (Dionysos Liknites) reflected a primitive matriarchal stage of society in which Dionysos was naturally seen as the son of his mother.[48] As civilization advanced, matriarchy gave way to patriarchy, and Dionysos was given new attendants and a new patrimony. The myth in which Dionysos was carried first in the womb of Semele, his mother, and then in the thigh of Zeus, from which he was eventually born, reflected the social shift in which the Father became predominant over the Mother.[49] In a similar manner Dionysos' supernatural attendants (the Maenads, Satyrs, and Kouretes) represented mythicized portrayals of the original historical worshippers.[50] Thus, in addition to showing how the Greeks conceived of Dionysos as a magical power within nature which could be compelled or supplicated to provide benefits, facts about Dionysos also preserved evidence about social development in Greece.

Dionysos was Harrison's favorite deity, and in him she saw more than the simple product of magical thought reformulated. Because of his nature he occupied a special place in the evolution of Greek religion. On the one hand, as a mental creation, he had progressed beyond the magical stage and attained personality. On the other hand, the Greeks had not 'crystallized' his nature into the aesthetically pleasing but religiously desiccated form of an Olympian deity. He had remained at the 'chthonic' level, the stage where *daimones* and gods stayed in touch with their worshippers, shared their life, and 'worked' for them, and at this level he preserved the truly religious impulse.[51] Coming from the more primitive culture of Thrace, his religion broke in on the Greeks at a time when their early cults had been superseded and the ruling Olympian religion had become moribund. The Greeks themselves had become weary of analytical clarity and welcomed Dionysos as the harbinger of 'a "return to nature", a breaking of bonds and limitations and crystallizations, a desire for the life rather of the emotions than of the reason, a recrudescence it may be of animal passions'.[52] They still expected him to deliver magical benefits, but they relished equally the thrill of escaping the tiresome bonds of civilization.

Dionysos represented even more than the release from conventions; he represented 'an impulse really religious' as over and against other mythical figures.[53] This 'really religious' quality sprang partly from the emotional nearness of Dionysos to his worshippers, but it derived more from the fact that Dionysos actually pointed to a genuinely mysterious element of life rather than being simply a spirit of magic or a projected supernatural man. For Harrison, the true mysteries of life were what Murray had called 'Things which Are', the things in which man sees himself lost to a larger life. Dionysiac religion and its Orphic reform were the currents in Hellenism which gave access to these true mysteries. Like Eros, Dionysos was a spirit of 'Life and of Life's ecstasy'.[54] The Orphic reform took the crude primitiveness out of Dionysiac religion by spiritualizing the Bacchic intoxication and by ennobling the idea of god and man, but it preserved the authentic religious kernel present within Dionysiac religion. 'The religion of Orpheus *is* religious in the sense that it is the worship of the real mysteries of life, of potencies (δαίμονες) rather than personal gods (θεοί); it is the worship of life itself in its supreme mysteries of ecstasy and love'.[55]

From *Prolegomena* it is not clear exactly what Harrison meant by this allegedly mysterious quality of life. Obviously it meant something to her, but she never explained its place in the total context of her analysis.[56] *Prolegomena* evidently began as a genealogy of Greek religion out of magic,[57] and only as Harrison worked on Dionysos and Orphism did she add the positive evaluation of religion as the expression of mysterious potencies. Later, in *Themis* she would use ideas of Bergson and Durkheim to show the truth expressed behind religion, but in *Prolegomena* her brief attempts to translate religion into some legitimate expression merely interrupted what otherwise was a consistent genealogy. Harrison seems to have tried to mesh together two not easily reconciled interpretations: Dionysos as a fantasy figure thought by his worshippers to confer material blessings and Dionysos as a symbol of life itself.[58]

In the context of *Prolegomena* as a whole one fact stood out: religious conceptions and practices were conditioned by the needs and situation of the worshipper. Needs for food, shelter, and sex plus major intellectual limitations gave rise to magic as man's first technology. Improvement in man's intellect and in his physical situation led to the creation of mythical beings and, eventually, gods. Dionysos too was shaped by the needs and circumstances of the Greeks. As long as mechanical magical techniques sufficed, the Greeks did without him. Once they had emerged from the purely magical stage into a more animistic level, they began to conceptualize him in their own image. As long as they had not realized their own distinctness from plants and animals, they portrayed him in the form of plants and animals; once they had perceived their own human uniqueness, they conceived him as human. His nature changed as their social structure changed. Under the matriarchy, he was Son of the Mother; under the patriarchy, Son of the Father. Throughout the shifting conceptions, they offered him sacrifice and worship because they thought that he would satisfy their need for the continued fertility of man and nature and for joyous intoxication and respite from sorrows through 'possession'. Sometimes they used frankly magical means, such as the omophagia or the liknon[59] to attain these ends; at other times they relied on reverent supplication. When they had forgotten the original reason for a ceremony, they made up reasons and added to the store of his myths.[60] Half-

remembered historical facts about his origin and his original worshippers also were transmuted into myth and further elaborated his
portrait. Yet no matter how complex Greek conceptions about him
grew, the essential fact was that he was an imaginary creation of
men who were trying to deal with practical problems but laboring
under erroneous thought patterns. Only with Harrison's shift to
another mode of analysis would Dionysos emerge as the Greeks'
most profound expression of man's self-transcendence in the other.

Dionysos in Harrison's *Themis*

Prolegomena grew out of the productive ferment of late nineteenth
century British evolutionism. Harrison published it in 1903, a tour
de force of massive erudition and enthusiastic speculation that
would have satisfied lesser scholars as the capstone of their careers.
Yet before the end of the decade she had encountered and adopted
a new method, the sociological evolutionism of the great French
theorist Emile Durkheim. She greeted the new approach as revolutionary, as indeed it was, and attempted to use it to rewrite
completely the history of Greek religion, showing the latter's origin
out of social processes.[61] In the years after 1909 she labored on this
project and in a surprisingly short time produced another *magnum
opus* on the same scale as *Prolegomena*. In 1912, the year that
Durkheim's *The Elementary Forms of the Religious Life* first appeared in France, she brought out her own application of Durkheim's theory, *Themis. A Study of the Social Origins of Greek
Religion*, and inaugurated a new approach for British classicism.[62]

As in the case of the other works considered here, *Themis* is best
understood as a reaction and a contribution to a new interpretation
of cultural products. *Prolegomena* had followed the evolutionary
positivists' refinement of the utilitarian model of man. Since man
was practical and, where possible, rational, one understood human
action by looking at the thought processes which fueled the vast
engine of human civilization. Where man thought well, civilization
progressed at respectable speed; where the logic was faulty or the
cognitive data insufficient, civilization sputtered and coughed and
sometimes did not advance at all. In this basically intellectualist or
mentalist conception of the moving force behind human behavior,

religion and magic, because intellectually indefensible, had the status of 'clinkers' in the fuelbox. 'Intelligible' behavior corresponded to what Pareto would later call 'logico-experimental' behavior, behavior which was rational and purposive in the utilitarian, scientific sense. Religion was unintelligible, based on error, and thus had to be treated genealogically.

There were always people who objected to this too intellectualist portrayal of man. Most of these, however, also objected to the effort to study man exhaustively in a scientific way, that is, to explain him as moved by causes. At the end of the nineteenth century, a profound shift began in the human sciences, motivated by the criticisms of the positivist vision as too intellectualist. This shift was to strengthen the possibility of a total science of man and make objections to the superficiality of scientific analyses harder to maintain. In the 1890's several important thinkers from diverse fields began independently to explain human behavior in terms of non-rational factors. Something beside reason fueled the machine; but (and here is where they diverged from the more conservative critics of positivism) *this something could be analyzed scientifically.* That which was 'below' reason, like reason itself, seemed to have its own 'logic', in the sense that actions driven by non-rational forces followed certain regular patterns, which lent themselves to theoretical generalizations. Laws seemed to apply to non-rational behavior as to the rest of the natural world so that what had been thought of as irrational in the sense of 'random' and 'free' now came to be viewed as but a complex extension of the causal chain. This conceptual revolution had the effect of 'thickening' man, of drawing a model of human nature in which more than rational instrumental thought went into the determination of any particular action. Theorists such as Freud, Marx, Pareto, and the mature Nietzsche argued (and, many felt, demonstrated) that motivational forces deeper than conscious thought were at the base of human action and culture. These forces—techno-economic determinants and psychological and biological drives—shaped human action; conscious thought was a later rationalization. Therefore, the way to understand culture was not to examine it in terms of its intellectual propositions but in terms of these infra-intellectual forces. Religious studies followed the same reaction against 'intellectualist' interpretations. The earliest shift occurred with R. R. Marett's identification of 'mana' as the basic element in religion, even before spiritual beings. Harrison was to be deeply influenced by Marett's claim that emotion was the well-spring of religious life.

Durkheim belonged to this new orientation, but he brought an important difference in perspective to his interpretation of culture. This difference can be summed up in his assertion that society is a *sui generis* reality. In his view, human reality certainly had a biological and a psychological foundation, but it was not exhausted on these levels. Because man lives in groups and externalizes his thoughts, desires, and emotions in ways that communicate them to others, a new reality is created: the social fact. Rules, values, beliefs, knowledge, indeed whatever may be considered as part of culture as opposed to man's biologically inherited endowment, all are produced through the collective interaction of men living in society. More important, once created they are present to man with the same denseness as physical data; they have their own external facticity and can be transmitted to others. Indeed, when the society is functioning efficiently, they can be *imposed* on others, not as propaganda or as a possible orientation to the world, but as the inevitable shape of reality. The total social environment surrounds man, and he, in his development, internalizes that part of this environment which will represent reality to him. Without consciously realizing it, man takes in part of the social order and makes it part of his own being. In so doing, man makes himself double; in addition to the individual nature composed of organic drives and processes, there is also his social nature, locus of his moral and intellectual life. Because of this duality, culture cannot be exhaustively understood, as previous thinkers had suggested, as the result of individual, instrumental behavior.

> This duality of our nature has as its consequence in the practical order, the irreducibility of a moral idea to a utilitarian motive, and in the order of thought, the irreducibility of reason to individual experience. In so far as he belongs to society, the individual transcends himself, both when he thinks and when he acts.[63]

Thus there is operative in human action something more than either practical rational thought or the subrational drives of the organism. The vast network of social facts existing in the consciousness and conscience of each participant also provides motive power for human behavior. Internalized social values, knowledge, etc. *con-*

strain man to act in certain ways and, as determinants, are just as powerful as are biological drives. In submitting to social constraints and in experiencing moments of 'effervescence' in the collectivity, man participates in a scientifically verifiable transpersonal reality and achieves the transcendence mentioned above.

For Durkheim, religion was the most profound and, at the same time, the most transparent manifestation of this *conscience collective*. It was not based on an error or lie but expressed its own truth. Interpretation was then a matter of finding the truth enclosed in religion and making it intelligible.

Doubtless, when one considers only the letter of the formulae, these religious beliefs and practices sometimes seem disconcerting; and one may be tempted to attribute them to a kind of deep-seated aberration. But it is necessary to know how to arrive at the reality beneath the symbol which the symbol represents and which gives the symbol its real significance. The most barbarous and bizarre rites and strangest myths express (*traduisent*) some human need, some aspect of life, be it individual or social. The reasons which the believer gives to himself to justify them may be, and in most cases even are, erroneous; nevertheless true reasons do exist. It is the concern of science to discover them.[64]

Eventually, in *The Elementary Forms of Religious Life* Durkheim would translate God as 'society', and claim that religious rites are really celebrations of the collectivity and its ideals.

Harrison took over from Durkheim the belief that religion had grown directly out of collective experience, that is, collective feeling and collective thinking, and that mythical beings—gods and *daimones*—were but ritual groups projected. Unlike *Prolegomena*, *Themis* did not expose religion as merely the result of erroneous thought patterns but as the result of legitimate emotions which had been objectified in such a way that each member of the community could participate in and embody them. On the level of human action, *Themis* presented religion as an acceptable expression of authentic human urges. Religion's theoretical superstructure obscured the reality behind it, but with proper methods one could penetrate behind this veil and uncover the truth which was expressed so confusedly. In this process of interpretation, Dionysos was crucial because 'nowhere so clearly as in the religion of Dionysos do we see the steps of the making of the god'.[65]

If *Prolegomena* had ignored many of the tenets of traditional historiography, *Themis* abandoned virtually all that remained. Again Harrison presented her analysis as a history of Greek religion, but even more insistently she modelled this history on an evolutionary scheme. Therefore, the chronology in *Themis* had virtually nothing to do with the dates of classical materials and was purely a function of 'parallels' she found between Hellenic data and the changing stages of primitive religion. Her presentation essentially was that of an 'ideal' development of Greek religion; the 'stages' described in *Themis* have struck most classicists as having little relationship to accepted chronologies, but Harrison seemed convinced that they were arranged in the proper 'logical' order.[66] Arranging events in terms of a hypothetical 'logical' order rather than in terms of history meant that whereas Dionysos had been the last god analyzed in *Prolegomena*, he was the first to be treated in *Themis*. Since he supposedly represented the clearest example of the origin of a god, Harrison simply omitted any discussion of his relatively late intrusion into Greece as an alien deity.

The change wrought by Harrison's shift in methods was thorough-going. Out of the vast and often contradictory evidence about Dionysiac religion she focused on new materials for her analysis. She continued to explain the prehistoric Greeks in terms of primitive mentality, but her image of the primitive mind changed to fit the new sociological paradigm. Ultimately, on the basis of new facts and a different understanding of the moving forces of human action, she produced a new image of Dionysos.

In *Prolegomena* she had seen the keynote of early religion as magical exorcism based on ignorance and fear, a mentally guided activity undertaken by individuals trying to control their world through pseudo-scientific means. In *Themis* the keynote of religion became collective emotion. As she later specified, *Themis* was 'in a word a study of herd-suggestion, or, as we now put it, communal psychology'.[67] Dionysos, accordingly, was now seen as the projection of authentic social realities. To be sure, early man, in confronting basic biological drives, especially hunger, had used rituals which were unscientific and, thus, inappropriate for manipulating the natural world. Nevertheless, the collective expression of the feelings and desires served a purpose other than the acquisition of food-stuffs; it served to solidify the identity of the group as an integral unit. By sharing his emotions with others, early man participated in a reality deeper than his own individual life, a reality which he would come to institutionalize through the process of initiations. Religion was inefficient as technology, but it was indispensable for social identity. Dionysos had been the earliest and the most legitimate representation of that identity for the Greeks. Among the social processes which led the Greeks to invent him, initiation had played the most important role. As a result, one of Dionysos' most important functions was to symbolize the group of initiates (and their emotions and drives) to themselves. Yet before they invented Dionysos, the Greeks had to pass through stages in which an intense emotional activity was only slowly supplemented with an intellectual dimension. Like *Prolegomena*, *Themis* portrayed Dionysos as a middling stage in the evolution of religion and explicable only in terms of his antecedents.

Harrison portrayed primitive man confronting essentially the same physical situation in *Themis* as in *Prolegomena*. He was faced with the fundamental problems of sustaining life; he needed food, protection from an often hostile nature, and other basic necessities. What distinguished *Themis* from *Prolegomena* was the way Harrison portrayed primitive man as meeting these needs. Where in *Prolegomena* Harrison had talked about the 'haze' of primitive thought, she had meant that it was muddle-headed but, except for its inexperience and its penchant for false associations, basically similar to modern analytical thought.[68] In *Themis* she treated the haze of early thought as a function of the primitive's social emotion.[69] Whenever primitive man gathered in groups, he became very excited, and affective states dominated analytical thought. 'Herd-suggestion' was at the basis of religious behavior, not erroneous ratiocination.

For primitive man, then, the basic problems of life had not been occasions for reflection but for tension and terror. This tension and terror elicited vivid reactions; the primitive had to express (in the cathartic sense of 'press out') these emotions in motor activity, which, once socialized, became ritual. 'Tension finds relief in excited movement; you dance and leap for fear, for joy, for sheer psychological relief. It is this excited doing, this dancing, that is the very kernel of both drama and dromenon', (i.e., ritual).[70]

Though she was not always consistent on this point, Harrison distinguished specifically religious emotion from emotion in general by stating that the former was always characterized by 'sacredness' or sanctity. The 'sacred' was made up of two essential components: awe and power.[71] A social dimension also seems to have been essential: the seed of religion was not the awe of the individual but collective awe, 'qualified by a sort of social sanction'.[72] Indeed, it seems that the individual at this stage of mental development did not yet have a separate identity and could deal with reality only as part of a non-differentiated collectivity:

> First, primitive man, submerged in his own reactions and activities, does not clearly distinguish himself as subject from the objects to which he reacts, and therefore has but slight consciousness of his own separate soul and hence no power to project it into 'animated nature'.... Second, man felt himself at first not as a personality separate from other persons, but as the warm excited center of a group . . .[73]

Early man felt himself real only when he participated in a collectivity, and it was the emotions experienced in such a state that formed the basis for religion. When these emotions were projected into external nature, the 'sacred' came into being.[74] Eventually all mythical beings would be projected out of these initial group emotions.

As described in *Themis*, religion originated more legitimately than as described in *Prolegomena*. According to the earlier work, the primitive, faced with a practical problem, had thought up the wrong solution; religion had been abortive from the beginning. According to *Themis*, the initial aspect of religion—the powerful emotions of anxiety—were appropriate to the primitive situation. By his vigorous activity primitive man had found an effective way to express these emotions and gain relief from them. Thus far, primitive religion had been acceptable. However, because his emotions overwhelmed his reason, he reified the former and mistakenly gave the status of reality to this new imaginary construct (the sacred; later, daimones and gods). By projecting his emotions onto external nature he transgressed the bounds of legitimate expression and began his concern with a false 'knowledge'. This reification had been the first step in creating the ideology of religion with which theologians would exercise themselves so fruitlessly for so many centuries.

From this point religion became increasingly distinct and rational. As primitive man evolved, he generalized the individual experiences of sacred power or *mana* into a continuum which he thought existed throughout all nature. Within this continuum magic and mysticism were supposed to take place. Because practically all of his thoughts were undifferentiated, the primitive did not distinguish himself from other beings. As a result he pictured himself as brother to certain plants and animals or as a plant or animal himself. Harrison identified virtually every association between gods and the biological realm as evidence for what anthropologists had classified as totemism, arguing that the latter was 'a phase or stage of collective thinking through which the human mind is bound to pass'.[75] According to Harrison, in this phase of deep feeling and wooly thinking, primitive man had acted out the roles of plants and animals which he needed for survival; he had 'participated' in the life of these beings so as to insure their abundance. Once he finally came to distinguish between himself and them, he recognized that he was not, say, an ostrich but only *imitating* one. From this realization came the invention of imitative magic, a higher stage than pure totemism.[76] Magical rituals then provided many of the social occasions from which deities would be invented.

As had been the case with *Prolegomena*, *Themis* was based on pure assertion. Harrison provided no evidence for her conclusions except primitive parallels. As before, her analysis is convincing only if one has a firm faith in the evolutionary model. For this faith one must accept three fundamental assumptions for which she offered no support: (1) that the sequence of development postulated by the evolutionists[77] reflects the evolution of religion from its origin to the present, (2) that the explanations offered by the evolutionists for the various rites and beliefs do correspond with the actual reasons these beliefs were held and these practices were carried out, and (3) that the primitive phenomena are relevant for the Hellenic material. Since all three of these presuppositions can quite legitimately be challenged, *Themis* is perhaps best categorized as a 'just-so-story', to use E. E. Evans–Pritchard's apt phrase.

Nevertheless, within the limitations of the genre, Harrison did offer some new arguments and a few very suggestive scenarios of how Dionysiac religion developed. Up to this point we have seen how collective emotion produced collective representations (such as mana, totemism, and magic) and essential social rituals through which man could act out these representations. According to *Themis*, Dionysos emerged out of the confluence of fundamental social practices—magic rites, sacrifice, and initiation—and the ill-defined collective representations centering around the sacred.

The ritual of initiation was the first process which Harrison discussed as creating Dionysos and the other Greek deities. Initiation was a basic part of primitive life since it was the means by which the child was socialized and received a larger identity as part of the tribe, the ancestral community, and totemic life in general. What happened to this straightforward social act to turn it into a religious act was fairly simple and seemed to have arisen naturally and inevitably out of the primitive situation in the normal course of evolution. The actors in the initiation ceremony were, obviously, human; yet due to the emotional power of the roles and the presumed power of magic, along with the repetition of the rite, the actors were turned into mythical figures.

> Gradually the chorus loses all sense that the god is themselves, he is utterly projected. . . . Strong emotion collectively experienced begets this illusion of objective reality; each worshipper is conscious of something in his emotion not himself, stronger than himself. He does not know it is the force of collective suggestion, he calls it a god.[78]

Dionysos was then the projection of the group's emotional unity during the initiation ceremony.[79]

Harrison organized most of her exposition of Dionysos on this basis. She questioned extant material not to find out what the Greeks thought they were doing but to answer what to her was the more profound question of what it all meant at the beginning. Conceptions about Dionysos had emerged out of social practices; but, as time passed, people had forgotten about this. Therefore, Harrison's task was to organize facts of Dionysiac religion to show their connections with these alleged primordial initiation rites. In accordance with this perspective she offered a new theory of the myth of Dionysos' double birth. She relegated the explanation put forward in *Prolegomena* that the myth represented the shift from matriarchy to patriarchy to the status of partial but inadequate truth. Now she interpreted the myth as reflecting a tribal rite of initiation, with rites of both infancy and adolescence intermixed.[80]

The blasting of Dionysos' mother, Semele, by the lightning of Zeus reflected an initiation of the child by fire for purification and strengthening,[81] while the passing of the child from mother to father reflected the adolescent's initiatory rebirth from the childhood world of his mother to the mature world of his father.[82]

Harrison acknowledged that this theory that initiation practices stood behind Greek religion had some weaknesses. The 'Hymn of the Kouretes' discovered at Palaikastro portrayed Zeus as a child attended by mythical guardians, but it did not present his death, dismemberment, and subsequent revivification as would be called for by the hypothetical initiatory pattern.[83] Therefore Harrison had to go to the Zagreus myth in which the infant Dionysos was devoured by the Titans in order to flesh out the pattern. Thus, the hypothesis depended rather heavily on establishing that the various phenomena of Dionysiac religion reflected initiation. But then how did one explain the fact that the ritual congregation (the *thiasos*) from which Dionysos was supposedly projected was made up of women? 'How can a thiasos of young women project a young male god'?[84] Harrison responded with her customary ingenuity, but her answer was not particularly compelling. She argued that such a projection occurred because the religion of the female thiasos was the religion of the Mother and the Child. The Maenads were the projected mothers and therefore nurses of the child; Dionysos was the child.[85]

Even if one were to accept the argument that the religion encompasses both mother and child, one would still be left with the question of what role the actual human child played in the hypothetical initiation. If it is 'manifest that Dionysos is but his thiasos incarnate',[86] then Harrison should have pointed to some evidence of an actual initiation involving a child in some way. Yet she never did.

Harrison's account of the origin of Dionysos was nothing if not multifaceted. She postulated not only initiation as the occasion for inventing Dionysos but sacrifice as well. She considered the Bacchic omophagia or raw flesh feast the prototype of all sacrament and sacrifice,[87] and the most instructive place to see the god emerging. Originally the Greek ate the sacrificial bull not to please some supernatural being but to obtain the bull's *mana*. Since the early Greek thought totemistically, he saw no barriers to acquiring the strength of an entirely different form of life. All he had to do was eat it and its mana became his. Yet in devouring the slain beast, the members of the group had been swept away with powerful collective emotions. It was at this point that Harrison offered one of the most delightfully improbable explanations in all of evolutionary theory: meat, for those who rarely eat it, 'has the effect of a mild intoxicant'[88] and therefore caused the Greek to think that he was possessed by some vague external sanctity. The end result of the collective emotions experienced during the rite was that the slain animal was 'sanctified, sacrificed, then divinized'[89] and Greek religion gained a new mythical figure added to its stock: Dionysos Tauromorphos, Dionysos in the form of a bull.

The sociological perspective influenced Harrison's total interpretation of Dionysiac religion. Whereas in *Prolegomena* Harrison had identified Dionysos' connection with intoxication as one of the most important features of his cult and, indeed, the reason the Greeks accepted him into their pantheon, in *Themis* she almost never mentioned his connection with alcoholic beverages. Instead, the emotional frenzy required to generate the idea of Dionysos was supposed to have come from the 'intoxication' of collective emotion in ritual. Given the prominence ordinary intoxication achieved in her early explanations, its relative absence in *Themis* is striking testimony to how much the new model had shaped her focus.

We have seen enough of her method of analysis to step back and examine some of its implications. The most original part of *Themis* was its fully developed myth and ritual hypothesis. The basic idea of this thesis was that mythical figures arose from rituals which had come to be misunderstood or changed. Harrison, with her customary lack of consistency, phrased the hypothesis much more blandly (and more defensibly) in certain programmatic statements but then contradicted those pronouncements in her actual explanations. Her first statement on the subject asserted that ritual was not prior to myth but that they arose together, one expressing emotions in action, the other in words.[90] However, as soon as she began describing the origin of religion, it was clear that she saw myth as only secondary in terms of both chronology and importance.[91] Every mythical being that she described was supposed to have been a projection of the actors of a ritual group.[92] The conclusion is inescapable that the main thrust of *Themis* was to show that myths were secondary and that gods arose out of rituals which had produced such intense emotions that the participants created stories about supernatural beings to account for their own temporary exaltation. Therefore, as in *Prolegomena*, *Themis* involved a genealogy of religious *conceptions* out of error. The difference between the two works was that, in asserting the priority of ritual to myth, Harrison had a basis for claiming that the ritual itself was not necessarily tied to specious ideas and may have expressed authentic human feelings.

In Harrison's view there were a number of things which primitive Greek man needed to express: his social identity, his deep emotions, and the dramatic process of yearly renewal which he saw and felt within and around him. Dionysos expressed these realities better than any other deity. Because Dionysos kept his link with his thiasos (the group of his worshippers), he showed the collective nature of early religion and demonstrated transcendence through social participation. Because his cult retained the dimension of genuine ecstasy, he was the Greek's access to an emotional richness (again connected to social reality) otherwise unavailable. And as the clearest example of what Harrison called the 'Eniautos Daimon',[93] Dionysos also expressed the universal yearly cycle of decay, death, and renewal, which took place not only in the natural world but in initiation as well. More than anything else this cycle of decay, death, and renewal was what lay behind the ritual and the subsequent mythical pattern of separation, killing and dismemberment, and revivification and reappearance. Since Dionysos preserved the elements of this pattern more clearly than any other god, he was the best example of the initial phases in the making of a god. Harrison believed that other gods had once conformed to the same pattern but had evolved into more static and eventually sterile religious forms. The history of Greek religion after Dionysos was the story of its progressive individualizing and rationalizing. Other gods withdrew from the cyclical growth and decay and achieved luminous personalities that remained the same, supposedly for all eternity. They grew increasingly distant from the lives and concerns of the people who had invented them, until they were eventually devoid of all but aesthetic content. They became 'gods' in the strict sense of the term, the playthings of theologians.

Dionysos, on the other hand, kept the fluidity and the emotional substance of a daimon, not yet ossified into an Olympian. Harrison explained what this quality of Dionysos meant in considerable detail in a work entitled *Alpha and Omega*, written three years after *Themis* but from the same perspective. According to this work, Dionysiac religion was 'aneikonic' in spirit; that is, it did not attempt to define the unknowable dimension but rather respected its otherness. Eikonic thought as represented by the rationalized Olympian stratum of Greek religion thoroughly defined the unknown and unknowable realm (which, by definition, is impossible in any legitimate sense) and therefore led to theology and other forms of false knowledge. Because Dionysiac religion did not make such unreasonable claims, it retained an appropriately vague and ever-changing character and represented a legitimate traffic with the unknown realm. It leaned towards more emotional impulses, towards immanence, mystical submergence in the other,[94] and monotheism and pantheism (in the sense of non-definite world-spirits as opposed to the well defined individualized figures of polytheism).[95] Dionysos was a 'life spirit', one of the 'Things that Are' in that he represented the mysterious force of the universe.[96] On the psychological level, he expressed subconscious urges which made for fusion, union, emotion, and ecstasy, as opposed to the conscious urges toward individualization and analysis.[97]

It is clear that Harrison had expanded the bounds of the positivist interpretation to the breaking point with this new dimension in her interpretation. Here she asserted, now in congruence with the bulk of her actual analysis in *Themis*, that there was a larger whole to which religion referred. The referent was not supernatural as the theologians would have it, yet it did transcend what was attainable by the analytical, discursive intellect. This intuitively sensed force which ran through the world of life[98] could find expression only through some sort of ritual action. Beneath all the false theological aspects associated with Dionysos, Harrison saw a legitimate truth: Dionysos represented the Greek's 'instinctive attempt to express what Professor Bergson calls *durée*, that life which is one, indivisible and yet ceaselessly changing',[99] Dionysiac religion was the way in which the Greek participated in this indivisible universal life.

According to Harrison's analysis, this life was most richly experienced in its social aspect; Durkheim rules the pages of *Themis* much more than does Bergson. All in all Harrison portrayed Dionysos more as the expression of social emotions than of the 'unknown'. In a 1913 article, 'Unanimism and Conversion', she expressed this judgment more forcefully than she had in *Themis*: at its beginning religion 'is not the aspiration of the individual soul after a god, or after the unknown, or after the infinite; rather it is the expression, utterance, projection of the emotion, the desire of a group'.[100] Religious conversion represented the socialization of the individual spirit;[101] conversion was 'not to God, but to your fellow-man'.[102] According to this view, Dionysos represented not an image of magical fantasy but the rich social matrix in which a person might find a larger life.

The relationship of *Themis* to *Prolegomena* is more complex than this last single dichotomy. Both works shared a basic evolutionary perspective that gave them an important solidarity. For example, in both works primitive mentality accounted for the differences between the 'primitive Greek' world-view and that of modern man. In both works gods were merely the outcome of a certain phase of primitive thought and not an essential part of religion.[103] Both works also portrayed the Greeks as, at some point in their development, thinking that religion was of practical use.

Once these commonalities are recognized, the importance of Harrison's shift from genealogy to translation is more evident. In both of these methods the basic presupposition is that the supernatural beings which the Greeks worshipped were not credible enough to justify religion as a human activity. The distinction between genealogy and translation is that where the former attempts to debunk religion by showing its mistaken foundation, the latter attempts to find some natural reality to which it refers and therefore to distil the legitimate aspect of religion from the illegitimate. In the present context this shift meant that for Harrison it was no longer adequate to interpret Dionysiac religion as pseudo-utilitarian behavior. To be sure, primitive naiveté did enter at a certain point, taking the authentic expression of emotion and trying to apply that to alter the world for man's benefit. Nevertheless, the original kernel of Dionysiac religion had represented something considerably more intelligible. As long as the projection of the collective emotion remained amorphous and indistinct, Dionysos represented the genuine expression of the larger social unity through which each worshipper found his greatest sense of reality. It was only when he was taken seriously as a supernatural figure independent of the emotions of his worshippers that he lost his justification for existence. Once the Greeks thought of him as separate from the collective emotion, they appealed to him for what he could provide them in material benefits. In so doing, they turned religion into the same kind of pseudo-scientific behavior that Harrison had portrayed in *Prolegomena*. Harrison's interpretation in *Themis* attempted to restore the authenticity to Dionysiac religion which it had lost in assuming the trappings of traditional theology. In this sense, even though *Themis* discredited belief in supernatural beings, Harrison saw the work as a religious testimony. In later works she attempted to integrate yet more evolutionary methods into her continuing analysis, but she never again devoted so much time to the religious significance of Dionysos, nor did she maintain the already modest level of consistency found in *Themis*.[104] *Themis* was her most original work and her greatest contribution to classical religious scholarship.

SOME CONCLUDING REMARKS ON JANE HARRISON

What are we today to make of Jane Harrison? As a human being she was one of the most arresting figures of her era, blending erudition, passion for the discovery and dissemination of new knowledge, and willingness to make bold hypotheses into works which bear the most personal stamp in all of classical studies. Yet she herself thought of her conclusions as increasingly verified by the advancing human sciences, and surely she would choose to be judged on the lasting merit of her work rather than on her own intellectual biography. What then is left of her theories?

Not a great deal. Harrison was such a vigorous partisan of the evolutionist model that she has shared its fate. Moreover, she championed the weakest aspects of the evolutionist theory, though it may have been impossible for her to recognize this at the time. It is hard to imagine any creative intellectual working in the milieu of the 'Cambridge school' who would have not taken the support of brilliant classicists like Cornford, Cook, Frazer, and, at Oxford, Murray as confirmation of his theories. In the excitement of taking part in an avant-garde interpretation of early culture, Harrison chose to analyze Greek religion by means of the most tendentious

and questionable theses of evolutionism. The evolutionist reconstructions of the origin and successive stages of religion were pure
speculations and ultimately as unscientific as the theories of primordial monotheism. In the early years of this century when primitive
parallels seemed to offer a convincing way of discrediting an
outmoded supernaturalism, this was doubtless not apparent, but
today such reconstructions are generally disregarded.

Harrison compounded the weakness of these speculations by
conflating competing varieties of them into a methodological pas-
tiche. She then attempted to force classical materials into this
schema without regard for established chronology or, in many cases,
for traditional interpretations given by the Greeks themselves.
Essentially, she based her inferences not on established facts but on
her own earlier suppositions. This procedure, combined with her
tendency to assure the reader serenely that the results were quite
scientific, lends to her works a never-never-land quality and makes
reading them one of the most intellectually exasperating experiences in modern religious studies. As one reviewer, noting the
combination of vivacious style and a priori argumentation, effectively expressed it:

> We are continually being 'surprised and delighted'; it is with
> 'amaze and delight' that we discover this and that. One suspects
> that as most of the delight is certainly the writer's, most of the
> amaze and surprise is the reader's,—that Miss Harrison has found
> about what she was looking for, and sometimes we must suspect,
> largely because she was looking for it.[105]

Having filtered virtually everything through the evolutionary perspective, Harrison never did the nuts and bolts type of classical
history which would have outlasted the demise of evolutionism.
Here the contrast with Rohde is striking. Writing more than a
decade before Harrison, he too had used evolutionism to explain
Greek religion. Yet he used it in an extremely restrained way,
applying it only after he had situated the fact to be explained in a
historical context. Since evolutionism did not supply the framework
for his portrayal of the sequence of Greek religion, its dissolution
did not discredit *Psyche* as acceptable history. The evolutionist
hypotheses, of course, remained in Rohde's work but in the status of
possible explanations of outdated beliefs and practices. These
beliefs and practices themselves could, even without evolutionary

theories, be arranged in such a way that the logic of transition from one movement to the next was quite clear. As a result, *Psyche* still rewards close attention in a way that Harrison's works do not.

This much said on the negative side, there remains the substantial positive legacy that Harrison left classical religious studies. If her reconstructions hold our interest only as historical specimens of an abandoned hermeneutic, the perspective we work with today is still indebted to her insights. Behind the evolutionism-run-riot were several ideas which supported broad changes in what classicists were to consider the really important phenomena. Harrison played a leading role in conditioning scholars to think of the 'lower' strata of Greek religion as of equal importance with higher forms.[106] The attention given to the stately balance of the *polis* cults and to the elevated religious concepts of the philosophers and literary geniuses of Greece had hidden the massive presence of beliefs usually associated with the folk stratum and identified as superstitious. Not only did Harrison demonstrate the importance of these phenomena, but, with her evolutionary perspective, she offered an alternative to the view that they were mere degenerations from a higher tradition. Even scholars who dismissed her hypothesis that the 'lower' religious forms preceded and gave birth to more advanced concepts such as gods were compelled by her analysis to devote more attention to the chthonic element.

In much the same way she drew attention toward ritual as one of the most crucial ways in which the Greeks constructed and expressed their religious world. Countering a widespread tendency to rely on literature in order to understand Greek myths and theology, she argued that rituals could explain their meaning just as effectively. Again, even where scholars are no longer prone to accept her hypothesis that ritual was the causal basis for religious conceptions, they still treat ritual as of great importance.

It should be noted that in both of these cases what Harrison accomplished was not what she set out to accomplish. For her the 'lower' elements of religion and of ritual represented indirect evidence that beliefs about Dionysos emerged out of fundamental misconstruals of reality. In *Prolegomena* the 'lower' elements were supposed to show that Dionysos was but the refinement of magical theories designed to insure natural fertility and, to a lesser extent, to account for the strange power experienced by Greeks during moments of intoxication. Harrison, however, never did demonstrate the causal line between magic and conceptions about Dionysos, so that her contribution lay in pointing out the mutual presence of both magical and religious elements in the same structure rather than in deriving the latter from the former. The same holds true of her contribution in *Themis*. The net effect of this work was to show the importance of ritual for Dionysiac religion, not to prove that Dionysos was merely the projection of the group emotions generated during cultic action. Largely because she was so excessive in applying the evolutionary perspective, she lost any chance of winning large numbers of scholars to her interpretation. It was left to other proponents of the evolutionary school to argue this perspective with less flamboyance and more cogency. Of these, Martin P. Nilsson, the scholar to whom we now turn, offered the most substantial analysis.

4

Martin Persson Nilsson and the Study of Dionysos

Among professional classicists and historians of religion, Martin P. Nilsson[1] is generally considered this century's leading scholar on Greek religion. Over a sixty-seven year period he published an extraordinary number of substantive works, primarily on Greek religion but also on primitive culture and folklore. Within this massive *oeuvre* Dionysos occupied a central place. Nilsson's first published work, his dissertation, dealt with Dionysiac religion in Attica, while his last work treated the Dionysiac mysteries of the Greco-Roman age. In other more general works he analyzed Dionysos within the context of Greek religion as a whole. By treating Dionysiac religion in several different contexts, from meticulous articles on vase symbolism to panoramic works locating its changing nature in the sweep of Hellenic religious development, he left the fullest account of Dionysos that we are likely to get.

Since Nilsson's career spanned decades of rapid development in both classical and religious studies, his discussions and documentation covered essentially all of the facts known about Dionysos. Always attentive to new archaeological perspectives, he did groundbreaking work on Minoan and Mycenaean religion. In addition to being current with developments in classicism itself, he also followed the different methods which emerged in the general study of religion and tried to apply from them aspects which he felt were legitimate.

Yet with all of the advantages conferred by his painstaking, lifelong thoroughness, Nilsson, like every other scholar, was forced to adopt a particular methodological stance. As we shall see, he responded to this inevitable limitation by providing the most complete version of the evolutionary interpretation of Dionysiac religion ever attempted. Through an ingenious historical reconstruction he was able to combine aspects of the explanations of both

Rohde and Harrison, while being more complete than Rohde[2] and more responsible than Harrison.[3] Like them, he used the perspective of evolutionary anthropology as the backdrop for explaining allegedly irrational phenomena and invoked primitive mentality to account for basically erroneous beliefs and inefficient activity. Yet unlike them, he did this in an era when evolutionism was under serious question and no longer provided the only acceptable version of interpretation. Ultimately, in spite of his erudition, Nilsson never came to terms with other interpretations which saw religion as intelligible behavior, and his understanding of Dionysos was always bounded by that limitation. In terms of the present study, Nilsson is best understood as the refiner of the evolutionary efforts of Rohde and Harrison and as the opponent of the reviving view that religion was a legitimate expression of metaphysical insight. (This view was propounded by the subject of the next chapter, Walter F. Otto, Nilsson's bitterest antagonist.) Nilsson's opposition to this new perspective was partly based on his exceeding care in handling historical materials; but to some extent, it was based on an unwillingness to see religion as comprehensible behavior in its own right. In any event, the existence of this alternative method forced Nilsson to be even more explicit in his method than Harrison. What was new about Nilsson's analysis was not so much what he said about Dionysos as the care with which he integrated previous evolutionary results into a more complete and plausible presentation. As well as defending evolutionism against its adversaries, he also wanted to protect it from the excesses of its more flamboyant practitioners like Harrison, who threatened to bring it into disrepute by wild claims and misapplication of its methods.

NILSSON AND THE RESTATEMENT OF THE EVOLUTIONARY METHOD

One of Nilsson's most basic hermeneutical strategies was to insist on the distinction between *Religionsgeschichte* (the historical treatment of religion) and *Religionswissenschaft* (the 'scientific' treatment of religious 'constants' based on the results of ethnology and psychology).[4] Jane Harrison's works represent what happened when this distinction was ignored: the historical sequences which were obvious to anyone vaguely familiar with the material were subordinated to an extrinsic sequence supplied by the social sciences. Under the guise of writing a history of Greek religion, Harrison had forced selected facts from Hellenic culture onto the Procrustean bed of the evolutionists' account of the development of primitive religion. As Nilsson insisted repeatedly, though Greek religion had its roots in primitive religion, it was not equivalent to primitive religion.[5] It had reached a fairly advanced level and had a history of its own which did not necessarily parallel that of primitive religion. Once one recognized the distinction between *Religionsgeschichte* and *Religionswissenschaft* though, this twisting of the material would become unnecessary. The investigator first had to do the job of the historian in detailing chronological and causal sequences based on the available facts. *Religionswissenschaft* was no shortcut to *Religionsgeschichte*; one had to do the same painstaking investigations as any professional historian. However, once the historical sequences were clear, *Religionswissenschaft* took over. It was the task of the science of religion to explain the meaning of archaic behavior. History could relate that the Greeks did this and believed that, but it could not explain why, because the 'why' was buried in prehistory. *Religionswissenschaft* represented a body of theories and 'laws' which concerned cross-cultural constants in religion and which could explain otherwise unintelligible behavior by relating it to the earliest stages of human evolution. Ultimately the laws of *Religionswissenschaft* were the basis for understanding religious facts, but these facts first had to be arranged in their own spatio-temporal sequence, not arranged to fit the laws.

Rohde had already understood this in the previous century. In *Psyche* data from primitive societies were not the key for reconstructing the history of Greek religion. They were useful only in providing a way to understand Greek religious behavior by comparison with primitive phenomena. Rohde clearly believed that explanations adduced by anthropologists to understand these primitive phenomena held true for Hellenic materials, but he acknowledged that the chronological sequences did not necessarily follow the same order. Nilsson's dichotomy between *Religionsgeschichte* and *Religionswissenschaft* served to give theoretical underpinning to this important insight and to render primitive parallels useful without allowing them, as had Harrison's approach, to swamp historical exposition. It was, Nilsson felt, the one sure way to insure the legitimacy of the evolutionary approach.

It was necessary that Nilsson concern himself with this issue. Since his career spanned the first two-thirds of the twentieth century, he saw a considerable backlash against evolutionism from several different sides. In anthropology the anti-evolutionists had built an increasingly impressive case to prove that the original stage of religion had been quite elevated and that religion could not therefore be dismissed as the outcome of primitive blundering. Anthropologists more skeptical of our ability to recover the original stages of religion or culture attacked the attempted reconstructions of evolutionists and anti-evolutionists alike as unverifiable speculations. In classicism itself, anthropological theories had lost much of their luster, and scholars could in good conscience deal with the philological and literary problems of Hellenism without feeling that they had to trace everything back to its prehistoric stage.

Almost anachronistically, Nilsson held out against these currents to the end. He ignored several of the new approaches, perhaps mentioning them but quickly adding that they were not necessarily relevant to the study of Greek religion.[6] In a more direct fashion he spoke out in opposition to the anti-evolutionists. (However, as we shall see, his refutations often dealt with something other than their actual argument.) And although he had great respect for literary criticism and the study of the great works of Hellenic culture, he consistently felt that studying the masterpieces entailed starting at the wrong end of Greek culture and ignoring the roots from which the later products had grown and which made their meaning intelligible.[7]

The battle which Nilsson conducted represented one skirmish in the twentieth century conflict over the proper way to understand culture; and, as has been the case with others, Nilsson's interpretation of Dionysos depended on his stance in the larger conflict. Throughout this epoch, the rejection of evolutionism in part reflected a return to a type of historical particularism. In several different contexts scholars went on the attack claiming that cultural products should not be explained in terms of their origins but in terms of an environing body of contemporary facts. In America, Boasian anthropology shelved the comparative method on the grand evolutionary scale for more modest explanatory contexts. The functionalist schools in Great Britain explained the meaning of any particular phenomenon in terms of its relationship to other working parts of the operative system. Classicists themselves grew more aggressive in their exhortations to 'Think Greek' and interpret Hellenic materials only in terms of facts from Greek civilization. And much of the impact of anti-evolutionism was to isolate religion itself as a separate, some claimed *sui generis*, field for which many of the concepts of evolutionism, for example, magic, were simply irrelevant. In each of these movements the net effect was to offer an alternative argument against what William James called the 'genetic fallacy', the attempt to explain a thing (often to explain it away) by means of revealing its (often discreditable) pedigree.

To Nilsson such a retrenchment meant abandoning the true goal of science: the search for the cause of a phenomenon.[8] Rohde and Harrison had assumed this goal as a matter of course; Nilsson had to fight for it. Nilsson's antagonists were claiming either that they could explain a phenomenon by showing its rationale in the larger system (how it 'worked') or that a total explanation was impossible and that one had to settle for merely exploring whatever was being investigated. Yet to abandon the 'total' explanation would mean that fundamental questions which seemed to have been answered definitively, such as the role and legitimacy of religion, would again be open to dispute. To avoid this equivocal situation, Nilsson tried to fight off the critiques of evolutionism. Since internal divisions within evolutionism precluded allegiance to any single evolutionist theory, Nilsson became methodologically eclectic. (While his use of several types of evolutionary theory was not as jarring as Harrison's had been, largely because he tended to blur the different theories into a kind of lowest common denominator sameness, his arguments often gained their plausibility from vagueness.) In the end, he did help support the evolutionary perspective by producing what might be called a common-sense version of it.

Nilsson challenged the implicit elitism involved in studying the highest products of Hellenism and asserted that to understand the original meaning of Greek culture one had to study the so-called 'average man'.[9] This claim was not without its advantages for his evolutionism. The idea that the views of the average man were more sociologically significant in actual Greek life is, of course, acceptable, provided that the investigator has access to this hypothetical figure. However, consistent with his genealogical approach, Nilsson implied that the average man was not merely the most statistically significant believer and practitioner of Greek religion, he was also its creator. Though, beyond the usual comments about the poverty of primitive mentality, Nilsson never said this explicitly, it is clear that he saw the originator of religion as a person of low to middling intelligence. That this may actually have been the case is, of course, possible; what must be noted, however, is the fact that this assertion is an assumption. Others have argued for the opposite assumption, that it was one of the cultural elite who originated religion. Neither hypothesis, of course, can be proved; but by choosing one as opposed to the other, the investigator has already done a great deal to determine his interpretation. Once Nilsson assumed that the most important actor to be understood was the average man, he had an implicit justification for presuming that religion was the creation of a deficient intelligence. Coupled with his demand for a fully causal explanation of religion, this presumption led him to look to primitive mentality as the source for the errors of Dionysiac religion. In Nilsson's view only the evolutionary theory of 'primitive logic' was an adequate explanation for the illogic of Dionysiac religion. To treat Dionysiac religion other than genealogically would be to describe it rather than to explain it, and mere description would leave its essential strangeness unresolved.

NILSSON'S EVOLUTIONARY INTERPRETATION OF DIONYSOS

Since Nilsson returned over and over to Dionysos throughout his career, his description of phenomena associated with this god was exceedingly rich. The following paragraph summarizes the main facts which he interpreted. One should note the numerous facets of the Dionysiac cult with which he dealt; but, more important for present purposes, one should note that these facts do not explain themselves and that they do not appear meaningful from within a purely rational or scientific context. Hence, from Nilsson's perspective, they required explaining.

Nilsson gave considerable attention, as had Rohde, to the ecstatic cult of Dionysos, portraying it in all of its emotional excitement:

Women are seized by a mental disturbance, sometimes despite resistance at first; they abandon their occupations, hurry out into the woods and fields, and wander about among the mountains, dancing and waving torches and thyrsi, the latter being sticks wound with ivy and having a pine cone at the end. Milk and honey spring up from the ground, we seldom hear of wine. The god Dionysos in person reveals himself. As the ecstasy reaches its climax, the maenads, as they are called, seize a beast, tear it in pieces, and devour bits of its flesh raw. Those who resist or try to hinder the ecstasy are severely dealt with.[10]

Nilsson also described features of Dionysiac religion having to do with nature, especially fertility. Dionysos played a role in several spring festivals and, through them, was associated with the blooming of the new vegetation, the tasting of the new wine, and the return of the souls of the dead. The phallos was a constant feature in his processions; and although Dionysos was never portrayed as carrying a phallos himself or as ithyphallic, his companions, the Silenes and Satyrs, often were. In some cases the phallos was pictured beside Dionysos as an independent deity. In another sexual association, during the Anthesteria, a spring festival at Athens, Dionysos was believed to make love to the wife of the Athenian archon, the Basilinna, in a special holy marriage. Whereas in the above instances Dionysos was presented as mature, in other instances he was conceived of as a child. One of the duties of the college of Thyiades at Delphi, for example, was to 'awaken' the child Dionysos, the *Liknites*. Furthermore, Dionysos was not always thought of as human; sometimes he was portrayed in animal form, most notably that of the bull, and he was associated with other animals as well, e.g., the goat, the deer, and the snake. These associations with plants, animals, and sexuality linked Dionysos to nature; yet he also had firm ties with civilization. His cult gave birth to both tragedy and comedy, two of Greece's most revered cultural products. In addition, private Dionysiac mystery cults led to well developed teachings about the fate of the soul after death. This tendency culminated in Orphism, a reform movement within Dionysiac religion.

From Nilsson's perspective it would have done little good simply to report these facts in their proper chronological order. The point of investigating them was to ascertain what the Greeks thought they were doing in worshipping this god and, still more important, why. Nilsson was firmly convinced that the Greeks wanted some material benefit from this worship and that, since science was the only effective way to change the world to fit one's wishes, some intellectual short circuit must have lain behind these beliefs and practices. Therefore he looked for the Greeks' rationale for Dionysiac religion and what gave rise to this rationale.

His most important interpretive category to explain Dionysiac religion was vegetation magic. To the end of his career he used this concept to account for various practices associated with Dionysos (as with Greek religion in general), but at the start of his career he used it almost to the exclusion of other explanations. Though he modified his account of the logic of vegetation magic to accommodate changes in the field of *Religionswissenschaft*, his general hypothesis remained the same; that practical problems plus mental incompetence yielded impractical methods of dealing with the external world. And though he made his accounts increasingly complex (and more diffuse), he relied primarily on Frazer for the explanation of magic to the end. His earliest explanations quite explicitly derived most Dionysiac rites from a pre-scientific magical world-view. As time passed and as the Frazerian model lost prestige, Nilsson did not use the theory of the illogical and pre-scientific magical world-view as extensively as he had originally, but he continued to employ it.

Thus, in his early works, Nilsson explained almost every connection between Dionysos and the natural world as an instance of fertility magic. Through 1925 Nilsson explained the climax of the ecstatic cult, the omophagia, in which worshippers dismembered and devoured live animals, as a magical act supposed to compel nature to be more fruitful.[11] Dionysos' associations with festivals were designed to help magically drive away evil forces and impel the growth of nature, whether this be through apotropaic magical practices in the Aiora[12] and the Anthesteria[13] or through the scourging of women in the rite of the Skiereia in Alea.[14] His sexual associations performed the same task, largely on the theory of sympathetic magic: if that which creates fertility in some aspects of nature was mimicked or presented in the cult, its creative power would spread throughout nature and bring fertility to all realms. Thus the presence of the phallos in many of the rites of Dionysos was supposed to increase fertility,[15] while the god's sacred intercourse with the Basilinna of Athens was an even more concrete magical attempt for the same goal.[16] The reason the Silenes and the

Satyrs with all of their sexuality were associated with Dionysos was that since they too were fertility producing vegetation daemons,[17] their presence would help compel nature to be fertile. In the early works, Nilsson explained the rites associated with Dionysos Liknites, the child god awakened by the Thyiades, as a magical imitation of the recurring fate of nature designed to help the growth of the crops.[18] Dionysos' incarnations in animal form were further examples of his nature as a fertility god,[19] as were epithets that associated him with trees, branches, twigs, and the like.[20] Even his associations with Greek drama originated in fertility magic; some of the cultic forerunners of tragedy were masked dances and ritual combats associated with Dionysos that were designed to impel fertility by imitating the changes of the seasons and facilitating their proper succession.[21]

Nilsson changed his interpretation over the years by broadening his ideas about the purposes of Dionysiac religion and explaining numerous Bacchic rites without reference to fertility magic. However, this shift was only partial; he continued to offer Frazerian interpretations for many phenomena to the end. The major shifts concerned his analysis of the ecstatic cult, especially the omophagia, and the rites relative to Dionysos Liknites. These reevaluations led Nilsson into a new presentation of Dionysiac religion and then, although he never fully acknowledged this, out of it again. The history of these shifts requires substantial explanation, but basically what was involved was that by reinterpreting the ecstatic cult, Nilsson separated it from fertility concerns and traced it to a different geographical source. Once he had separated the ecstatic cult from the vegetative cult, he was able to organize the materials relative to the latter into an extremely clear and ingenious reconstruction which did much to explain the background and rationale of Dionysiac religion. Years later, however, his reinterpretation of Dionysos Liknites undercut the main evidentiary support for this artful reconstruction and left the utility of the earlier separation in some doubt.

Nilsson's first reinterpretation allowed him to incorporate the results of both Rohde and Harrison into a synthesis which he felt was more historically accurate. He admired elements of the work of both scholars, but he had felt that Rohde's interest in immortality had led him to overemphasize the Thracian ecstatic cult to the detriment of the connections with fertility[22] and that Harrison's preoccupation with vegetation led her to attribute to wine, the product of nature's bounty, too great a role in the ecstatic cult.[23] The problem was to articulate a schema which by separating the ecstatic from the vegetative cult would preserve the autonomy of each and yet which could relate them in some meaningful way.

It took Nilsson over a quarter of a century to find such a schema. He had just finished a major summary of the field, his *A History of Greek Religion*, in 1925[24] and was turning his attention to the Minoan and Mycenaean background in an attempt to bring his research up to date with the archaeological discoveries made under the leadership of Sir Arthur Evans. The result of these investigations was *The Minoan-Mycenaean Religion and its Survival in Greek Religion*, his most important work until the publication of the first volume of his massive *Geschichte* in 1941. By isolating a specific Minoan religious pattern related to Dionysos' vegetative cult and by tracing its origin to Asia Minor, Nilsson had discovered a way to separate it from the Thracian ecstatic cult. From this point on he would speak of two Dionysoses, one from Thrace, the other from Phrygia, and would describe how Greece received the two different Dionysiac impulses, ecstatic and vegetative, from these two locations.

According to his reconstruction, the Thracians to the northeast had produced the mystical Dionysiac religion of orgiastic celebrations culminating in the omophagia. Yet these Thracians had not been a sedentary people, content to watch their influence radiate out from their homeland. At some point during prehistoric times a substantial number of them had migrated to Asia Minor and formed the civilization later known as Phrygian. They had brought the worship of Dionysos with them, but their conceptions of the god were to be changed through contact with the highly developed culture of Lydia. This Lydian influence infused Dionysiac religion with notions about the yearly death and revivification of nature and led to the conception of Dionysos as a Divine Child sharing this cyclical fate. Whereas the Thracian stream of Dionysiac religion entered Greece overland from the north, the Phrygian stream came by sea from the east, crossing the Aegean via the islands. At some point in prehistory these two cults were united. The Greeks applied Phrygian ideas about the yearly death and renewal of natural life to their conceptions of the human soul. Later, they combined these ideas with the ecstatic states they experienced during the Thracian cults and from this combination derived their ideas about the blissful immortality of the soul. In this regard Nilsson's portrayal of the developed Dionysiac faith in immortality did not differ radically from that of Rohde, especially as concerns the two scholars' presentation of the belief system of Orphism, but Nilsson was convinced that these beliefs resulted only after a synthesis of two originally autonomous cults.

This hypothesis was truly ingenious and represented one of Nilsson's most creative scholarly reconstructions. By means of this dual derivation of Dionysos he was able to present unified portrayals of both the Thracian and Phrygian cults which respected the specific environment from which each derived. Earlier he had analyzed the Thracian ecstasy primarily in terms of its vegetative associations and, correspondingly, had been unable to treat the intrinsic religious satisfactions of the mystical cult as more than an epiphenomenal outgrowth of magical practices. With this new dichotomy he was able to treat the religious satisfaction of the Thracian cult as primary without totally abandoning his use of vegetation magic as an explanation for other aspects of Dionysiac religion. It was now quite simple to treat the vegetative aspect as the legacy from the indigenous Minoan culture and its Anatolian kin.

In treating the two cults Nilsson assumed that they had each been more complex in their native habitat than they were in Greece where only selected elements could be incorporated into an ongoing religion. In Thrace Dionysos had undoubtedly been more than simply a god of ecstasy; but this ecstatic element, by predominating over other aspects of the original cult, assured his victorious entry into Greek religion.[25]

The main events involved in the ecstatic cult have been described above,[26] but there are other facts which deserve notice. For one, the maenads dressed as did Dionysos, wearing fawnskins. Since the fawn was one of the animals regularly torn apart and devoured during the omophagia, some scholars have assumed that the maenads thought Dionysos was incarnated in the fawn and that by eating the animal they would be taking the god into their possession. Nilsson sympathized with this approach but cautioned that there was too little evidence to guarantee that the Greeks thought

Dionysos to be in the fawn. He argued, on the other hand, that there were sufficient testimonies identifying Dionysos with the bull to warrant this interpretation for the devouring of the bull in the omophagia.[27] Another significant indication of the nature of the cult was that the worshippers often wore masks either of Dionysos or of the sacrificial animals.[28] Both the devouring of raw animals and the masked impersonations seem to be means of drawing the worshippers close to the god.

The most complete descriptions of the Bacchic orgia occur in mythical and literary accounts, but several historical witnesses confirm these descriptions. We know from several sources about the maenadic celebrations held every other winter on the top of Parnassus by the Attic Thyiades and the women from the sanctuary at Delphi. There were state cults as well which involved ecstatic rites in honor of Dionysos. These were widespread and well-known, being found in various places on the mainland, on the islands, and in Asia Minor. In almost all of the testimonies, historical as well as mythical, one can find the elements of ecstasy, madness, and bloody sacrifice.[29]

How to interpret these orgiastic rites is not self evident. Once Nilsson had separated the Thracian and Phrygian cults, he dropped the connections between the orgia and vegetation magic. In the *Geschichte* he included the Frazerian interpretation as one of the four classically given for the omophagia,[30] but this seems to be due to the nature of the *Geschichte* as a handbook rather than due to any continuing allegiance to this explanation. He did not interpret the omophagia as fertility magic either in *The Minoan-Mycenaean Religion*, written before the *Geschichte*, or in *Greek Piety*, written afterward.[31] Basically, after having dismissed the fertility magic theory, Nilsson interpreted the omophagia in terms of 'mana', religious power.[32] By eating the animal, one ingested the power of the god and this power produced the ecstasy. The exalted state of mind experienced during this rite was its own reward. One need not gain any material benefit from this power; simply to feel it was enough.

Rohde had believed that the Bacchic ecstasy had given the Greeks the idea that the soul was destined for a greater, never-ending existence as soon as it would divest itself of its bodily prison. Nilsson was in no way convinced that the ecstatic cult carried with it

such a heavy intellectual content. He wondered aloud 'whether the
Dionysiac ecstasy was anything more than an elemental outburst of
religious excitement or brought with it certain religious ideas'.[33]
Earlier he had believed that the original ecstatic cult did include
'ideas of life and death, germination and decay'.[34] However, once he
had located the vegetative aspect of Dionysiac religion in Phrygia,
he challenged his earlier assumption that ideas about life and death
were part of the original Thracian cult. All that could be said about
this cult was that it was highly emotional and that during the ecstasy
the worshipper felt lifted above the human sphere and filled with
divine power. He experienced both *ekstasis* and *enthousiasmos*: he
had been taken out of himself; he had been filled with the god.[35]
Thus Nilsson affirmed Rohde's sensitive treatment of the mystical
cult but rejected his thesis that the ecstatic cult had been the origin
of ideas of life, death, and immortality.

Those ideas had come from the influence of the pre-Greek
vegetative cult, and it is to that cult which we must now turn.
Nilsson's reconstruction is rather complicated, but basically he
wished to show that pre-Greek Minoan religion contained conceptions related to fertility and the natural world which eventually
formed a particular understanding of Dionysos in Anatolia and that
the Anatolian Dionysos reimported these conceptions when he was
brought to Greece.

Nilsson was struck with the ubiquitous occurrence of phenomena
related to the life of vegetation and the earth in the original Minoan
cult. He saw this religion of the earth as distinct from the martial,
aristocratic religion represented in Homer and felt that the two
religious impulses clearly had come from two distinct cultures. Thus
like other scholars before him[36] he juxtaposed the 'chthonic' ('of the
earth') religion of the pre-Greek civilization to the 'Olympic' (of
Mount Olympus, i.e., heavenly) religion of the basically Indo-
European Hellenic civilization. The former religion had to be
reconstructed from archaeological remains, but Nilsson felt that we
could be certain of its main features:

> We may reasonably suppose that these people believed in various
> daemons and nature gods of which some were raised up to
> Olympus, while some, like the corn-goddess Demeter, were not
> presentable in the Olympian court; also that they favored certain
> rites and beliefs tinged with mysticism (e.g., the ascent of the

daughter of the corn-goddess from the subterranean siloes at the autumn sowing, and the conception of the Divine Child which, abandoned by its mother, was nurtured by the powers of Nature); and that they revered the heroes of the upper class so much that they even worshipped them at their tombs.[37]

In all these elements one can see the characteristics of the chthonic cult: interest in the life and powers of nature and graveside concern for the souls of departed heroes.

Nilsson interpreted Dionysos as one manifestation of the Divine Child motif. According to Nilsson's reconstruction of this pre-Greek mythologem, a Divine Child was born of his mother but then quickly given over to someone else to nurse. After his youth he died or was killed. Nilsson interpreted this hypothetical mythologem as belonging 'to one great cycle of religious ideas, the annual coming to life and decaying of the Life of Nature'.[38] The mother of the child represented the Earth, who gave birth to vegetation and animals but then handed them over to other attendants for care. After its growth for a season, the child, representing the Life of Nature, died. By celebrating this religion the Minoans believed they were helping to bring about a good year. Nilsson thought of this interpretation as self-evident[39] and believed that it accounted for much of Dionysiac religion.

Dionysos himself, of course, was not Minoan. What then was his connection with pre-Greek religion? Nilsson's reconstruction was complex but not implausible: racial and cultural ties existed between Crete, the center of Minoan civilization, and southwest Anatolia, near, if not including, the area to which the Phrygians had brought their god Dionysos.[40] The Dionysiac cult had already been penetrated with vegetative associations through contact with the Phrygian religion of the Great Mother. From the Lydians the Dionysiac worshippers probably derived specific conceptions of Dionysos as a Divine Child, whose brief life cycle was a mystical imitation of the life of nature. (The Lydians, it should be remembered, were either related to the Minoans or in close contact with people who were.) Once the Phrygians added these conceptions, they linked Dionysos closely with vegetation and brought this association to Greece as the paramount concern of their Dionysiac cult. Ironically, although it ultimately originated in Minoan civilization, this Phrygian cult had no great success on Crete itself because the role that would have fallen to the child Dionysos was already filled by the Cretan Zeus.[41] On the mainland, though, this cult was active and left considerable evidence of its importance. Though there was no direct testimony from the Greeks about the Divine Child as a formal type, Nilsson felt that it was legitimate to use evidence from the mainland Dionysiac cult to help reconstruct the original Cretan Divine Child mythologem because he believed he could parallel the structure of the Dionysiac mythologem with that of other Cretan divinities—the Cretan Zeus, Hyakinthos, Ploutos, and Erichthonios—who also seemed to be born, be turned over to other persons to nurse, and die.

Nilsson's hypothetical Divine Child, like Jane Harrison's *eniautos daimon* with which Nilsson equated it,[42] was the result of a speculative reconstruction. Accordingly, as he explained the content of this mythologem, Nilsson was at the same time trying to prove its historical actuality. He began by pointing to Phrygian and Lydian cults which he argued were Dionysiac. Since the ceremonies involved were celebrated in the spring, he took them as vegetation rituals. For example, according to Himerios, spring brought Dionysos and his revels to the Lydians. Galen reported that snakes were torn apart in honor of Dionysos when spring changed to summer, and, in Nilsson's view, he was probably referring to Anatolian customs. Plutarch recorded the conception among the Phrygians and Bithnians that 'the god' slept or was chained during the winter but awoke or was freed in the summer. This god was, Nilsson argued, Dionysos and clearly represented an image of the life of nature, following its course both as he rested (or was chained or 'died') and as he woke (or was released or 'resurrected').[43] Also the importance of the Phrygian earth goddess connected with Dionysos, whether Meter Hipta (the nurse of Dionysos according to one Orphic hymn) or Semele (the mother of Dionysos) indicated fertility connections of Dionysos. The identity of Dionysos with the important Phrygian god Sabazios also corroborated the presence of the Divine Child Dionysos in early Phrygia.[44]

Nilsson also tried to demonstrate the elements of the Divine Child motif in the Greek Dionysiac religion. He interpreted the tradition of Dionysos Liknites as evidence for this motif. From Delphi the Thyiades, female attendants of the god, performed a ceremony in which they awakened the Liknites, the child in the winnowing basket. The fact that the child was transported in a winnowing basket (that is, an agricultural implement) indicated to Nilsson clear vegetative concerns.[45] Traditions of the death of Dionysos and his burial at Delphi added the third element of the mythologem of birth, growth, and death.[46] Evidence for the second theme, Dionysos' being reared by persons other than his mother, had been present in sources as early as Homer's reference to the god's 'nurses' (*tithenai*), while later the common myth of Dionysos' birth corroborated the pattern of the Divine Child being left by his mother and nursed by nature beings.[47]

Naturally, we do not find a unified account in the sources identifying Dionysos as a Divine Child, nursed by persons other than his mother, and killed in his youth; if we did, Nilsson would not have had to reconstruct the pattern. Much of our knowledge of antiquity has come through such reconstructions, where a scholar has perceived some organic structure behind a disparate mass of facts which no one had previously thought to connect. What necessitates such reconstructions is the fact that in numerous cases events have developed in such a way as to obscure the facts, even from the ever-curious historians of the classical age. Only by ingenious deductions from limited documents can the modern scholar discern the pattern. Nilsson postulated such cultural change to account for the fact that classical authors nowhere identified the Divine Child as a unified mythologem. Whereas he thought he could point to explicit connections between Dionysos and the seasonal fate of vegetation in Anatolia, he acknowledged that in Greece the Dionysos child appeared without relation to the changing of the seasons.[48] He explained this by asserting that the contrast between the suspension of vegetative life in winter and its renascence in summer is not as marked in Greece as in Anatolia and that, as a probable consequence, the Greeks let the connections between the child Dionysos and the phases of the year recede behind other rites.[49] Nevertheless, Nilsson felt that the weight of evidence concerning not only Dionysos but, as well, other gods in the form of children associated with Cretan religion established the existence and nature of the Divine Child mythologem as he had described it. The cumulative evidence, he felt, justified interpreting one of the two major manifestations of Dionysos as the personification of the cyclical life of nature. This personification itself performed a basically magical function since in representing and celebrating the birth, life, death and new birth of Dionysos the Greeks had tried to guarantee the orderly and productive succession of the seasons.

Nilsson never explicitly abandoned this reconstruction, but his reinterpretation of Dionysos Liknites in 1951 effectively undercut its main support. Earlier the tradition of the child Liknites periodically awakened and carried in the winnowing basket had been Nilsson's clearest evidence for the connections between Dionysos and the yearly fate of the crops. Actually, the sources themselves had not indicated that Dionysos' 'awakening', which Nilsson interpreted as his birth, was a yearly affair; Nilsson had supplied that information deductively. He spoke of 'the conception of the newborn child in the winnowing fan and of the death of the god. Here he is clearly the spirit of vegetation, and as such *must* be born and die annually'.[50] The circularity of this reasoning seems to have escaped Nilsson for many years; but he was an extremely probing and conscientious scholar, and in 1951 he repudiated this understanding of Dionysos Liknites (though not of the Divine Child motif).[51] What led Nilsson to reverse his position was his conviction, based on the 53rd Orphic Hymn, that the rite of awakening the Liknites was part of the trieteric (biennial)[52] ceremonies celebrated by the Delphic Thyiades. This cult belonged to the Thracian orgia, not to the Phrygian stream. Furthermore, since the child is awakened only every other year, he can hardly be a mythical representation of the yearly birth of vegetation. Thus, in the second edition of the *Geschichte* Nilsson dropped all discussion of the relationship between Dionysos Liknites and fertility and interpreted the awakening as the god's return from the underworld.[53]

Though Nilsson never admitted it, once he had removed this linchpin, little remained to hold the Divine Child structure together. It had been the supposedly 'obvious' fertility character of the Liknites rites that had allowed Nilsson to connect traditions about Dionysos' death (all of which, incidentally, were related to Dionysos's dismemberment by the Titans, part of the trieteric orgia) to the references about Dionysos' birth and childhood.[54] Now there were no reasons to group these two disparate traditions together and certainly none to justify the assumption of a yearly death of Dionysos.

To a large extent, Nilsson had justified the projection of this mythologem on Greek religion because of its supposed prior existence in its Phrygian homeland. But even here the reconstruction could be contested. The reference Nilsson cited for the child Dionysos having an Anatolian nurse (Meter Hipta) came from an Orphic hymn, a late source.[55] Inscriptions to Meter Hipta and Zeus Sabazios[56] did not establish anything about a child Dionysos and his fate. The most important evidence, Plutarch's statement about 'the god' asleep in winter and waking in summer, did not necessarily refer to Dionysos.[57] Thus, if one was not predisposed to agree with the hypothesis from the start, Nilsson could not be said to have established the existence of the mythologem for Anatolia any more than for Greece proper. What seems to have happened is that separate elements from both Greece and Anatolia (with the tradition of the Liknites paramount) coalesced for Nilsson into a meaningful complex, and he then projected this composite complex back onto each of the two geographical areas.[58] Once there is reason to doubt the complex, as when Nilsson states that the Liknites is not related to the Divine Child motif, the different pieces of circumstantial evidence are not terribly convincing.

If one disputes Nilsson's presentation of the Phrygian Dionysos as an example of the Minoan Divine Child motif, what is the value of his separation of Dionysiac religion into two streams? Originally the primary utility of the separation had been for establishing a pattern, since a separate Phrygian cult could have been in contact with Minoan and related Anatolian ideas and would have been more clearly related to fertility concerns than the Thracian cult with its biennial orgia. This separation, though, had other implications which transcended the acceptance or rejection of the Divine Child mythologem. Its most important contribution was that it allowed Nilsson to differentiate between the orgiastic and the fertility cults, something he could not effectively do as long as he interpreted everything from a Frazerian perspective. Using the Thracian/Phrygian dichotomy, Nilsson interpreted the Dionysiac orgia as produced by autonomous religious urges unrelated to the desire for a bounteous harvest. Consequently, he portrayed the orgia as more serious rites than had many scholars. Because he had another context in which to discuss Dionysos' associations with wine, he pointed out that we rarely hear of wine in the orgia and that the ecstasy was not the result of simple intoxication.[59] Because he could relate Dionysos, associations with the phallos to the Phrygian side of the cult, he could point out that there were no indications of sexual relations or phallic worship occurring in the Hellenic orgia.[60] These disclaimers guaranteed Nilsson's seeing the ecstatic orgia as a serious mystical cult directed toward bringing the worshipper into close contact with his god, rather than as ritualized fertility magic. In this regard, the separation helped Nilsson go beyond his earlier Frazerian interpretation. It also meant that he would be a strong voice arguing against the simplistic interpretation by many not familiar with the actual nature of the Hellenic cult that Dionysiac orgies (orgia) had been merely drunken exercises in sexual licence.

Furthermore, regardless of the fate of the Divine Child hypothesis, Nilsson was clearly correct in drawing attention to numerous connections between Dionysos and fertility. In refining his analysis, Nilsson narrowed the range of these connections, until he had restricted Dionysos' associations to a special domain of nature's growth, specifically that of the vine, trees, and flowers.[61] Nilsson felt that, practically speaking, Dionysos' identity as god of wine was his most important natural association in the Hellenic age, but that originally he had been a vegetation god attached to a tree cult.[62] Only after his cult had entered Greece and developed there had he assumed the patronage of wine. Throughout Greece celebrations were held and offerings made to him in honor of his power over the life of nature. Associations with various types of mayboughs and with the phallos strengthened his nature as a vegetation deity, while an imposing number of ceremonies and practices were carried out to honor his lordship over wine.

The organization of the *Geschichte* forces one, in a sense, to reconstruct Nilsson's interpretation from different portions of the text. The section devoted to Dionysos consists predominantly of statements of historical sequences with little explanation of the meaning of Dionysiac phenomena for the Greeks. In the theoretical sections, however, Nilsson had set down his understanding of the reasons behind Dionysiac religion or, more accurately, behind religion as a whole. From these sections it is clear that, like Harrison, he explained Dionysos ultimately more in terms of primitive mentality than in terms of classical materials themselves, though from a historiographical point of view his organization of those materials was much more orderly than hers.

Nilsson saw the Dionysiac cult, especially in its ecstatic form, as a regression from a higher level and, like Rohde and Harrison before him, argued that the Greeks had resisted Dionysos' incursion. First of all, the Greeks disliked emotional excess. Like some other Indo-European peoples, they disparaged ecstasy and unhealthy psychic conditions and discouraged the expression of the dark side of the human soul.[63] The wild nature of the Dionysiac orgia then quite naturally aroused their disgust.[64] In addition to greater emotional stability, the Greeks had also attained a higher intellectual level than societies which nurtured the Bacchic cult; they had developed beyond such irrational magical and religious conceptions on their way to a scientific view. Their thought had thus overcome almost all of the fantastic elements which occupied the imaginations of surrounding cultures.[65] Having rationalized and anthropomorphized the supernatural forces with which they dealt,[66] the Greeks had learned to be much less cringing before the gods and much more willing to examine the natural world scientifically.[67] As heirs to this great advance, the Greeks who witnessed the incursion of Dionysiac religion rejected the new cult as an atavistic regression.[68]

Nilsson's explanation of what led to Dionysos' victory was even richer than his explanation of why the Greeks resisted him. First, as suggested by his hypothesis of the Divine Child, Dionysiac religion had similarities to, if not roots in, pre-Greek Minoan religion.[69] Besides the Divine Child complex, other pre-existing fertility cults of an ecstatic and phallic nature may also have facilitated his entry.[70] For example, the cult of Artemis had surprising resemblances to that of Dionysos. Both included the phallos, wild circle dances of women at night, association with trees, and a retinue of followers.[71] The earlier presence of Artemis in Greek religion could have mitigated the shock of Dionysos' entry.[72] Having struck responsive chords in existing Greek religious cults, especially those of the aboriginal peoples who had been suppressed by the Homeric nobility, Dionysiac religion gained entry more easily than if it had been a totally new phenomenon.

In addition to previously existing religious factors, Nilsson advanced racial factors as a partial explanation for the status of Dionysos within Greek religion. At the time of the Dionysiac incursion, the races which were to form the Greek people had not yet been completely assimilated. In a milieu of racial instability the new Dionysiac movement represented the recrudescence of older, more emotional religious ideas which had been suppressed by the rational, sober-minded Indo-Europeans.[73] Nilsson believed that the alleged racial superiority of the Indo-Europeans partly accounted for the advance of their religion over that of the pre-Greeks. Variability of intelligence and volition and the ability for cultural and political development were, in his view, all 'properties which vary with the race'.[74] Since the Indo-Europeans were genetically more steady-minded and intelligent, they resisted Dionysos; since the aboriginal Mediterraneans were more emotional and prone to irrationalism, they welcomed his arrival.

In addition to his racial explanation, Nilsson also used a somewhat sexist and elitist explanation of Dionysiac religion's victory. He asserted that women 'are more inclined than men to an emotional religion and more easily got hold of by one.'[75] He also dealt with this cult as an essentially lower class phenomenon. Thus he showed Dionysiac religion to have had an important constituency ready made for its spread: Mediterraneans, women, and lower class persons, all of whom would be disposed to follow an extremely emotional mystical cult which produced intense, easily attained religious gratification.

Furthermore, historical conditions in the archaic age were right for Dionysos to appeal to the Greeks. After the nobility overthrew the monarchy, 'the humbler population found itself practically and economically in an oppressive state of dependence rendered still more vexatious by economic distress'.[76] In response, they turned to two major religious movements: Apollinian legalism in which they scrupulously observed all religious injunctions and Dionysiac mysticism in which they could be lifted from the everyday level into contact with the divine. In the heightening of religious feeling offered by Dionysos, the Greek sought 'oblivion of the miseries of life and the worries of the day'.[77] Even apart from economic distress, many Greeks found their individual religious needs for intimate communion with divinity unfulfilled by the state religion. The growing Dionysiac cult was the most effective answer to this need.[78]

The momentarily weakened condition of Greek civilization helped explain how Dionysiac religion spread across Greece with such vigor. Here, like Rohde, Nilsson relied on impressionistic metaphors to communicate his meaning rather than spelling out in concrete detail how he thought the Dionysiac orgia were transmitted from place to place. They spread like 'wildfire';[79] they 'swept over Greece like a river in flood'.[80] Using Rohde's medical analogy, Nilsson characterized the spread of the cult as a '*religiös-psychopathische Epidemie*',[81] 'a violent psychical epidemic almost like St. Vitus dance'.[82] The cult was transmitted from person to person and from community to community because it was 'infectious'[83] and impossible to restrain.[84]

Unable to resist Dionysos, the most Greece could do was to moderate his cult. Nilsson agreed with Nietzsche, Rohde, and Harrison that in the face of the ungoverned Bacchic phenomena sweeping over Greece like the waters of a river in flood, Apolline religion had been the 'counter-current strong enough to dam them and lead them into ordinary and quieter channels of Greek religion'.[85] Apolline religion regularized the Bacchic ecstasy by restricting its celebration to official, numerically small communities of maenads.[86]

Even as the Dionysiac cult was being taken into the 'official' state religion, it was undergoing significant change, picking up new features and shifting emphases, and it continued to develop throughout its long life. Nilsson, more than any other scholar, tried to clarify this development. In addition to the elements already discussed, there were four main aspects of Dionysiac religion's development which he treated: wine, drama, postmortem beliefs, and the sect of Orphism.

As has been noted, Dionysos' most important association as a vegetation god was with the vine and its product, wine. Originally a god of trees and flowers, he had gained lordship over wine only after he had entered Greece. The early wine ceremonies in his honor involved dedicating the new wine, celebrating its miraculous origin,[87] and lifting the taboo placed on it before its consecration to the god.[88] Later, when Greeks reflected on the suffering of Dionysos, they interpreted the treading of the wine press as the god's dismemberment. However, this theologizing was restricted to the late classical and Hellenistic times.[89] 'Wonders' involving wine proving the god's power were also reported, but these too were probably late, as were most of the mythical accounts of Dionysos' associations with wine.[90] In the Hellenistic and Roman eras the Bacchic cult became increasingly more luxurious, and the symposia or drinking parties became well known.[91] Thus the main direction in which Dionysiac religion changed with respect to wine was from an early, rather staid patronage to the hedonistic, more religiously frivolous sponsorship of later times.

Dionysos' evolving relations with drama had been healthier. The Dionysiac cult gave birth to both comedy and tragedy. The jokes and humorous songs of those who carried the phalli in Bacchic processions gave rise to comedy, while the Dionysiac cult of Eleutherai gave rise to tragedy.[92] In the latter cult, a ritual combat took place between 'the Light One' and 'the Black One'.[93] (Nilsson interpreted this combat as a representation of the battle between summer and winter.)[94] The ritual actions and the lamentations over Dionysos, the dying god (believed to rise again), supplied the basic form for tragedy: struggle, defeat, and lamentation. Then the biographies of dead heroes were fitted to this form, giving it variety of content, and this combination produced tragedy as we know it.[95]

As with wine, Dionysos' associations with the realm of death were later developments which evolved with the Greeks' changing concerns. Nilsson rejected Rohde's belief that Dionysos had brought ideas of immortality from Thrace,[96] even though in his early works he had attributed ideas of germination and decay, life and death and new life to the original Thracian cult.[97] Once he had bifurcated Dionysiac religion into Thracian and Phrygian branches, he no longer attributed even these basic ideas to the Thracian cult.[98] Only after the union of the two cults was the Thracian mysticism combined with the Phrygian beliefs of the dying and rising vegetation god to produce a mythical prototype of the fate of the human soul.[99]

To be sure, Dionysos did play an important role in certain Greek festivals for the dead or for souls, but this participation had been a late development. Both the Anthesteria and the Agrionia, festivals for the dead under the ostensible patronage of Dionysos, seem to have predated Dionysos' arrival in Greece.[100] Furthermore, on the last day of the Anthesteria when the dead were thought really to be active, Dionysos played no role, whereas Hermes was paramount.[101] Nilsson felt that these facts disproved any early identity of Dionysos as 'Lord of Souls'. He suggested instead that Dionysos' patronage of the Anthesteria was probably due to his associations with fertility and to the fact that fertility and the underworld were closely related in the minds of the Greeks.[102] Dionysos had been affiliated with the Agrionia probably because it was an orgiastic festival.[103] It was only later, perhaps towards the end of the archaic age, that Dionysos assumed the role of 'Lord of Souls', largely on the basis of mystical teachings added to his cult.[104]

In time Dionysos became closely associated with the realm of the dead. Orphism, a Dionysiac reform group originating in the archaic age, had the post-mortem fate of the soul as its primary concern. From the late fifth and early fourth centuries B.C., Dionysos was increasingly associated with the Eleusinian Mysteries, also concerned with the fate of the dead.[105] Later, in the Hellenistic and Roman ages, anxiety about death increased and became one of the chief reasons for the great popularity of Dionysos.[106]

In Nilsson's view the Orphic reform represented the greatest and most ennobling change undergone by Dionysiac religion. Nilsson's understanding of the Orphic cosmogony and anthropology paralleled that of Rohde. The thrust of the Orphic myth was that man had been created out of the ashes of the Titans whom Zeus had destroyed after they had killed and eaten Dionysos. Though man's body was his Titanic, hence evil, portion, his soul represented the small portion of Dionysos which had been ingested by the murderous Titans and which yearned for release back to its divine home.[107]

Unlike Rohde who had seen Orphism as the logical extension of Dionysiac religion, Nilsson saw it as at least in part a break with the early cult which he did not interpret as world-denying. The Orphics transformed the conceptions of Dionysos, intensifying his association with the underworld and hailing him as the ruler of the universe.[108] They also attempted to reform other aspects of Dionysiac religion, exhorting man to regain his divine stature through asceticism and ritual catharsis. Though there were a number of possible explanations for Orphism (intense feelings of guilt in the face of excessive rules, a bifurcation between divine and human aspects created by the experience of Dionysiac ecstasy, and the tendency for asceticism due to the new belief in transmigration), Nilsson asserted that it was best understood as the creation of a religious genius.[109]

Nilsson's description of Dionysiac religion was remarkably complete and sensitive to the changes this cult had undergone throughout antiquity. Yet Nilsson was as concerned to explain as to describe, and for this he had to go beyond historical narrative. In his view only *Religionswissenschaft* could clarify and explain *Religions-geschichte.*[110] The historical behavior of the Greeks had been the result of certain traditional beliefs and practices transmitted from a more primitive epoch. Certain psychological or 'logical'[111] structures described and explained by anthropologists had been the ultimate causes of these traditions, and adequate interpretation involved showing how these primitive structures had operated to produce the actual historical situation of Dionysiac religion.

In order to understand Nilsson's strategy, one must recognize his conviction that between Dionysiac religion and intelligible contemporary behavior there was an immense gap created by a great intellectual advance. Therefore, the point of interpretation was not to recapture the experience of being a worshipper of Dionysos but to see where this intellectual advance originated and how it progressed.

Nilsson assumed that all persons acknowledged the legitimacy of the scientific world-view. The earlier pre-scientific view, on the other hand, was, he believed, difficult to understand rationally. To explain this background, the spawning place of religion, was the task of the science of religion. Like Frazer, Nilsson believed that the proper data of *Religionswissenschaft* were beliefs and practices which could not be explained as rational.[112] As soon as a conception or action could be explained as rational, it was no longer religious.[113]

Nilsson obviously continued the longstanding positivist tradition that intelligible behavior was necessarily guided by science and reason. Accepting the idea that everything man did was in some way utilitarian, he incorporated a vague kind of functionalism into his explanation. This was not the functionalism that studied cultures in their complex interrelationships to see processes of maintenance and change but the simpler generalization that people do things because of needs. Hence, in his total interpretation of Dionysiac religion, Nilsson's general strategy was to present humanity's most basic needs and to show how primitive man dealt with them, given his then current abilities. What follows will spell out Nilsson's understanding of those needs and then his understanding of the mental equipment with which early man tried to meet them and through which he came to believe in Dionysos.

First and most important, religious phenomena including gods like Dionysos were the products of man's fundamental *practical* needs.[114] On the most basic level man had to fulfill certain biological demands to survive. Above all, it was necessary to eat to insure one's own existence and to propagate in order to insure the continuation of the tribe. Thus, for man living in simple and archaic conditions, 'blessing' had been largely expressed in the word 'fertility'.[115] Yet man had needs not only for food and sex but also for security and relief from stress, and these needs too caused belief in gods.[116] His need to satisfy his powerful curiosity also created deities and other religious concepts.[117] Even man's need for recreation played a role in a number of religious ceremonies like fairs for the gods.[118] And finally, in circumstances of great distress, there was the very basic need to escape from too much pain; one of the important functions of Dionysiac religion in the archaic age was to provide 'oblivion of the miseries of life and the worries of the day'.[119]

The important thing to notice about all these needs is that they were natural, or perhaps better said, naturalistic. All humans shared the need for food, sex, security, relaxation, relief from pain and satisfaction of curiosity. Religious and non-religious persons did not differ on these needs, only on the means to satisfy them. For Nilsson it was self-evident why non-religious, scientific man relied on empirically established causal relations to obtain his wants; what was not obvious was why religious persons tried non-scientific, non-logical means for attaining practical ends.

Primitive mentality was the answer. Nilsson returned to it over and over in his works to explain the irrational behavior of religious man.[120] Helpless and confused in an overpowering world, primitive man's attention had been drawn to unusual phenomena; such phenomena manifested the power of the universe.[121] What resulted from this initial perception was 'mana', not simply a *belief* in power but a predominantly emotional appreciation of that power and response to it. Respect and awe before this power then was the first moment of religion.[122] Nilsson felt that mana, in fact, in its twofold content as a positive relation to power through magic and a negative relation to power through taboo, could serve as a satisfactory minimum definition of religion.[123]

Magic and taboo resulted from the limitations of primitive

mentality once it tried to work with this initial response to the awesome but uncomprehended power of the universe. Nilsson borrowed Lucien Lévy-Bruhl's terminology to explain this mentality, altering the latter's meaning where he thought necessary. First, primitive thought was 'mystical' in that the associations that primitives made about their world were often irrational and different than those of the educated. Second, primitive thought was 'prelogical' not in the sense that the primitive followed another system of logic than we but in the sense that his logic was undeveloped and not always used consciously to deal with the facts of experience. Third, the 'law of participation', which held that in primitive representations the part is equal to the whole, was due simply to the primitive's inability to make logical associations.[124] In all of these characteristics primitive thought showed itself to be confused and inaccurate, as one would expect of the first bungling steps of intellectual advance.

Unable to think abstractly,[125] unable to distinguish between human and animals,[126] between real action and a copy,[127] between dream and actuality,[128] primitive man turned to magic to gain his ends.[129] As had Frazer, Nilsson saw magic as the result of confused associations. Thus it was a malfunctioning logic which led the Greeks to expect numerous aspects of Dionysiac religion to provide improvement in their material conditions. This was the essential reason for the ceremonies, the carrying of the phallos, the associations with sexually potent animals and fertile plants, and so forth, not the fact that vegetative associations may have been added to Dionysiac religion in Phrygia. The historical facts about Anatolian forerunners only pushed the puzzle back one step. By specifying the logic of magic, Nilsson explained the *real* cause of many of the elements of Dionysiac religion.

What of Dionysos himself? What accounted for him? Like all gods, Dionysos resulted from the development of the earlier, more fundamental religious categories. As mistaken associations had produced magic, so they produced more complicated concepts as well—the soul concept,[130] fetishism,[131] taboos regarding the dead.[132] Once current, the soul concept in particular evolved quickly into other religious forms. Extrapolating from his belief that he had a soul, primitive man soon peopled the entire world with imaginary spirits, then further anthropomorphized them until they became gods.[133] A later creation than magic,[134] gods were supposed to furnish those changes in the natural world which magic could not.[135] They were also supposed to account for things which the primitive could not understand; since in the primitive mind, 'the incomprehensible is supernatural, and the supernatural is divine' (*göttlich*).[136] The great gods like Dionysos usually came from smaller daimones and numina who had achieved individuality and prominence,[137] but sometimes they arose directly from the personification of some power or natural phenomenon.[138] Nilsson interpreted the Phrygian Dionysos in this manner, as a copy of the life of nature given human characteristics.[139] In fact, a god generally represented a combination of several earlier religious components, each one of them the response to some original need. In understanding a god like Dionysos one must acknowledge his composite nature and seek to discover the origins of the individual elements.[140] Dionysos would then have been in part the mythical portrayal of the life of nature, in part a structured religious form around which to constellate various magical practices intended to help fertility, in part an explanation for the psychological exaltation of the mystical state, and, later in the god's career, in part the psychic precipitate of man's instinctive fear of death and delusive hope for postmortem survival. Taking the concept of Dionysos as the Divine Child in particular, two things were at work which made the Greeks think that Dionysos was instrumentally useful. First, by representing the cyclical passing of the seasons in the mythical life cycle of the child Dionysos, the Greeks thought they were magically guaranteeing the fertility of nature and their own propagation. At the same time as this mythologem supposedly gave the Greeks some control over events, it also explained the succession of seasons, something they were unable to comprehend naturalistically.

It should be readily apparent that from this perspective the way to understand Dionysiac religion is 'from the outside', not from empathically sharing the subjective world of the Dionysiac worshipper. The Greeks' beliefs and practices did not bring the results wished; they were mistakes, wastes of time. Looking at the alleged aims of Dionysiac religion, one could always envisage naturalistic science having more success. In this sense, behavior centered around the cult of Dionysos had been unintelligible, since it was irrational and did not work. As a fruitless attempt to satisfy man's practical needs, it could only be understood by tracing the causes of the error.

Nilsson, however, did not analyze religious behavior as entirely utilitarian. He believed that it began that way, but, like Rohde, he was sensitive to the autonomy religion attained once it effectively formed part of the 'known' world of a people. Thus he spoke frequently of 'religious needs' as distinct from practical needs. By this he meant that once someone had come to believe in a god, then he needed the presence of that deity in and of itself apart from any empirical benefits. Hence one of the motive forces behind the success of Dionysos was this religious need, this urge to be close to the deity. To a significant extent the smaller gods had filled this need by not being as august and distant from man as were the more sublime great gods.[141] Of the important gods, however, Dionysos responded to this need the most effectively. His ecstatic cult answered the individual's emotional needs for the presence of the god in a way the state cults never did.[142] Mystical experience was something, Nilsson felt, that man had needed at all times and in all religions.[143] In fact, if the emotional side of religion were suppressed, it would break out even more explosively than if left to its own course, so strong was this general need.[144] Thus, it was easy to see why Dionysos would have become popular once he became known and why the priests of the Apolline cults had been wise in not trying to suppress the Dionysiac cult altogether but in merely regulating it. As a creation of mistaken thought and fantasy, Dionysos was imagined as very accessible to his followers and therefore gave them a generalized sense of security and significance. Men needed him. Of course, he was there for them to need only because earlier errors of judgment had led them to fabulate his existence, but they did believe in his existence and they needed him all the same.

Late in his career and completely apart from the theories spelled out so far, Nilsson enunciated another interpretation of religion which was considerably less positivistic. In an article entitled 'Religion as Man's Protest against the Meaninglessness of Events',[145] he portrayed the purpose of religion not as utilitarian manipulation of the world but as the search for cosmic significance. According to this article, religion provided man a total orientation towards his experienced world—either it showed that the world had meaning, despite apparent evils, or it admitted that the world was meaningless and provided techniques of salvation to help man escape.[146] Thus the protest could cut either of two ways. In optimistic religions, the protest was against the *appearance* of meaninglessness; what appeared to be merely random or mechanical events were shown, usually by way of mythical paradigms, to cohere into a larger meaningful order; or, failing that, where the injustice was too glaring, post-mortem restitution was predicted— punishment for sinners and rewards for the righteous. In pessimistic religions, the protest was against the *actuality* of meaninglessness; given an evil, painful, or absurd universe, the only proper response was to employ religious techniques to free oneself from the limitations of incarnate existence.

In this perspective Nilsson postulated a new purpose for religion. As a protest against meaninglessness religion represented a way of understanding the world so as to make sense out of the brutal facts of lived existence. Here the implicit model of man was no longer a creature of solely practical drives. In this view man had needs for meaning, for satisfaction of his ethical sense. By postulating that where man found the world meaningless, he could give all his energies to winning salvation, Nilsson pointed to a highly significant drive which transcended utilitarian concerns and reached to the most serious metaphysical level. The hypothetical everyman of the 'Protest' article was really much closer to the hypothetical actor of the theories of Max Weber than to those of Tylor, Frazer, and Marett.

Yet even in treating religion as non-utilitarian behavior, Nilsson contrasted it with science and judged it inferior. As opposed to many scholars describing religion as a totalistic orientation to the world and its difficulties, Nilsson did not maintain a phenomenologically neutral stance toward the truth value of religion. Whereas most phenomenologists dealt with religion simply as an alternative orientation with different concerns than science, Nilsson judged it essentially as a mask to cover up the truth of science or allied visions of the world. He assumed the indifference of the universe and the meaninglessness of existence as givens and saw religion as a veneer designed to render life bearable. Hence its value was more that of an anodyne than of a defensible understanding of the world.

Nilsson never applied this theory to Dionysos, but one can easily see elements in Dionysiac religion which would fit it. First, on the most world-affirming, utilitarian level, Nilsson portrayed seasonal rites as designed to prevent meaningless interruptions of the ordinary course of Life and Nature.[147] Thus, in part Dionysos would represent a guarantee of seasonal and economic stability, helping man to the extent that man worshipped him properly. When conditions deteriorated, as they did in the archaic age, the fact that the ecstasies of the mystical religion granted man oblivion from the miseries of life represented an important protest against distress. The hope for immortality which formed such an important part of later Dionysiac religion was another obvious answer to the problems of life's pain and transience. And finally, Orphism, Greece's closest approximation to Buddhism, did actively promote the view that earthly existence was a meaningless trap to which man would be condemned until he purified and freed his soul by leading an Orphic existence. In these later aspects of Dionysiac religion what was at stake was essentially an attempt to trade a painful and meaningless existence for something both more real and more enduring.

Since Nilsson never integrated this perspective into the rest of his work, it is impossible to say whether he believed religion could have originated as protest or assumed that function only after it had already been in existence for some time. Probably he would have argued that religion began in the way outlined in his earlier works: pressing needs drove unenlightened man into specious concepts like magic, spiritualism, and worship of divinities. Only after these concepts had given man the sense of a supernatural presence environing the world and of a possible existence after death would religion be an effective protest against meaninglessness. Almost certainly Nilsson would have continued to derive religion ultimately from man's attempt to control his world.

Nilsson and the Critique of Evolutionism

Nilsson's advocacy of evolutionism is interesting because of his awareness of methodological counter-currents and his attempts to answer critics of his position. Rohde and Harrison had both worked during a time when evolutionism was sufficiently dominant that they could ignore non- or anti-evolutionary perspectives without being irresponsible. Nilsson properly and conscientiously acknowledged the existence of these later alternative positions and their challenge to the legitimacy of his own. His counterarguments, as a consequence, serve as a good index of the increasing difficulty evolutionists were experiencing in justifying their method.

Scholars reacting against evolutionism had begun to criticize the entirely speculative character of earlier accounts of the evolution of non-material culture and to apply to evolutionist works pejorative epithets such as 'armchair' and 'scissors and paste' to connote artificial reconstructions cut off from the reality of pre-literate societies. Successions of stages thought of as 'inevitable' or 'regular' by the evolutionists were dismissed by later anthropologists as at best purely hypothetical, often as highly improbable. These later anthropologists insisted that there was no proof that development had taken place in a uniformly or even consistently progressive direction, especially in areas involving human values. Barring such proof, they invited evolutionists to cease inventing unverifiable sequences of development. For the study of religion this turn away from evolutionism was crucial, since if these sequences of development were valueless, it was illegitimate to derive phenomena such as the worship of deities from 'simpler' phenomena such as magic, soul-belief, mana, totemism, and so forth.

Nilsson recognized the implications of these arguments. On the one hand, he knew that it was fruitless to argue that the evolutionary sequences of religion had been demonstrated in the same way as had, for example, biological sequences. Thus he could not appeal to these schemata as historically verified. On the other hand, if they did not have some sort of authority, then it would be impossible to explain the 'higher' phenomena on the basis of the 'lower'. Clearly he had to find some middle course which would not violate the generally accepted criticisms of evolutionism but which would preserve evolutionism's central tenets.

The compromise which Nilsson struck was, to put it bluntly, something of a mess. At times he admitted that the evolutionary sequences were valid only as logical, not as historical, series. This said, however, he would consistently ignore the admission and use the series to explain the origin of gods and other phenomena as refinements and transformations of earlier, simpler, and more patently illusory conceptions. At other times, he would redefine the anti-evolutionist argument and then refute the argument as he had redefined it. At still other times, he would acknowledge the uncertainty of the different evolutionary theories and try to compensate for this by blending them together into a lowest-common-denominator vagueness.

Nilsson's most explicit attack on the anti-evolutionists came in his 'Letter to Prof. A. D. Nock on Some Fundamental Concepts in the Science of Religion', written in 1954.[148] His first argument was that in denying evolutionism the anti-evolutionists were denying that religion had developed.[149] To do this was to deny the obvious historicity of man in the most obtuse way. Certainly any theory which cannot take change seriously did not deserve attention.

The problem with Nilsson's refutation was that the anti-evolutionists had never denied change or development; all they had denied was that religion had evolved from 'simple', 'rudimentary' conceptions to more complex ones. Even Lang and Schmidt and their followers of the 'High God' school gave considerable attention to the development of religion. Where they differed from Nilsson was in claiming that this development represented a conceptual *decline* from elevated theistic concepts to superstition rather than a progressive advance. One could argue that their reconstruction was inaccurate, but it was hardly fair to label it ahistorical.[150]

In his own definition of evolution Nilsson attempted to avoid any semblance of doctrinaire rigidity by asserting that 'evolution may go in either direction to higher or lower forms, the latter is called degeneration'.[151] Yet he still argued for progressive evolution: 'On the whole evolution goes from what are in regard to formalities and concepts, more elementary forms to purer and more complicated forms, just as material evolution does'.[152]

Yet on the next page he denied historical progressive evolution, asserting that it was a mistake to take what he called the 'common series' (power, taboo, magic, daemons, gods, religion) as a historical sequence. These ideas, he acknowledged, were found in all stages of religious evolution, and historical development did not necessarily entail moving from one of these stages to the next. This series should be understood as a logical, not historical, one.[153] In these statements Nilsson seemed to agree with critics of evolutionism, and few could have quarrelled with the way in which he identified himself as an evolutionist: 'for I acknowledge the logical series, going from lower to higher ideas, but as conceptual, not as historical'.[154]

The problem was that Nilsson did not take these claims seriously or, if he did, he never put them into practice. If one accepts his concessions to criticism of evolutionism, the rest of his *oeuvre* makes no sense. His entire interpretation consisted of explaining phenomena genealogically, showing how after a birth in primitive error they underwent rationalization and became more elevated. Such an interpretation could be justified only if the proposed series-power, taboo, magic, daemons, gods, religion—was taken as an historical sequence, not as merely logical.

In the face of this problem, Nilsson appealed to the evolutionary sequence but only 'in general'. That is, while he acknowledged that the actual historical evolution is unknown, he seems to have believed that the sequence presented by the evolutionists was 'more or less' the way religion evolved and was therefore still useful for our understanding.[155] For example, in the *Geschichte*, twenty one pages after asserting that the evolutionary series should be understood as logical, not historical, Nilsson presented religion as generally developing from soul-belief to spirit-belief, to polydemonism, to polytheism, to henotheism, to monotheism. He said that this reconstruction (which makes no sense other than as historical) fitted Greek religion 'to some extent' (*einigermassen*) and qualified it only by the statement that some people did not worship demons and that the Greek situation was somewhat more complicated, since dynamism and animatism had also been involved.[156] The net effect of this vagueness was to render Nilsson's reconstruction considerably more flexible and less vulnerable to disproof than those of more dogmatic evolutionists. Obviously Nilsson hoped that this elasticity would allow him to retain the basic evolutionary interpretation. If he admitted that the specific developments may have varied from culture to culture, this did not necessarily disqualify the theory that the general development of religion had been from simple to complex.

It is a rather exasperating argument, partly because of its surface plausibility. Nilsson had taken the entire list of alleged origins of religion proposed by evolutionists and had, in effect, said 'Choose one or more of the above'. If one considered this choice as sufficiently broad, then it was still obviously correct to explain primitive and therefore Greek religion as the product of the inherently deficient primitive mentality.

Thus, for example, when the worshippers carried the phallos in the Dionysiac procession, it was because the original logic of imitative magic claimed that a representation of a source of fertility would mystically cause fertility throughout nature. If women were whipped in another Bacchic rite, it was because the Greeks thought the scourging of women would magically drive away evil influences and impel fertility, again according to mistaken logic. If Dionysos was worshipped as lord over vegetation or over the grape, it was because certain natural processes has been personified. If Dionysos was the one great god who blessed his worshippers with his intimate presence, it was because those who experienced the powerful exaltation within themselves could explain this strange and foreign power only in supernatural terms. It was not necessary to specify the exact order of stages, only to show that the deistic stage embodied by the fully formed Dionysos succeeded more rudimentary phenomena and represented a more complex attempt to satisfy basic needs.

The tactic had an obvious appeal. On the one hand, it implicitly acknowledged that the attacks on the evolutionary method had merit insofar as they demystified certain speculative reconstructions which had been taken as established fact. While evolutionary sequences presented credible portrayals of what may have given rise to religion and were helpful antidotes to the assumption that religion represented revelation from on high, they did not represent the discovery of 'laws' and could not be guaranteed to be true. On the other hand, to dismiss evolutionism completely, Nilsson felt, would be to abandon a genuine advance in our understanding of cultural development. Progressive intellectual evolution could be demonstrated for scientific and technological matters; surely, he believed, the same thing had occurred in religion. In his view it would be an obscurantist skepticism that denied all discussion of religion's evolution just because one could not specify the different stages. Nilsson's response to this situation was extremely pragmatic. He blurred the lines of the different classical evolutionary theories until he was able to bring them together into a predigested, common-sense compendium. If one had a difficult time understanding why the Greeks would carry phalloi, thyrsi, and snakes, why they would rant and rave about on the mountaintops, terrifying the women and children and livestock, sometimes to death, and why they spent considerable time and resources to honor this thing they called Dionysos, whose existence was disproved by contemporary thought patterns, then Nilsson had a no-nonsense explanation which would account for most if not all of this strange behavior.

The issue, as is the case with many hermeneutical problems, boiled down to one's choice of presuppositions. If one assumed that primitive man in his concern to ameliorate his material condition devoted all of his energies to utilitarian pursuits, then the phenomena associated with Dionysos probably were best explained as Nilsson proposed, as traditions based on primitive attempts to control and explain the world through non-logico-experimental means. Whether Dionysos was the result of the refinement of magic, or a substitute for magic, or an explanation for psychological states, or the personification of nature, what the Greeks were up to when they worshipped him was transparent enough. One might disagree about the sequence in which mistaken associations led to the developed religion of Dionysos, but one understood this religion as the result of errors made in the dawn of human existence and propagated by each generation.

Nilsson's treatment of the *history* of Dionysiac religion had been the most complete one available, partly because he wrote full-length works both on Dionysos and on Greek religion as a whole in which he situated Dionysos in a wider context. As already mentioned, he had been sensitive to historical development and to the differences in the cult at different locations, and his treatment of Dionysos will probably always be of use to historians. For those who accepted his presuppositions, not only his historical work but also his total interpretation was a landmark contribution to classicism, since it certainly represented this century's most refined and sophisticated treatment of Dionysiac religion from the evolutionary perspective.

Yet if one was inclined to accept the critique of evolutionism at its full value, then Nilsson's interpretation became much more questionable. Contemporary primitive peoples engage in utilitarian *and* symbolic activities with equal seriousness and refinement, and there is no evidence that this has not been the case for as long as man has been religious. If technological knowledge is not the paradigm for all other knowledge, then one can no longer say that worship of deities like Dionysos is simply the compounding of a pseudo-scientific error. If primitive mentality itself is no longer considered as *ipso facto* infantile, then to trace religion back to primitive mentality no longer has the same devastating implications Nilsson thought it did, nor, ultimately, does it explain religion. Since primitive thought patterns which differ from Western thought patterns are no longer necessarily to be explained as the result of mistaken associations, they require some other explanation. Scholars increasingly see great metaphorical and metaphysical sophistication in pre-literate cultures; the question seems totally open whether these metaphysical concerns originate independently of more pragmatic concerns or are merely extensions of initial misdirected practical responses. Skeptics of evolutionism see no way in which the latter theory could be proved and therefore dismiss evolutionary reconstructions, even those as loosely defined as Nilsson's, as indefensible.

Once one has rejected evolutionism, there are two basic options left open. One of these is most clearly represented by the structural-functional approach, where the question of origins becomes irrelevant, since the scholar investigates the interrelationship of different elements in an ongoing system. He examines the religion to see how it works in society, how society impinges on it, how religion and society reflect each other's reality, and so on.

The other option is to deal with the religion as an independent orientation toward reality which makes a truth claim believed to be more than a reflection of the social and cultural context. One understands religion by reconstructing not its genealogy but its insight into the nature of existence. From this perspective Dionysos was something very different than what Nilsson thought. The subject of the next chapter, Walter F. Otto, was a perfect foil for Nilsson, because his diametrically opposed presuppositions about religion led to a radically different understanding of Dionysos.

5

Walter F. Otto and the Study of Dionysos

The work of Walter F. Otto[1] represents a violent break with the interpretations which we have considered up to this point. Whereas Rohde, Harrison, and Nilsson saw Dionysiac religion as based on a faulty conceptualization, Otto argued that it disclosed a profound truth about the nature of the universe. As a result he interpreted it by spelling out the content of this authentic vision of the Divine rather than by tracing its genesis or translating it into some natural referent. Otto was a vigorous polemicist and defined his position in opposition to evolutionists and others who, in his opinion, were blind to the legitimate truth of Greek religion. On almost every issue—the nature of historical understanding, of religion as a human phenomenon, of Greek religion as a specific example of religion, and of Dionysos as a unique Greek god—he took an antithetical position to that assumed by the evolutionists.

As with the evolutionists, there are different levels of seriousness with which one can take Otto. Ultimately, his intention in writing on Greek religion was homiletical; he thought that Greek religion was the most authentic way of understanding reality and should replace both modern scientific freethought and Christianity as man's orientation to the wider universe. While this aspect of his argument is always interesting and frequently powerful, it is not the sort of thing that professionally engages classicists and historians of religion. Some scholars have viewed Otto's exhortations as discrediting his interpretation and have ceased to pay him any attention. This is understandable; but it is also regrettable, because behind his passionate advocacy for Greek religion there lies a very useful and carefully articulated exposition of the role of world-view (or what has come to be called, in a value free sense, ideology) in shaping culture and human behavior. In addition, he provided one of the earliest explanations of how rituals, social groups, cultic paraphernalia, and other facets of religious life convey information about a culture's stance in the universe. Even without accepting Otto's belief in the superiority of the Greek world-view, one can learn how to interpret myths and cults as religious communication from a distant culture more effectively after having read him. In addition to describing his argument for Greek religion, this chapter will, where possible, indicate those aspects of his analysis which are separable from his own religious vision and which can be profitably applied in any interpretation.

Of the scholars examined here, Otto was easily the most vigorous partisan of the hermeneutic of rearticulation. Heavily influenced by Frobenius and culture-morphology, he argued that religion sprang from a deep insight into the nature of reality experienced when the universe seemed to disclose its essential secrets to a perceptive and creative spirit. Assuming that man's capacities at the time of religion's origin were basically comparable to those of today, Otto held that the creator of any specific religion was best understood as a genius who had been able to give form to an entire culture's understanding of reality by his imaginative and visionary power. Originating from such an insight, religion initially had nothing to do with utilitarian concerns and existed solely to express man's relation to the universe and the divine reality which sustained it. Because religion revealed the absolute horizon of being and the divine order which founded human and universal reality, it defined the nature of authentic human existence and therefore shaped the nature of culture. Since Otto believed that Divinity did reveal itself in various forms in different peoples' religious orientations to the world, he retained the language of Divinity and supernaturalism in his analysis. In his view the language of the Sacred was neither an error nor a mask for natural reality tinged with emotion but was the only means of doing justice to the sanctity of reality in its entirety. Accordingly, the only legitimate way to treat Greek religion was to take its content seriously as an alternative understanding of reality and see what could be learned from it.

OTTO'S UNDERSTANDING OF INTERPRETATION

For the evolutionists, who believed that intellectual evolution had resulted in man's increasingly adequate comprehension of the world, interpretation and historical understanding involved evaluating as defective intellectual constructs which differed from Western conceptions and explaining the situation which accounted for their inadequacy. The movement of interpretation was downward; one descended to the level of premodern religious thought in order to explain the error involved.

For Otto, historical understanding demanded that the interpreter suspend faith in the adequacy of his own view of reality in order to be open to the possible truth of another vision of things. For him history was not a storehouse of past errors or of dead facts but the record of man's confrontation with Being. Otto clearly presumed that in any era these expressions could be appropriated as viable and could lead the interpreter to a meeting with Being in its divine aspect. Thus, one should confront a religious fact on the same level as one accepted one's own perspective and even allow for the possibility that one would be convinced of the truth of this heretofore alien world view. Otto felt that by acknowledging the profundity of religious worlds and also the frequent difficulty of penetrating them, one avoided the flatness of the evolutionist perspective, which reduced religion to its lowest common denominator of intelligibility and thereby deprived it of its richness and integrity.

In Otto's view, legitimate history entailed portraying the enduring values of a particular culture. In this case that meant delineating the essential form of the Greek religious world seen as a very specific phenomenon. History had to maintain and display the specificity of the culture being investigated, but it also had to reveal the aspects of that culture which were timeless and spoke to the human condition across cultural boundaries. Legitimate understanding was legitimate because one respected the autonomy of the culture; it was understanding because one saw the universality of that particular religious world.

Otto rejected evolutionism as having failed at both of these levels. In the first place, by examining Greek religion as simply an example of a generalized 'primitive religion', evolutionists had ignored its particularity. Then by relegating Greek religion and its hypothetical primitive background to the status of mental infantilism, they had denied it any enduring value which might have manifested ultimate truth to contemporary man. Otto's response was to contrast to other religions what he took to be the central religious content of

Hellenism, thereby showing its specificity. At the same time, he attempted to present this religious content in a way that revealed its continued religious and philosophical relevance.

Otto openly admitted the difficulty of penetrating an alien culture's mind-set. He agreed with the evolutionists that Greek conceptions about reality were different from modern conceptions, both Christian and scientific. Yet he argued that scholars had to acknowledge the remoteness of Greek religion from Christianity and other religions of salvation and not explain this difference away as merely the result of undeveloped religiosity.[2] At the same time he considered it inadmissible to explain the difference between ancient man and modern scientific man by assuming that archaic man had been like his modern counterpart, interested primarily in materialistic gain or in causal or logical thought, but simply inaccurate in his thought processes.[3] In either case, by picturing the Greek as striving to be like modern man but lacking the necessary equipment, one was not really dealing with the actual phenomenon but merely brushing it aside in order to set up something else in its place that was more easily explained.[4]

For example, it was, Otto held, a mistake to try to interpret myth as a variant of our ordinary manner of thinking and living. Myth for the Greeks had been a response to the primal world. Since modern man had turned away from this primal world, the myth no longer made sense as it had for the Greeks. Not understanding the structure of reality in which the Greeks thought and lived, modern man cast about for some way to relate myth to the world with which he was familiar. However, rather than explaining the content of the myth, all he did was call attention to the fact that he had lost touch with this primal dimension and no longer saw reality in such depth.[5] Otto argued that by using modern conceptions we could not return directly to myth; therefore we should understand it indirectly in its type and in its effects on human existence and thus get a clearer notion of its contents.[6] In his analysis of Dionysos he attempted to resurrect the primal world made accessible to the Greek by the myths and show how religious behavior made possible the entrance into a different level of reality than that of the ordinary 'natural attitude'.

The distance between archaic religious phenomena and modern conceptions was due to what we have called the specificity of cultures. Since each culture has had its own systematic integrity, one could not simply assume some sort of easy commonality by which everything could be interpreted. For example, to claim that there was some fundamental religious experience with its own intrinsic content common to all men and to arrange religions according to how fully they had apprehended and expressed this experience was to misinterpret non-Christian religions and ignore the diversity of man's religious experience.[7] At the same time, for modern (rational-ist) scientists to present Greek religion as equivalent to that of any primitive society was also to obscure the specific nature of this religion.[8] The only proper response to the data was, Otto claimed, to take into account the fact that 'to each people, corresponding to the special quality of its nature, there is revealed a special quality of the Divine'[9] and to elucidate the form Divinity had taken in a particular culture.

Thus, rather than trying to reduce the language of supernatural-ism to the status of error, Otto attempted to explain the content of the Greeks' perception of Divinity. Since he believed the Divine manifested itself wherever men were perceptive, he treated it as a primary datum in all cultures and not as a fantasy which required a naturalistic causal explanation. He felt that historical investigation should open the modern historian to the 'great truths' about existence from past cultures which had an internal authenticity equal to truth claims of the modern West.

Scholars who insisted on pedantic objectivity and treated Hellen-ism as of only antiquarian interest ignored the true purpose of history.[10] The cultural legacy left by the Greeks represented, Otto insisted, 'the self-attestation of an eternal truth which revealed itself to them and ever since waits to be recognized anew'[11] and history's task was to mediate this renewed recognition.[12] For Otto, authentic history was existentially relevant.[13] To give true knowledge the past had to awaken the self-consciousness of the present and show the present its own being in the world.[14] Thus he claimed, history was as necessary for the modern man as myth was for the primitive.[15] Classical history was especially significant in this process of self-understanding, since Hellenism had provided the basis for modern European culture.[16]

Yet if history was a necessary enterprise for modern man, it was still a delicate task, and not everyone was equally well equipped for it. To understand truths of high creative magnitude one had to have some affinity with them. The definition of understanding (*Verstehen*) which Otto described as Nietzsche's was also his own: 'What is understanding? . . . The understanding of the living is no mere auditing and combining of facts, but the response of related life; and only fullness (*die Fülle*) is capable of responding to the fulfilled (*das Erfüllte*)'.[17] The interpreter had to be willing to lift his own thinking to a level commensurate with that of the material and even to learn from the cultural creators of the past.[18]

In making such heavy demands on the interpreter Otto was implicitly raising a long-standing dispute over the nature of scientific understanding. If science was the empirical investigation of phenomena, there was still a question about how best to be empirical. One might have an impeccable method in the sense that the questions one asked about the material might be very well defined and the model used for explanation might be quite clear and helpful for certain situations, and yet one could still ignore empirical evidence which, though not fitting into one's methodological framework, in fact constituted the heart of the phenomenon. What Otto did, in contrast, was to loosen his historiographical rigor and to employ intuition and creative, almost poetic, insight to get at aspects of the material which eluded clearer scientific paradigms. Theorists have sometime noted that one frequently has to choose either impeccable rigor and clarity, leading possibly to trivial results, or intuition and partial obscurity, leading possibly to more profound results. Otto consistently opted for the latter.

Thus, whereas the evolutionists had followed the models established by Enlightenment thinkers, Otto preferred the Romantics. In his view, they had been more open to the potential grandeur and truth of religious phenomena like myth. 'Instead of, as was previously done, approaching the myth with preconceived opinions, they first sought to raise themselves to its height in order to understand its language'.[19] Since rational science, both history and psychology, had failed to tell us what the gods were, he argued that we needed to listen to figures such as poets who themselves had been struck by the Eternal.[20] These figures, through their reflection on and dealings with the Greek gods, had been able to perceive something of the truth of the Greek myths and had mediated this truth to the modern period. Otto's most blistering condemnation of the methods employed by evolutionists and his strongest exhortation to follow more sympathetic expositors occurred in his attempt to define myth and cult in a different way than had the evolutionists:

> If then the cults are no utilitarian actions but powerful creations, called into life by the afflatus of the Divinity who reveals himself, and the myths, no fables but witnesses to the same encounter with the Sublime; if, therefore, it is valid to acknowledge *primal phenomena* and to do justice to great realities, then the study of psychology and logic, of which everything has been expected, can no longer be of use to us. Instruction can come to us only from the Being of the world itself; and instead of the most narrow-minded and petty type of man from whom we have previously derived our orientation, our qualified leaders must now be the greatest spirits who have looked deepest into the world and who have been most powerfully seized by reality.

> It is time again to remember the words of Schelling: 'It is not a question here of how the phenomenon must be turned, twisted, limited, or curtailed in order to be explicable in any case by principles which we once resolved not to go beyond, but rather how must our ideas be expanded in order to come to terms with the phenomenon'.[21]

Otto felt that the specifically religious character of Greek religion, its traffic with Divinity, had been misrepresented by those who could not deal with such concepts within their own frame of reference. Other thinkers, however, who had been seized by reality could deal with ideas of the Sacred as meaningful and not merely as, to use Parson's phrase, 'a residual category'.

Otto's desire to penetrate to the central insight of Greek religion as a meaningful expression of metaphysical truth led him to do history in a radically different manner than had the evolutionists. For the latter the essential task had been to trace the evolution of religious ideas and practice through time in order to clarify the objective situation which caused and shaped them. According to evolutionism there was continuity in the chain of events (knowledge increased as a function of time) but discontinuity in the knowledge possessed by respective cultures (modern culture was qualitatively superior in its understanding of the universe than traditional Greek culture). Otto ignored the continuity of the causal chain in order to focus on the abiding ideological essence of Greek culture, which, he contended, maintained its integrity throughout the archaic and classical periods. Studying cultures as organic units, he then treated the Greek view as of equal stature with the contemporary view in terms of its fundamental knowledge of the world. He clearly believed that if one comprehended the intention of Greek religious expression, the Hellenic view would manifest its own autonomous cogency and make naturalistic explanation unnecessary.

Otto's Understanding of Religion

One of the most important areas of debate between Otto and the evolutionists was in the understanding of religion as a general phenomenon. Much of the disparity between Otto's interpretation of Dionysos and those of the evolutionists can be traced back to this issue. Otto believed that one of the fundamental reasons that the evolutionists propounded erroneous theories was that they had misconstrued the nature of religion and had evaluated it in terms of how well it performed tasks for which it simply had not been designed. Naturally, if one explained religion as a poor substitute for some other, ostensibly more legitimate human behavior, one would as a matter of course treat traditional cultures as backward and be disinclined to seek any profound truth in their ideology. Otto held that only by coming to a more adequate understanding of what religion was really all about would one ever be able to interpret correctly a specific religious form like Dionysos.[22]

His primary criticism of the evolutionist interpretation was that it mistook religion for utilitarian activity. The reason the evolutionists had been able to make this mistake was that they had drawn their evidence from certain primitive groups which had ceased to understand their own customs.[23] Otto subscribed to the culture-morphologists' view that cultural forms were analogous to living organisms, with a period of health and a period of decay and eventual death. As time passed and people grew distant from the initial inspiration of an idea or a behavior, the phenomenon in question, for example, a ritual, would undergo a process of semantic depletion in which people would forget its original expressive meaning and increasingly expect it to yield some material reward.

From this perspective Otto could acknowledge that numerous people did practice religion for many of the reasons suggested by the evolutionists, but he claimed that this depleted state was inadequate evidence from which to explain the original religious institutions and cults.[24] He argued that some contemporary primitives still carried out religious practices which manifested the genuine nature of myth and ritual and adduced these practices and beliefs to contradict the interpretation that religion was instrumentally oriented.[25]

Otto felt that the evolutionists' interpretation was based on a prejudice. Since they themselves were limited to logical and causal thought and practical activity, they were unable to grasp modes of thought and behavior which were not dedicated to manipulating external reality to man's advantage. This limitation lay behind their difficulty in understanding many aspects of Hellenic civilization, for example, Sophoclean tragedy. The driving force in these dramas, Otto argued, was the protagonist's passion for self-recognition. This recognition was not for the purpose of adjusting more effectively to the world but for the pure, disinterested knowledge of Being and the protagonist's relationship to it. The fact that the Sophoclean hero would seek this knowledge when it was not to his advantage and even when it led to tragic consequences demonstrated the insufficiency of utilitarian motives as an explanation.[26] Otto clearly presumed that man's need for the truth in the widest sense was as important in human behavior as the desire for comfort and pleasure, and he insisted that religion was better understood as a statement about this universal truth than as practical behavior.

Otto hoped to reverse the evolutionists' presuppositions about man in order to allow religion to appear in a different light. Evolutionists had accounted for religion by presuming that religious man used rational and scientific techniques as best he could until he reached the limits of his scientific knowledge, at which point he relied on myth to fill in the gaps.[27] Since, in their own scientific thinking, the evolutionists had relied on mechanistic thinking, they had taken it as 'the simplest, most self-evident, and most original' pattern of human thought and seen it, or a flawed form of it, at the basis of religion. But projecting the thought of the nineteenth century back onto primitive man ignored cultural changes which had intervened and unfairly limited legitimate human behavior to that practiced by 'educated' Europeans.[28]

In *Dionysos* Otto used this criticism against Nilsson's interpretation of religion. In this instance the phenomenon over which the two scholars disagreed was the Greek ritual involving the *pharmakos*, a criminal who was led around the city and then killed for its purification. Nilsson had asserted that the *pharmakos* functioned to cleanse the city just as a sponge is used to wipe off a dirty table and subsequently thrown away. He labeled the thought behind the rite 'thoroughly primitive and comprehensible'.[29] In answer, Otto remarked bitterly that 'a ceremonial custom of antiquity is "comprehensible" to the modern scholar as soon as he thinks he recognizes the characteristics of the same way of thinking that directs our everyday life', and suggested that the ethnocentric arrogance of this interpretation was even more astounding than the alleged superstition of the primitive.[30]

Otto countered Nilsson's interpretation by saying that the Greeks killed the *pharmakos* not because they could not distinguish between sponges and people but because such a serious sacrifice was the only way they could give an adequate expression to a grim presence they perceived working behind and through the world. The sacrifice both expressed this sinister presence and freed man emotionally from its grip by giving it a cultic form. Later, when the original grandeur of the perception had been lost, more utilitarian explanations were offered by Greek commentators and readily accepted by the evolutionists.[31] Yet if one wished to understand man in his fullest capacities, Otto argued, one had to take into account the creative moments of human culture when pure knowledge and expression free from practical concerns were paramount. Only then would one understand phenomena like the *pharmakos* or Dionysos. As he asserted in another context, there are non-utilitarian dances and songs even in the animal kingdom.[32] One should be able to presume the same richness in the nature of man.

On one and only one occasion Otto briefly suggested a framework which would have allowed him to integrate man's need to express the truth about reality into a causal explanation of human behavior. Arguing against a simple utilitarian view in the introduction to *Die Götter Griechenlands* (*The Homeric Gods*) he portrayed man as moved by more than material drives:

It is often said that it is the needs of human existence whose growth and change are expressed in the formation of the image of the gods. True enough; however, the requirements of thought and a way of looking at things also surely belong to these needs.[33] Otto explained that the formation of a *Weltanschauung* was the most significant event in the life of a people and that the need for each people to have a distinctive mode of thought and way of seeing the world was just as important as material needs which allegedly led to magic. In this view religion provided man with an orientation to the universe, allowing him to see the basic structure of Being and his own relationship to it. This orientation had both epistemological and ontological value: it provided a mode of thought which allowed man to perceive the depths of reality and it presented an ordered model of the universe which this mode of thought had allowed to emerge in the life of the culture.

This 'orientational' understanding of religion has been very important in recent studies of religion, especially in the second third of this century. Scholars from diverse fields have come to argue that man carries on his activities within a socially defined understanding of reality which specifies the limitations and possibilities of existence and on which man draws for his values, his sense of meaning, and his expectations. In this manner scholars, even those who are non-religious, have been able to describe the metaphysical activity of mankind as something which plays an important role in shaping human behavior and which should be understood as a social fact among other social facts. Acknowledging the human need for some ultimate context of meaning, these scholars interpret religion as a type of 'world-building' which has its intrinsic satisfaction. Man, because he foresees his own death and experiences existence as both grandiose and morally out of joint, needs an articulated horizon for his thoughts, wishes, and actions.

The young Rohde, following Schopenhauer, had pursued this interpretation, though more from a philosophical than an anthropological perspective. He had even integrated this view into *Psyche* to some extent, but only after deriving religion's origin from misdirected curiosity. Nilsson had hinted at this approach in his article 'Religion as Man's Protest against the Meaninglessness of Events', but he seemed to treat this function of religion as epiphenomenal as compared to more practical concerns. From the opposite side Otto approached the same perspective, but he chose not to pursue the explanation of religion as 'orientation' in terms of human needs. Perhaps he felt that to the extent such orientation corresponded to a need, its truth value would be suspect. Nilsson's portrayal of religion as a metaphysical anodyne certainly had such a 'demystifying' effect. In any case, in other works Otto emphasized religion's purely expressive role as opposed to the way it satisfied needs.

Once familar with the work of Leo Frobenius, Otto appealed to the tenets of culture-morphology as a background for understanding the place of religion in culture. While he seemed to use culture-morphology as a scientific justification for revelation, his statements on the formative power of ideology could be rephrased so that they would be quite acceptable to any secular sociologist who acknowledged the dialectical nature of thought and praxis.

The first stage in his exposition was to derive religion from a different origin than had the evolutionists. Whereas they asserted that it sprang from simple, indeed confused beginnings and only gradually evolved into maturity, Otto argued that it sprang from a fully formed discovery about reality at its deepest level, just as biological life must spring from some structured kernel or embryo.[34] In religion the equivalent of the embryo was a manifestation (or revelation, *Offenbarung*) of the world upon which everything else was dependent.[35] This creative event was the basis for the entire culture.

On several occasions Otto utilized Frobenius' notion of *paideuma*[36] to explain how cultures derived their shape from the initiating vision. *Paideuma* was the essence of any particular culture. Objectified in the products of society and publicly shared, it incarnated the manner in which the world encountered that people. As the deposit of an entire culture, it was above the inorganic and organic realms, in a realm all its own, though still a genuine form of nature.[37] Constituted by the interrelationships of the entire culture, this *paideuma* stood over the people of a society, shaping them according to its form both as individuals and as a community and thereby realizing itself through them.[38]

What distinguished Frobenius' notion of *paideuma* from other social scientists' treatment of the molding power of culture was his insistence on ideology as the motive force in the process. In the final analysis, *paideuma* was primarily *idea*. Furthermore, it was an idea which had not arisen from practical experience and which had not

been directed to producing anything immediately useful. Its value was entirely intrinsic, in giving man his authentic bearing. Ultimately *paideuma* was a culture-wide metaphysical testimony to
the *meaning and spirit (Sinn und Geist)* which draws man up from the nature of a mere creature of drives (that is, from the 'animalistic') to that which he is *supposed* to be—to *man*—to that being for whom the world is more than a playroom for his life needs, for whom the world in its deeper ground is itself *meaning and spirit.*[39]

As opposed to the evolutionists' view, this perspective held that man gained his true humanity only when he was more than a practical problem solver and confronted the world as ontologically meaningful. *Paideuma* was the socially sedimented result of that confrontation. Objectively speaking, it was a picture of the world, yet not simply a disembodied thought but a world-view presented through all the cultural manifestations of a people. Thus, man, as he was shaped by his culture, was inevitably being formed by its *paideuma*; and as he acted out his role in the culture, he continued to objectify it. In this sense one could describe man's entire existence as giving form through various cultural expressions to this conception of the being of things. Put subjectively, one could say that human existence was, in its essence, man's creative answer to the manifestation of sacred reality.[40] Since the awareness of this sacred reality penetrated every aspect of each culture, Otto called religion 'the unending foundation of [a culture's] creative power'.[41]

Thus, culture was born out of the meeting of man and the Divine. As Otto conceived it, man was not the conscious originator of this meeting but felt himself seized by some wonderful otherness which was, in fact, the presence of a higher being.[42] The god stood at the beginning of religion, and it was his presence which initiated man's profound knowledge of the world.[43] Otto denied that one could derive this belief in gods from earlier conceptions and ideals, since all of man's conceptions and ideals themselves had come from his meeting with divinity. The appearance and form of god was not a result of human thought but a presupposition for it and all of the ways man fashioned his world. This confrontation between man and Divinity was thus something non-derivative and irreducible.[44] Not until it had occurred did man have the context in which to organize the particularities of his existence, since only the ultimate horizon

provided by this confrontation could give ordinary reality its accepted contours and significance. In other words, Otto was arguing
that cultures operated with fundamental paradigms of reality and
that the creation of such a paradigm was the determinative event for
a culture, much in the same way that it has been argued that sciences
are dependent on basic paradigms and perform day-to-day opera-
tions only within them. What made Otto's analysis unique was his
insistence that it was a religious experience which established the
paradigm.

Otto was not content to allow religious experience to be analyzed
in the same manner as ordinary experience, so he invoked a
presupposition to establish the irreducibility of gods. He claimed
that gods could not just be invented but must be experienced.[45]
Since the reality of a god could not be compared to anything in the
profane realm, there was really no way to explain it to someone who
lacked all awareness of Divinity. 'The god can only appear and be
experienced or not'.[46] There might be those to whom the god did
not appear, but it was false to attempt to explain Divinity to them as
some 'ordinary' phenomenon which had been understood in an
eccentric manner. One could adequately interpret the god only by
rearticulating the culture's use of supernaturalistic concepts until
one understood the reason why these people accepted them as
defining the shape of reality.

On occasion Otto did try to explain the meaning of Divinity. He
argued that even though the Divine could be known only by direct
experience, such knowledge was always available because super-
powerful Divinity was ever striving to show itself as primal life.[47]
Where man was receptive, Divinity illumined the entire world and
man saw the god as 'the magnificence and holiness of Being'.[48] Each
god then expressed the entire world from a particular perspective,[49]
or, put another way, 'To be a god here means to carry the entire
meaning of a realm of existence and to rest as glory and grandeur on
all its creations'.[50]

Otto had a tendency to be both oracular and rhetorical, so that
many of his explanations are obscure; but what he proposed here
was an interesting alternative to the evolutionist analysis of gods.
Unlike the latter, which saw gods as cultural figments thought up for
the purpose of helping man by interfering with the order of the
universe, Otto was claiming that they in fact represented and

expressed this order. In the final analysis the gods were not devices to change the world but were focussed images of the world through which existence could be perceived in all its majesty and darkness. Thus, they aided man's perceptions of reality, not man's workaday activity or curiosity. If one accepts this viewpoint, it is easier to sympathize with Otto's frustration with evolutionist interpretation. Its assumption that the Greeks were trying to perform practical activity through religion ignored the possibility that their religious vision and behavior might have given their experience an entirely different texture than that of modern man,[51] just as poetry can impart to ordinarily unnoticed things an unexpected richness. If there was any alchemy involved in religion, Otto would have located it at the level of perception instead of at the level of objective fact. Yet from Otto's viewpoint, this was sufficient alchemy, since he believed that the richness of a person's world was a function of his creativity and perceptiveness. It was almost as though the world itself was of unlimited 'thickness' and the only variable was the mode of experiencing it. Logical and causal thought opened up one layer of the world so that man could perceive spatiotemporal relations with great clarity. However, religion opened up an even more ultimate layer so that man could experience and participate in the beauty and terror at the very heart of existence. From Otto's viewpoint the 'flatness' of the evolutionist interpretation resulted from its inability to deal with different levels of experience.[52]

Thus religion was in part man's expression of the deepest level of reality in which he lived. Otto also saw a supernatural content in religion and portrayed the Divine as existing independently above and beyond the world. He spoke of this transcendence only infrequently, but on at least one occasion he said of the gods that they 'signify the entire being of the world and *above and beyond that* the inexpressible magnificence of *the Divine as such*'.[53] In specific cultures Divinity manifested itself in various ways. For the Greeks, divinity manifested itself through Being and was thus very close to the natural world; for the Romans, it revealed itself as power and will standing *over* the world.[54] In Asian religions it revealed itself as acting in man's inner self and ignoring the outside world.[55] Common to all of these cultures was the supernatural confronting man in some part of his experience.

To define a god as a supernatural being was relatively common.

The evolutionists had defined Divinity in more or less the same way. Yet for them, since 'supernatural' meant *ipso facto* 'non-existent', the question was how had such a mistaken concept arisen? For Otto, the reality of Divinity was never problematic. He believed that its existence was presupposed as self-evident by every reasonable man.[56] Since the reality of the Divine was evident to all clear thinking people, manifestations of Divinity to man needed no justification. In fact, the acknowledgement of the Divine was one of the oldest, most primordial realizations of mankind and, as such, was inextinguishable from human nature.[57]

Confronted by the manifestation of Divinity, what did man do? According to Otto, man's response to the Divine was to celebrate it, to give expression to it, to recreate it with his own form and in his own actions, and thus to enter into relations with it. Expressing its glory was man's way of communing with the Divine. He could give it nothing useful and he expected nothing in return. He could, however, re-present the structure of this great reality in a form in which he could participate and through which he would achieve his proper identity. At the dawn of religion man had stood before Being as its most effective self-manifestation since he, better than any other aspect of the world, could give form to its wonderful reality. Hence, religious cult was man's necessary response to the revelation of Being.[58]

It is relatively easy to understand how religious practices could be interpreted as celebratory when they deal with the magnificent or beneficent side of the supernatural realm, but what about those that dealt with the darker, more dreadful side? After all, as the work of Jane Harrison showed so clearly, the latter aspect had played an important part in Greek religion. Here too, Otto interpreted Greek religious behavior as the disinterested expression of a perceived reality. Myth and cult gave form to the dreadful as well as to the sublime, and through this expression religious man achieved a cathartic liberation from his dread.[59] Whether the truth being confronted was pleasant or unpleasant, Otto contended that religious man was driven to express it fully.

There were many ways in which religious man could express his insight. Otto took obvious pleasure in the fact that the Greeks looked to their artists rather than to their priests, prophets, or philosophers to mediate truths about Divinity. The Greek genius expressed its piety through literature, music, two-dimensional art and sculpture. But the most important forms of expression were myth and cult, and it was here in his discussion of these two interrelated phenomena that Otto made his greatest contributions to scholarship. By redefining their nature and role he made possible an entirely different understanding of the nature of the Greek gods. Thus, it was not accidental that his major interpretation of Dionysos begins with a long programmatic explanation of myth and cult.

As with so many issues, Otto's understanding of myth was diametrically opposed to that espoused by the evolutionists. For Rohde, Harrison, and Nilsson, myth and cult stood within the orbit of everyday life as inferior versions of science and technology which were supposed to help man's condition. Otto argued that myth and cult defined the horizon and significance of ordinary life rather than being simply two of its components. It was the myth that most explicitly communicated the great truth that the founding genius of a culture experienced when he was struck by the manifestation of Divinity, and it was cult which allowed later men to participate in this great truth. From this perspective myth was not just a part of culture but its origin and foundation.[60]

The primacy of myth in Otto's analysis had two important implications. First, as a presupposition for culture, myth was obviously not a later and derivative elaboration of religion thought. The evolutionists had argued that gods were secondary additions in religion's evolution, and one of their crucial assertions backing this argument was that myth, the language which told of the gods, was not in religion's original makeup. For example, Rohde had portrayed religion's first stage as a language of spiritualism concocted to explain psychological phenomena. Harrison had argued that cultic activity produced by inchoate emotions and desires had come first and that myth had been only a later rationalization. Nilsson had argued that the first stage had been mana and tabu, which only at a much later time had given rise to gods and therefore to myth. Even scholars like Ulrich von Wilamowitz-Moellendorf, who contested the evolutionistic explanation of Greek religion as based on error and argued that the gods had formed the major part of the original religion, dismissed myth as a secondary poetic elaboration which only veiled the original faith.[61]

Otto rejected these interpretations and argued that all of the activities which had been put forth as prior to myth (notions of souls, cultic activity, emotional experiences like mana or 'the numinous', and poetry). were possible only if there was some myth on which they were grounded.[62] On another occasion Otto even argued that it was myth as the expression of the primal experience which made rational thought possible.[63] Thus, myth, like the god, stood at the beginning of culture.

Second, myth was not, as Tylor would have had it, a superstition marked out for destruction. It was not simply an undeveloped stage of thought which could be sloughed off once man had made enough scientific progress. The evolutionists had taken the distance between myth and their own modes of thought as evidence that myth was *passé*. Otto denied this, holding that modern man's alienation from myth was not based on advancing truth but on man's turning away from the world and from Being into an encapsulated existence of his own fabrication.[64] Otto felt that myth was a permanent possibility as a form of knowledge. It lived alongside rational, practical, and playful thought and owed them nothing. If anything, it had given them their direction.[65] In any case, it was an autonomous mode of knowledge and still existed,[66] not as a survival but as legitimate insight into the nature of Being.

Otto described myth in several different ways. The simplest description was 'traditional peoples' conceptions of Divinity and its actions in the world'.[67] He also described it as immediate testimony about the self-revelation of Being,[68] a meeting with Being which presented man with the truth of reality directly through living experience rather than through reflection.[69] In terms of its content, myth was 'the form-possessing appearance of the Eternal'[70] and 'the true primal image'.[71] As the formed image of ultimate reality, myth revealed not only the nature of Divinity but also the paradigmatic model for man. Traditional man patterned all his actions and the modes of ordering his existence on the model of the myth.[72] Thus, genuine myth was the 'true word' for traditional man in a double sense as both reliable testimony (about the nature of the universe) and authoritative command (to man to assume his 'real' place in this universe).[73] In Otto's presentation, myth had the same function for those within its grasp as had the initial religious manifestation for the original genius. Its function was 'to announce the timeless, the eternal in the form of a narration of an occurrence in the primal world and to announce it in such a way that its truth grasps the entire man, forms him, and makes him what he should be from the beginning: an image of Divinity. A dialogue with God'.[74]

Myth, then, was more than primary religious language; it was the mode in which the god was ordinarily manifested to man. It was the expression of the first creative meeting between man and god, but for those who came later than the creation of this paradigmatic narrative and who were shaped by it, it was also the occasion to meet the Divine.

For most persons, the most forceful presence of the god would occur as they perceived the world in a different manner through the focus of myth. Therefore, Otto felt that to explain Dionysos and the other Greek gods, he had to (1) show myth to be an autonomous and valid way to apprehend reality and (2) reconstruct the edifice of Greek religion so that its metaphysical and existential values would be self evident.

Much of Otto's interpretation of Dionysos involved showing how the individual myths and cultic activities of Dionysiac religion expressed and even made possible the manifestation of Being at its most primordial level. To do this, he had to take a position on the relationship between myth and cult which set him apart from other classicists. One view had held that cult was just a reflection or imitation of myth; another, that myth was only a rationalization of cult.[75] Otto argued that myth and cult both had to be understood as autonomous expressions of man's being in the world and not as imitations of one another. To treat cult as imitative of myth was to ignore the fact that non-verbal behavior was as important for defining man's stance in the universe as discursive language. To treat myth as an explanation of a no longer understood ritual ignored the ideological importance of myth for religion. To be sure, from time to time one or another would be more helpful in interpreting a specific facet of Greek religion,[76] but for the Greeks themselves both had been indispensable.[77]

The reason that myth and cult were each autonomous was that both were called into being by the Divine's meeting with man. They were not reflections of each other but responses to an intuitive insight.[78] Myth recorded this insight and continually mediated its truth to man; cult expressed the insight in gesture and action. Both were culturally sedimented modes of revelation; the one through speech, the other through action.[79] As Otto phrased it, religious behavior was 'the becoming-manifest of the holy being of Divinity'.[80] That is, man's religious life was the expression of a truth about the universe which, except in those rare moments of revelation, was itself not available to man outside of religion. Here Otto's argument was much like that found in Archibald MacLeish's 'Ars Poetica': 'A poem should not mean/But be'. Religious behavior did not simply 'mean' or point to something but actually *was* the time when man met the Divine. For this reason, the evolutionist interpretation, which was not sensitive to the totally different form of experience mediated through religious behavior, had erred profoundly in looking for some extrinsic reason for religious beliefs and practices. The authenticity of religion was totally imbedded in the bearing it imposed on man. Consequently, proper interpretation involved explaining how Dionysiac religious behavior established a specific universe. The enactment of the ritual and the telling of the myth created for (or revealed to) Greek man a primordial, transcendent dimension of existence in which he could dwell. Furthermore, once the ritual and the myth were finished and sacred time again gave way to ordinary time, Dionysiac symbolism perpetuated this religious consciousness by disclosing that facts of the Greek's everyday experience (wine, certain plants and animals, masks, etc.) were ciphers for supernatural reality.

In Otto's view, since the separate facets of religion all testified to a discovery about divine reality, it was necessary to understand god, myth, and cult as inextricably bound together from the beginning.[81] Since each of the three elements implied the other two, Otto insisted on a synchronic rather than a diachronic interpretation. Religious behavior (which involved myth and cult in their diverse forms) was best understood in terms of the structured cosmos (grounded in Divinity) which it made experientially available rather than in terms of the historical conditions which had led to its production. Examined as a functioning structure, this world of the Dionysiac votary had its own intelligibility. Like the world of the person in love, it looked different than that of the sober thinker, but it was no less true. It was simply reality seen from a different perspective, at a different level of abstraction. One could deal with the Dionysiac world causally, just as one could analyze the state of the lover in terms of physiology, but this maneuver should be recognized as essentially the translation of one frame of reference into the terms of another. In its own frame of reference the truth of the experience of the lover or of the worshipper could only be understood by intersubjective participation. Because of this, the Dionysos that Otto presented would have to be quite different than that of the evolutionists.

OTTO'S UNDERSTANDING OF GREEK RELIGION

Dionysos occupied a unique position in Otto's presentation of Greek religion. In early works, when Otto was arguing against Christianity, he dismissed Dionysos as the product of a subjective, feminine religion as contrasted to the heroically objective and masculine Homeric religion. Later, when he argued against evolutionism as a greater threat than Christianity, he integrated Dionysos into his portrayal of Hellenic religion as part of its early foundation and analyzed him in the same manner as Homeric deities, as the formed image of the world perceived in a certain light. Since he always interpreted Dionysos in terms of the wider context of Hellenic religion, it is necessary to see what he thought distinguished Hellenic religion as a unique phenomenon.

One of the most striking things about his interpretation is its high level of generality. Otto was committed to disclosing the *Geist* of Greek culture, and this involved showing an organic ideological unity which ran throughout the diverse centers and epochs of Hellenic civilization. He was not concerned to trace the historical development of the 'hard culture' of Greece,[82] largely because he thought of it essentially as the medium for the Hellenic *ethos* or 'soft culture'. If one could understand the motivating spirit of Greece, one would thereby understand why the Greeks had objectified their spiritual life in the diverse manners we find in the historical evidence. Consequently he looked at religious artifacts to find shared ideological continuities rather than the circumstances which rendered each artifact unique within the Greek context. Thus, although he was reproached, especially by Nilsson,[83] for abandoning history, his task was still historical: to portray the essential characteristics of Hellenic religion as a holistically unified phenomenon. Obviously he had to be tremendously selective to integrate the multifarious facts available into an intelligible unity, but he felt that what might be lost in factual precision was more than recompensed by insight into the culturally shared foundations of the Hellenic *ethos*. From the evolutionists' perspective, Otto's scale of analysis was so general that it had minimal relationship to the facts of Greek culture; but from Otto's perspective, their scale had been more questionable. Either they had focussed on small historical connections which were too atomistic to be informative or they had conflated Greek and primitive practices in huge generalizations that he felt made his own look quite tidy.

In attempting to delineate a single *ethos* which ran throughout Hellenism, Otto portrayed the major mode of Greek religion as 'Homeric',[84] that is, as the clearly formed, objective, and somewhat rationalized religion found most openly in the Homeric epics but present throughout Hellenism. Phenomena which were not consistent with this Homeric ethos he classified as pre- or post-Homeric. Pre-Homeric religion was an elemental religion which venerated nature and its dark, implacable, and impersonal laws as a maternal and feminine cosmos. This religion was dominated by four great realities: earth, procreation, blood, and death.[85] Post-Homeric religion focussed on the hope for a blessed existence beyond the grave and turned man's interest away from the objective world to a self-centered desire for individual salvation.[86] Homeric religion distinguished itself from its predecessor by its greater clarity[87] and anthropomorphism,[88] its ability to transcend the vision of existence as ruled by impersonal laws and forces and to see personal forms behind the universe,[89] its lack of concern with the elemental realm and death,[90] and its disinterestedness,[91] as manifested by its having outgrown magic.[92] It distinguished itself from post-Homeric religion by its refusal to look past the world for salvation[93] and by its ability to see this world in the light of Divinity,[94] that is, to perceive the ideal in the real.

Otto's actual characterization of Homeric religion can best be described as a limited demythologization designed to render the Hellenic world-view appropriable in the contemporary period. He tried to present it in such a way as to neutralize the objections of naturalistically oriented critics while retaining its religious dimension. Thus, he described Greek religion as 'realistic': it focussed on perceptible data and events and did not invoke exceptional or miraculous events as proof of the presence of Divinity. 'The hand of Divinity accomplishes things here exactly as really occurs in the world of experience'.[95] Seeing all existence as grounded in Divinity, the Greeks were able to unite realism and idealism. That is, whatever was truest to nature was at the same time the most spiritual[96] since Divinity revealed itself in the natural rather than in the supernatural.[97] For the Greeks, the Divine was not the 'Wholly Other' but the 'Just This' (*Eben dies*),[98] 'just that which surrounds us, in which we live and breathe, which seizes us and becomes form in the clearness of our sense and our spirit'.[99] For the Greek the Divine was neither an explanation or justification of the natural course of the world nor its suspension but the natural course of the world itself.[100]

The thing that distinguished Greek 'realism' from naturalism was the fact that the Greeks perceived the Divine in the great forms of the world. Otto believed that 'form' (*Gestalt*) was an organic structure of the world which proceeded from the internal reality of nature itself. Each of the forms reflected in the images of the Greek gods was natural and yet more than natural, because through these holistic structures one could see what amounted to a kind of personality. That is, the Greeks' creative insight involved the perception of distinctive and meaningful patterns which the universe manifested to man. The naturalistic mode saw only the concatenation of cause and effect in an ever-changing and ultimately meaningless natural process. Otto claimed that the Greeks had been more perceptive because, although they acknowledged that everything individual was imperfect and perishable, they could see that within the maelstrom of change there were distinctive forms of reality which endured[101] and which pointed to an eternal spiritual content. When the Greeks looked at natural or historical events, they perceived the 'face' of Divinity illuminating the world and giving it significance. Thus, each god articulated an entire range of human existence and was the signature of a world complete in itself.[102] Since the totality of Being transcended any one of these forms and since the Greeks were committed to giving reverence to all of reality, they worshipped a number of deities instead of just one. Otto argued that Greek polytheism was not the result of religious frivolity but the most effective expression of the manifold and contradictory character of reality.[103]

Because the Greeks saw Divinity in the depths of man's perceived existence, Greek religion was 'world-affirming' in a way that Christianity and other 'Asiatic' religions were not. It did not look for authentic reality in some eschatological future but found it in this world. Seeing the world itself as the manifestation of Divinity, the Greeks did not have to deny earthly life for God.[104] Rather than longing for some other-worldly peace, they were free to test their powers within the arena of incarnate life.[105]

Otto argued that along with accepting the limitations of earthly existence the Greeks transcended concern for their own personal, individual fate. Instead they had focussed all their attention on disinterested knowledge of the being of things, whether this knowledge brought joy or suffering.[106] In fact, knowing that all individuals were ephemeral and that only the essential forms of the world endured, they necessarily had a tragic vision.[107] Yet even knowing that their destiny was death and without the security of some post-mortem recompense, they remained serene and noble. No matter what their own individual fate, they were happy in the knowledge that the gods *were* and that 'everything, whether good fortune or bad, joy or sadness, is of divine origin, indeed, in its profundity and truth, of divine Being'.[108] Thus their religion allowed them to participate in that which transcended their own limited existence and made that existence meaningful. Though their religion promised neither other-worldly salvation as did Christianity nor material benefits as did utilitarian behavior, it gave them a way to express the truth of Being and to attain their own authentic humanity.

OTTO'S UNDERSTANDING OF DIONYSOS

In his large monograph on Dionysos, Otto portrayed the god as one of the formed images of existence, just as he had portrayed the major Olympian deities in *Die Götter Griechenlands*. In other works where he was concerned to show the objective and 'rational' character of Homeric religion, Otto had treated Dionysos as pre- or post-Homeric, concentrating on the god's connections with older religious forms,[109] religious enthusiasm,[110] elemental life,[111] the world of women,[112] the dynamic, almost chaotic realm of becoming,[113] and the promise of perfected existence after death[114] as showing the difference between Dionysos and the other great Hellenic deities. On the occasions when Otto delineated Dionysos as non-Hellenic he was trying to safeguard Greek religion from charges of being subjectivistic, instrumentally-oriented, or world-denying. With *Dionysos, Mythos und Cultus* he was arguing against scientific naturalism more than against 'Asiatic' religions, so he could interpret Dionysos as a legitimate Greek phenomenon. Returning to the same appreciation of Dionysos which Nietzsche had displayed in *The Birth of Tragedy*, Otto analyzed the god as a necessary foundation for the rest of the Greek pantheon. Though not the same as the Olympians, Dionysos had been the legitimate portrayal of one of the chief forms of the world.

At the most general level Otto interpreted Dionysos as the religious expression of the world in its primordial aspect. The 'form' which Dionysos both reflected and stood behind was that of the universe in its most passionate and furious state, seen as it created and destroyed. Other deities presented other 'faces' of reality to man—loving, playful, ordering, etc.—but only Dionysos expressed the beauty and horror inextricably tied to the process of Becoming. Dionysiac religion was the paramount place where the Greek could directly experience and celebrate this aspect of the world.

Otto used the concept 'primordial' (the German prefix *Ur-*) in two divergent senses, each of which contributed to his meaning. In one sense he used the term, as had Goethe in his morphological works, to characterize certain universal forms and phenomena such as 'beauty'. Such things were primordial in that they were absolutely fundamental. They could neither be compared to nor derived from anything else. The primal phenomenon was a basic fact of the experience of being[115] and could not be defined in terms of something other than itself. Immediately behind it stood Divinity.[116] Otto applied this meaning of 'primordial' to show that the Greeks had been more effective than other peoples in delineating the fundamental structures of reality. Frequently coupled with the word 'form(s)' (*Urgestalten*), 'primordial' signified the formed expression of a true essence of the world and could be applied to other deities besides Dionysos.

As applied to Dionysos alone, the word 'primordial' carried

another meaning. Used in the sense that Nietzsche used it in *The Birth of Tragedy*, 'primordial' connoted 'original' rather than 'essential'. For Nietzsche, the origin had been a dark unity where pleasure and pain were joined in a titanic and fearful matrix which then formed the substratum of the brighter Olympian god, Apollo.[117] In this original unity all dualities—suffering and joy; life and death; etc.—were held together in a stormy chaos which preceded and underlay the emergence of discrete individuated forms.[118]

Thus, while Dionysos was primordial in the sense that he represented one of the essential forms of reality and was therefore akin to the Olympians, he was also primordial in the sense of being connected to the elemental level of the world where duality predominated and where death was as visible a reality as life. This second aspect of his primordiality often led Otto to withhold Dionysos from the Homeric sphere. Like the evolutionists he saw Dionysos as different from and to some extent 'earlier' than the Olympians; however, even in acknowledging this difference, he insisted on the legitimacy of the Dionysiac vision.

Since Dionysiac religion had been the Greeks' access to a specific kind of reality, Otto tried to *evoke* that reality for his reader as the only way to communicate the god's subjective meaning for the classical votary.[119] His monograph thus has a poetic, almost liturgical quality about it, as he was extremely careful in his use of words and images to create certain moods and associations. Though, like all poetic effort, the work loses much of its force in being summarized, basic images and motifs give a feeling for the ethos of Dionysiac religion as Otto conceived it.

The world of Dionysos was the world of the primordial Feminine, nourishing and fostering, enraptured in the wonder of all life.[120] It expressed creativity, the torrent of life that wells up from the motherly depths.[121] Yet, though motherly, it was also a world of madness, since the security of the routine world was abolished and everything was transformed. As the world revealed itself in its superabundant generative power, it revealed as a primal mode of being not only coming-to-be but passing-away. As Otto described the Dionysiac vision, it was similar to a 'time-lapse' version of reality where the rhythms of the world were speeded up so that reality revealed itself as a maelstrom of flux. As against the Olympians who represented forms of Being, Dionysos represented the world of vertiginous and maddening Becoming. Yet in this vision, coming-to-be and passing-away were not seen merely as discrete stages rapidly succeeding one another but as indissolubly linked at all moments. The Dionysiac world thus unified the dualities of existence which ordinarily were split apart because of their tensions and contradictions. In this world barriers were broken and reality lacked all boundaries.[122]

Reflecting this duality in his relations to men, Dionysos brought both joy and suffering. Many of his epithets expressed this contradiction, so that it was clear that the Greeks thought of him as both the most fearful and the most delightful of the gods.[123] He himself experienced the same contradictions by suffering and dying as well as being exalted. Ultimately, all the dualities of Dionysiac religion—ecstasy and horror; boundless fullness of life and savage destruction; wild noise and deathly silence; the god's supernatural presence which was paradoxically also an absence; the blessing and risk involved in his gifts of prophecy, music, and wine—expressed the opposition and unity of life and death.[124]

This fundamental perception fueled the Dionysiac world. Confronted with the realization that everything finite and created had within itself the seeds of its own death and disappearance, the Greeks had responded by expressing this hard truth as richly as possible and by celebrating the will to create in spite of the knowledge that creation implied destruction.[125] Hence what was usually thought of as the Dionysiac 'madness' was actually a truth which transcended all normal expression. In the primeval depths of the universe, death was seen as the other side of life's face.[126] Dionysos had been the Greeks' most effective expression of this mode of reality.

To a large extent Otto's analysis was an attempted vindication of Nietzsche's insights in *The Birth of Tragedy*. There Nietzsche had treated Dionysos as representing the eternally suffering and contradictory primordial unity where 'excess revealed itself as truth; contradiction, the rapture born out of pain, spoke of itself out of the heart of nature'.[127] This insight had revealed the duality of existence: both the destructiveness of history and nature and the ineradicable power and pleasure of life.[128] The superabundant fruitfulness of the world-will brought things into being and yet also caused their struggle, pain, and destruction.[129] Sensitive to this duality, Nietzsche had emphasized the contradictory nature of Dionysos as both a cruel, brutal demon and a mild, gentle ruler.[130]

Yet if Otto derived most of the substance for his interpretation from Nietzsche, he was not able to accept Nietzsche's atheism and therefore saw a different meaning in the content of Dionysiac religion. Nietzsche saw the world as devoid of any moral foundation and, therefore, justifiable only as an *aesthetic* phenomenon.[131] Otto admitted the moral ambiguity of existence but argued that the Greeks had nevertheless been able to see reality as redeemed by the majestic presence of the gods in the essential forms of the world. Thus, for Otto and, he argued, for the Greeks the world was justified only as a *religious* phenomenon, that is, as the finite manifestation of Divinity.[132] Otto acknowledged his debt to Nietzsche for the latter's insight that each of the Greek gods signified a world,[133] but he rejected Nietzsche's final explanation as being too influenced by the prevailing psychologism of the nineteenth century and insensitive to the Divine and to genuine myth and cult. Nietzsche had vitiated his interpretation by not seeing the importance which the certainty of the gods played in Greek religion.[134] He had been able to see the gods only as illusions which made bearable the terror of the world rather than as a true expression of existent Divinity. Reacting against Nietzsche's irreligious stance, Otto went back to the pagan piety of Goethe, which still held open the possibility of Divinity, and used this perspective to transform Nietzsche's insights into a more religious interpretation.

Another thing which distinguished Otto's analysis from Nietzsche's was the material out of which he drew his interpretation. Nietzsche had been concerned with Greek literature rather than with Greek religion *per se* and therefore had not dealt systematically with the multifarious facts of Dionysiac religion. Otto appropriated Nietzsche's insights about the Primordial, its duality, and the complementarity of life and death and applied this perspective to the entire range of Dionysiac religion. He then had a framework in which to explain the particular myths, cultic behavior, symbols, gestures, social groupings, and other phenomena associated with Dionysos as expressions of this insight into reality.

His exegesis began with an argument against the commonly accepted thesis that Dionysos was an alien god intruding his presence on the unwilling Greeks. The evolutionists had argued that

Dionysos had made his way into Greece as a deity with limited functions and had picked up additional characteristics merely because of the passage of time. If this were so, then it would have been impossible to argue that Dionysos represented a fully formed vision of the world. Only if the Greeks had always conceived of Dionysos in all his complexity as an integral whole could one argue that he represented the duality of life and death in its primordial unity. And only if he held these polar opposites together from the beginning of Hellenic religion could one argue that he represented the primeval matrix out of which the Olympian clarity sprang.

Otto argued that at the latest Dionysos was part of Greek religion toward the end of the second millenium B.C. This early dating meant that Dionysos would have been part of the decisive transformation which synthesized the separate elements of religions in Greece into authentic Hellenic religion some time before the Homeric corpus was written down. Otto also contended that Dionysos manifested signs of bipolarity and primordiality from the very beginning of Hellenism, since scattered references in Homer already indicated the god's basic modes of being as a mad god, a god of wine, a friend of the deities Thetis and Hephaistos, a lover of Ariadne, and a god associated with the waters of the sea.[135] The widespread celebration of the Anthesteria throughout the Ionian world also suggested Dionysos' presence before the dispersion of the Ionians.[136] Finally, Otto attempted, somewhat weakly, to turn arguments showing a Thracian or Phrygian provenance for Dionysos on their head by suggesting that the cult migration had been from Greece to Thrace and Phrygia rather than vice versa.[137] His arguments were rather defensive in *Dionysos: Myth and Cult*;. but after the discovery of the god's name on a Linear B tablet,[138] his assertion in *Theophania* about Dionysos' presence in Crete in the middle of the second millenium was quite confident.[139]

Having dealt with the question of the god's fully formed existence in early Greek religion, Otto attempted to demonstrate how specific phenomena like the myths and cults of Dionysos both expressed and made perceptible the primeval world of duality. Rather than relating facts to specific historical connections, Otto tried to show how the diverse facts referred to a level of reality which any era could appropriate. In his view the Greeks went to the trouble to worship Dionysos in various ways because this worship put them in contact with a meaningful and sacred aspect of the universe, not because of inertia or a desire to preserve some cultic recollection of past history. For this reason he rejected the historicistic explanation of the myth of Dionysos' double birth.[140] Some had interpreted the story as a conflation of a Thrako-Phrygian and a Greek myth in which poetic licence had reduced the Anatolian Earth Mother to the role of a mortal woman. This explanation assumed that the myth had been sufficiently unimportant to have been changed at will by the Greeks and that the most important information it conveyed was an historical recollection of a synthesis of Greek and foreign fables. Otto argued that the meaning of the story was rather a function of the religious life of the worshipper. It expressed the essence of Dionysos, revealing his spirit of duality and paradox. With chilling power it evoked a sense of divine bliss which was both creative and destructive and communicated man's nearness to but distance from the god.[141]

Otto took the same approach with the resistance myths about Dionysos, which told of Dionysos' appearance and call to mortals, their rejection of him, and his final vengeance by driving them mad and, in many cases, inciting them to murder. Rohde, Harrison, and Nilsson had seen these stories as the residue of a vain attempt by the Greeks to fend off the foreign Dionysian incursion.[142] For Otto these myths referred to something more essential than a specific moment in the development of Dionysiac religion. They reflected the violence of Dionysos himself. The more violently Dionysos encountered men and the more unconditional his demands were, the more they resisted him and the greater was their punishment. Thus inherent in Dionysiac religion were a violence, fearsomeness, and tragedy that both expressed and shaped the Dionysiac worshippers' perceptions of reality. These myths spoke of a terror at the heart of things, and they did this in terms not only of the fate of mortals but of the god and his mythical attendants as well. Otto noted myths in which Dionysos was defeated and his companions killed. The duality and tragic dimension of the Dionysiac vision was nowhere more apparent than in these stories where even Dionysos and his attendants suffered and died.[143]

Dionysiac religion had a tremendously strong non-rational component, which had led many scholars to interpret it as barbaric and intellectually defective. Otto celebrated this non-rationality as a conscious expression of transcendence of the commonplace. The Dionysiac cult was unusual because this was the only way to break pedestrian thought patterns and reveal a deeper level of reality. As the god of primordiality, Dionysos was naturally less tractable than other deities.

For example, his manner of epiphany was more startling and violent than that of other gods. All at once he would disappear incomprehensibly from his worshippers; then suddenly he would be with them again, making them rage in ecstasy. The Greeks even symbolized his presence in a different, more concrete way than that of the other gods. Instead of coming invisibly, he would enter his temple in a formed image. Once a year in Athens he would consummate his sacred marriage with the wife of the Archon Basileus, the most imposing display of his furious appearance.[144] Each element of these phenomena communicated some aspect of the primordial world—its disquieting change, its fury, its intimate connection with elemental life processes in all their concreteness.

Otto saw the Dionysian duality as especially striking in the use of the mask, one of the most important modes of the god's epiphany. Having a front but no back, the mask was perfectly suited to express the god's nearness which was paradoxically also a remoteness. As a god of the mask, Dionysos was a god of encounter; yet for the votary there was really nothing which transcended the moment of confrontation with the mask. Therefore, in the mask Dionysos was really as much 'not there' as 'there'. As before, Otto saw the specific data of Dionysiac religion opening up a level of reality otherwise closed. The two-dimensionality of the mask expressed the presence of the god with its front and his absence with its back and thus, once again, manifested his dual nature.[145]

The paradoxical duality was also displayed by the god's association with wild noise and silence. Often the pandemonium of the Bacchic cult brought horror as well as enchantment; yet the Greeks saw both emotions as appropriate for receiving the god. Many epiphanies were accompanied by bewitching music and loud sounds, while Dionysos himself was known as *Bromios*, 'the noisy one'. For Otto this auditory frenzy was an apt symbol for the supernatural onrush of the god. Yet if the loud din was an effective and composure-shattering symbol, so was the deathlike silence into which the noise suddenly changed. The Greeks portrayed the maenad just as poignantly in melancholy stillness and silence as in her revel rout, and both images belonged to the inner duality of the cult.[146]

The worshippers of Dionysos not only used unusual symbols for the god's reality; they also had experiences which transcended the ordinary. Here, rather than interpreting the Dionysiac *mania* from the outside, Otto attempted to participate imaginatively in the reality which those seized by the ecstasy must have experienced. In the exalted state the worshipper perceived the world bewitched. In his deeper gaze, he had pierced the well-ordered and antiseptic surface of the natural attitude and had seen the stupendous power behind existence. In this rapture he saw the depths of Being open and the primeval world appear with its creation and destruction, bliss and terror. In this state the earth gave forth its fruit miraculously. Barriers which seemed impenetrable to the everyday consciousness were easily dissolved so that man moved effortlessly through nature and saw into the future and into remote obscurity. In public festivals the Greeks also witnessed wine produced supernaturally. Here non-ordinary experience and cultic symbolism reinforced one another, since in addition to wine's 'miraculous' appearance in the world, its consumption led to the same transcendence of boundaries as did the ecstatic dancing. The Dionysiac experience in all its forms led the Greek to perceive the world as a furious but inexhaustible explosion of creativity and nurturing.[147]

However, if the Dionysiac world was creative, it also was a realm of destruction and of dark madness. The truth learned in the ecstasy enchanted, but it also made one shudder. Myths of the persecution of Dionysos and his worshippers by other Greeks conveyed part of this somber aspect, but there were more gruesome manifestations. In the ecstatic cult the women votaries frequently tore apart and devoured the young animals they had just suckled. The worshippers of Dionysos were often ritually persecuted by the Dionysiac priest himself, sometimes to the point of being hounded down and slain. There were even traditions of human sacrifice exacted in the god's name. The cruelty of the god was not glossed over but celebrated by portraying him as either accompanied by bloodthirsty predators or as one himself. In fact, part of his realm was the realm of death. Not only was he the supernatural patron of festivals for the dead, but he showed many similarities to Hades, Lord of the underworld. Heraclitus equated the two deities; many of the actions of Dionysos and his attendants were indistinguishable from those of underworld deities; and in some traditions Dionysos himself visited and even lived in the world of the dead. Yet the horror of death was not simply something he foisted off on mortals. Traditions told of his own grave and that of his lover Ariadne, and it was clear from numerous traditions that he too shared the same destructive fate as his victims.[148]

Clearly the violence of the Dionysiac realm was not simply an abstract concept, since Greek man took such pains to experience it through myth and cult. This religious behavior shaped his perceptions of the world so that he came to see many ordinary facts and events as empirical manifestations of Divinity in its primordial aspect. As he saw observable features of his environment in the light of myths that linked them to a supernatural origin, he saw them as having a different significance than they would have had in a naturalistic context. As he participated in the cult, he experienced bodily an openness to a higher dimension of things than was available through profane activity. Since it was the myths and rites that opened him to this particular form of divine reality, they had to be very specific and concrete, whether they manifested bliss or terror. Hence the cruelty of the Dionysiac cult was not a function of barbarity but of the Greek's commitment to an adequate expression of this colossal reality.

Here Otto's explanation was a very clear alternative to that posed by the evolutionists. They too had noted the motifs of life and death and of the cult's ecstatic 'madness', but they had always explained these motifs in terms of human needs. Otto argued that to explain them as imitations of vegetative life designed either to explain it or control it magically or as means to gain mystical power or have an ecstatic experience was to foreclose the possibility of seeing something much more important.[149] Greek myth seized and expressed the basic forms of Being, and these expressions could, Otto felt, still enable men to see an authentic aspect of reality. In actively celebrating the processes of life and death and in acknowledging the madness of the primordial realm, the Greeks had not been trying to gain some advantage, but rather to participate in an aspect of divine reality.

The madness of the worshippers reflected an *imitatio dei*. Once the world had revealed itself in its primeviality, the only proper human response was to share in this reality. The worshippers went mad and, in their madness, witnessed and even brought about life and death because this was what Dionysos, the mad god (*mainomenos*), did.[150] To participate in his reality was to transcend one's limited, compartmentalized fragment of existence and to enter the realm where creation and destruction sprang from the absolute foundations of Being rather than merely issuing out piecemeal as minor events in the cause and effect sequence.

The Greeks had several physical ways of both gaining access to and, at the same time, expressing the Dionysian world, including music, dance, and prophecy; but in Otto's view the most important of these was wine.[151] Wine contained the wonders and secrets, the wildness and boundlessness of the god. Like the god it gave man joy, dissolved the bonds of pedestrian habit, and brought the truth closer to man. Yet, of all the earth's products, wine was also closest to the god in its ambivalent nature. Though it could bless and comfort, in wine there slumbered 'also the madness of the god of terror' which could conquer and destroy. Thus, the drinking of wine, an act devoid of religious significance in many cultures, was for the Greeks a means of experiencing and even participating in the primordial realm of the god.[152]

The spirit of Dionysos pervaded other biological phenomena— not vegetation in general, but a 'mysteriously aroused element of life' manifested in certain plants as well as in the animal and human world. The plants associated with Dionysos shared the common characteristics of conspicuous moistness and procreative power. Whether the vine or the ivy, the tree with succulent fruit or the sap-laden pine, the fig or the myrtle, 'it is the life-giving element of moisture to which the plants sacred to Dionysos bear witness'.[153] Once again phenomena which on one level were thoroughly natural were able to reveal another level of reality and symbolize the primordial, generative force of the world.[154]

Even moisture itself witnessed to Dionysiac nature. 'For the mythical understanding, water is the element in which the primeval mysteries of all life dwell'.[155] Water expressed birth, death, past, present, and future, becoming, enchanting beauty, revival, refreshment, and nourishment for the entire creation. Just like Dionysos, water betrayed a double nature: bright, joyous, and animating; dark, sinister, dangerous, even murderous. Here, although the connections were not so direct as those with wine, Otto could still point to myths and cults which associated Dionysos with water, as emerging from it, riding over it, or escaping into it.[156]

Other associations expressed the generative aspect of Dionysiac reality. The phallus played a major role in Dionysos' cult, and sperm was seen as one of the forms of generative moisture over which he was sovereign. Highly sexual and prolific animals, such as the bull, the he-goat, and the ass, symbolized the god's nature.[157]

Dionysos was also always surrounded by women. In the myths they served as his nurses and his attendants; in the cult they made up the majority of worshippers. According to some traditions Dionysos himself had something feminine about him. The womanly character of the Dionysiac circle was not the erotic femininity of Aphrodite but the womanliness of nurses and mothers, expressing creativity and nurturing. Yet as part of the primordial realm, these women had a terrible side, killing those they nursed or dying violent and tragic deaths. For example, Ariadne, Dionysos' lover and wife, experienced the ecstasy of the god's love, destruction, then final elevation to divine rank. Ecstasy and woe were always conjoined in her biography.[158] Whereas the evolutionists had interpreted the preponderance of women in the Dionysiac cult sociologically, as a reflection of Greek woman's need to escape humdrum reality, Otto interpreted it as the expression of a metaphysical judgment about primordial duality.

The final constellation of religious facts which Otto saw as reflecting this metaphysical judgment was the Greek's portrayal of Dionysos as sharing the same fate as his followers. Tradition reported his grave at Delphi and told of his death as the child Zagreus at the hands of the Titans. On the island of Tenedos a sacrifice symbolized the god's violent death, as a calf dressed in the boots worn by Dionysos was slaughtered by an ax. 'The lord of dying and of the dead himself goes through the terrors of destruction'.[159] As the embodiment of Becoming, the god did not, however, vanish forever. Where he was thought to have died, he was also thought to be reborn again. In other cases he was thought to disappear suddenly without dying, only to reappear with equal abruptness. In both processes, death and rebirth and occultation and epiphany, Dionysos was the god of two faces, the spirit of presence and absence, the expression of the paradoxical unity of life and death.[160]

Thus the religious behavior of the Greek established a special kind of reality which could be experienced as metaphysically meaningful. By relating ordinary facts to Dionysos and by expressing the culturally shared truths about the god in myths and rituals, Greek man was able to perceive and, at least for a time, inhabit the world in its primordial state. Through his cultic behavior he both experienced and testified to this reality, whether it was in the mad dancing of the maenadic revel or in suddenly melancholy stillness, in the motherly solicitude for wild animals or in their savage destruction, in the implacable hunting down of victims or in the terrified flight from pursuing priests, in the worried search for the absent god or in the joyous proclamation of his reappearance. Natural symbols also made the worshipper conscious of the indirect presence of the god and of the death-touched generative abundance of primordial reality, whether these symbols were fiery wine or the cool, luxuriant ivy, the succulent fruit tree or the sap-laden pine, the juicy pulp of the fig with its rich sexual associations or the myrtle, with its underworld associations, the basic creative element of water or the more specifically creative moisture, sperm, animals associated with prolific generation or with violent hunting and death. Finally and most transparently, the myths manifested the primordiality and duality of the Dionysiac realm, whether they were of the god's violent double birth or of his violent death, of his sudden disquieting appearance or of his equally abrupt disappearance, of his vengeful persecution of his enemies or of his persecution by his enemies.

The means of evoking and experiencing the Dionysiac world were various, but the basic perception of reality which Dionysos as a focus made possible was coherent and consistent throughout Greek civilization. The Bacchic worshipper faced a world fresh from creation, a creation so rich and superabundant that it called forth its own destruction. In this reality man was but one part of the world's unity and enjoyed no special status. Since death was as real as life, man's death was just another aspect of the Dionysian realm. Unlike the more anthropomorphically structured worlds of the Olympian deities, the Dionysian world was an elemental world. It was the world of creation, the 'first' world; all things in it were seen in their most elemental modes, i.e., of coming to be and passing away; and the natural elements symbolized its character better than did the life of man. Its elemental quality set it apart from the Olympian religion; but, Otto argued in *Dionysos*, it nevertheless represented a valid perception of reality and a legitimate stance in the universe. Though the 'Homeric' gods had been purely anthropomorphic deities of light and life who shunned the dark elemental world of earth and death, their worshippers always respected the Dionysian sphere. The most vivid proof of this respect was the fact that Apollo and Dionysos shared cultic honors at Delphi. Otto countered the evolutionists' interpretation that this situation reflected an expedient solution for cultic antagonism by arguing that the Greeks saw the truth expressed in the Dionysiac vision as a necessary component in any adequate understanding of reality. Like Nietzsche before him, Otto argued that the light and spirit of the Olympian realm required the darkness and the maternal depths of the Dionysian realm on which all Being was grounded. In the union between Dionysos and Apollo and the concomitant tension between restlessly whirling elemental life and still, far-seeing spirit the Greeks expressed the entire range of existence.[161]

Otto's final position on the relationship of Dionysos to the rest of the Greek pantheon remained ambivalent. In his view, Hellenic religion had not focussed on the elemental aspect of reality, which Dionysos represented, nor had it been overly concerned with life after death. Both the Dionysiac emphasis on the elemental and the later concern for life after death were, even if complementary to the Homeric view, alternative positions, and Otto seemed always tempted to reject them as unhellenic. Since he believed so strongly that expression was religion's true purpose, he treated views that entailed a reciprocal relationship between man and deity as basically utilitarian degenerations. Thus to the extent that the Greeks looked to Dionysos as a savior, they were departing from the disinterested grandeur of the original faith.

Still, in the final analysis, apart from the eschatological dimension of Dionysiac religion, Otto saw Dionysos as an authentic refraction of the Divine in the world. Dionysos had been the ordered form in which the Greeks had seen reality in its most furious incarnation. As such he represented a legitimate metaphysical category which was experienced in the world but which also stood behind the world as a source of creation and destruction. Dionysos was one of the 'faces' through which Being expressed itself—to man and through man. That is, the Divine appeared to man and man expressed this appearance through Dionysiac religion. At this level man was not a seeker after supernatural blessing but a knower and a teller. Man's existence, with religion at its center, was simply the most poignant song of the universe to itself. Dionysos was the form through which the Greeks celebrated for themselves and for Divinity the primeval in all its beauty and terror.

OTTO'S CONTRIBUTION TO THE UNDERSTANDING OF DIONYSOS

Tendentious as it is, Otto's work has naturally evoked strong reactions, both favorable and unfavorable. In fact, both types of reaction can be justified, and in assessing Otto's contributions it is essential to understand the legitimate arguments of both admirers and critics.

On the positive side, Otto's analysis presented a rather compelling case for the need to understand a religious world 'from within'. The evolutionists had consistently derived the thoughts and feelings of the worshippers from conditions outside their religious life, such as social forces, intellectual and scientific limitations, psychological distress and the like. Otto argued forcefully that the conceptual, emotional, and volitional experiences which grew out of the cult itself were powerful factors in shaping Hellenic behavior and were dependent not on non-religious causes but on specifically religious discoveries. His claim that the religious orientation was always the absolute foundation for each culture is hardly tenable, but he did show how, once a 'revelation' has been accepted by a people, their actions and perceptions are directed toward the continued validation of and participation in this sacred reality.

A legitimate question, though, is whether the Dionysiac vision which Otto presented corresponded to the subjective experience of the Greeks themselves. Clearly Otto depended on nineteenth century German thought for his interpretation, and one could argue plausibly that his Dionysos represented German romanticism in Hellenic guise more than the lived experience of the ancient Greeks. On the other hand, much of the romantic tradition from which Otto drew his analysis was itself heavily based on a serious meditation on

Hellenism and obviously was intended to discover deep truths expressed by the ancient Greeks and apply them to the contemporary situation. Otto was willing to submerge the 'uniqueness' of Greek civilization, that is, its limitation to a specific place and time, in favor of what he felt was its universal character. In general, one will applaud or lament this maneuver according to whether one thinks it proper for the historian to make his material immediately 'relevant'. For those who find the practice defensible, Otto's depiction of the Dionysiac world is the richest account available, especially in its thorough explanation of how the different phenomena of Dionysiac religion all contributed to the creation and maintenance of an intense religious reality.

On the negative side, Otto can be seriously faulted for his inability to deal with historical change. In order to compose the total structure of Dionysiac religion, he took documents and materials from all ages and places where Dionysos was known. As a result his account is monolithic, allowing for no evolution of the cult and no local particularism. To a large extent this is a function of his choice to reconstruct a holistic system of meanings rather than to trace change; and, given the relative paucity of material, conflation seems a defensible strategy. Still, it is obvious that any totalistic system such as Otto's is achieved only at the expense of some, perhaps considerable, historical distortion.[162]

As a whole, Otto's method served a definite use in understanding Dionysos. More importantly, it provided a needed foil to the evolutionists' portrayal of the genesis and purpose of religion. By attributing religious and philosophical profundity to early man, Otto possessed a rationale for judging religion a legitimate enterprise, even if it was assumed to have originated among preliterate peoples. To some extent Otto portrayed the creator of religion unconvincingly, as a figure of apparently independent means with little concern for mundane matters like food, shelter, and sex, who spent most of his time articulating his *Weltanschauung*. Still, this portrayal was a useful balance for that of the evolutionists in which the creator of religion had bustled about in well-intentioned practicality but with fundamental misconceptions about the causal chain or the real purpose of his own behavior. Both positions were extreme, and in presenting another view of the original impetus behind Greek religion, Otto contributed to a richer understanding of Hellenism.

Man's inherent need to signify, to express himself and his sense of reality has won increasing recognition in the twentieth century, and Otto was the earliest classicist to show the relevance of this need for Greek religion. By interpreting Dionysos as the expression of a powerful metaphysical view, he again provided a helpful corrective to the evolutionists' overemphasis of ancient man's utilitarian drives. On the other hand, Otto's insistence on the non-utilitarian nature of religion was clearly too uncompromising. He generally ignored the Greeks' explicit desire to be blessed by Divinity and their equally explicit assumption that religious activity was effective in changing the course of things. Where he did not ignore this human desire for a reciprocal relationship with Divinity, he dismissed it as a degeneration. To be sure, there is a noble disinterestedness which runs through much of Greek religion, but it is hardly fair to label this normative and to reject everything else as unrepresentative. His unwillingness to accept Nilsson's hypothetical 'average man' (*Durchschnittsmensch*) as the originator of religion gave him a ground on which to build a useful interpretive framework, but he was surely wrong to dismiss this 'average man' as totally unimportant for Greek religion. He could have ceded the point that Dionysiac religion was frequently practiced for material or emotional gains without abandoning his major contention that for many this religion had its own intrinsic fulfillment in allowing them to dwell for a time with the Divine in its most primordial form.

Nevertheless, there is something to be said for drawing the lines of debate as sharply as possible, and one of Otto's merits is his lack of equivocation. He succeeded in presenting an arguable alternative to the evolutionist perspective; and, in a time when he stood practically alone in classical studies in this attempt, it was doubtless tactically wise not to blur his position. It has been the task for later classicists to moderate between hermeneutical extremes and to present a rich interpretation of Dionysos which would bring out the multiform values he had manifested to the ancient Greeks.

6

Scholarship since Nilsson and Otto

Dionysos is still a focus of classical scholarship, and other scholars have written major works on Dionysos which deserve to be treated in their own right. However, the primary interpretive options have been exercised by the four scholars previously discussed. What I would like to point to in this chapter is a process of moderation which has occurred following the explicit methodological conflicts between Nilsson and Otto.

As is most often the case, the shift in the interpretaton of Dionysos corresponds to a shift in religious studies as a whole. By and large, recent scholars have recognized that limiting themselves to any single interpretive framework eliminates certain important facets of the phenomena from consideration. As a result they have attempted to integrate different perspectives into their total framework so as to take into account several layers of human motivation.

Among the newer interpretations of Dionysos, two of the clearest examples of this trend toward moderation are the works of E. R. Dodds and W. K. C. Guthrie. Operating from a basically psychological perspective, Dodds has refined the basic position put forth by Rohde so as to give more weight to the emotional needs of man, while Guthrie has combined a sensitivity for the metaphysical values expressed in Dionysiac religion with an awareness of the cult's more practical dimension.

E. R. DODDS AND THE STUDY OF DIONYSOS

Although Dionysiac religion *per se* has not been Dodds'[1] central concern, it has exemplified his major interest: the place of irrational forces in the Greek experience. As a result, he has analyzed

Dionysos in the context of a wider investigation into the nature of Hellenism. As with the other scholars already treated, his interpretation of Dionysos can be understood only against this wider methodological background. His masterwork, *The Greeks and the Irrational*, a remarkable intersection of classical erudition with anthropological and psychological sophistication, represents his clearest exposition of the meaning of Dionysos and Dionysiac religion.

As Rohde's *Psyche* was ostensibly limited to the problem of Greek conceptions of the afterlife, so Dodds characterizes *The Greeks and the Irrational* as limited to a single issue: 'the successive interpretations the Greeks placed on one particular type of human experience', i.e., irrational experience.[2] But, like Rohde, Dodds has been too modest; the richness of the data treated and its methodological sophistication qualify it as one of the most outstanding monographs on the central problems of Greek religion. *The Greeks and the Irrational* presents not merely the Greeks' *judgment* about the irrational but also the active *role* the irrational played in Hellenism—how it confronted the Greeks and forced them to shape their culture so that the dynamism supplied by the irrational would be retained but also restrained. Since a great deal of the Greeks' cultural response was religious, Dodds treatment is in large part of a history of Greek religion.

Like the other scholars heretofore considered, Dodds wrote not out of a purely antiquarian interest but with an eye to the present. He took great pains to show the differences between the ancient Greek understanding of the irrational and a modern understanding based on a refined Freudian viewpoint. The implicit lesson in this contrast was that, although the irrational would always play a fundamental role in human life, modern society had the conceptual tools to free itself increasingly from irrational impulses and constraints and to act from rational (and constructive) choices. Thus, by acknowledging the power of the irrational without divinizing it, as had the Greeks, modern man might create a more 'open' and humane society.[3]

Where Walter Otto saw in Dionysiac religion patterns of universal reality which had been discovered by or revealed to man and which gave him an authentic human essence, Dodds saw a single and not terribly attractive cultural configuration among an unrestricted number of other possibilities. In his view it had been imposed by traditions which themselves were based on intellectual limitations, and it, in turn, imposed undesirable behavior patterns on the ancient Greeks. Obviously Dodds' attempt to demystify Dionysiac religion derived from a moral commitment as deep as Otto's; but, like the previously examined evolutionists, he saw the human cause served more effectively by critical reason than by religion.

Dodds explicitly stood in the same tradition as Rohde, Harrison, and Nilsson; yet in several ways his analysis was more complex than theirs. Though he acknowledged a tremendous debt to Rohde, he had integrated elements from other interpretations into his treatment of Dionysos; and the resulting synthesis was a creative contribution to Hellenic studies.

On the question of the origin of Dionysiac religion, Dodds' essential independence from Rohde was apparent. Rohde had accepted the late nineteenth century's fundamentally intellectualist portrayal of man; in his view religion originated as a response to cognitive problems that were to be solved correctly only by modern biology. As cultures evolved and as historical exigencies and religious traditions exerted their weight on successive generations, emotional impulses which were not well understood were also interpreted according to the logic of animism, and Dionysos was invented to explain certain extraordinary states. While Rohde described the remarkable tensions generated around Dionysiac religion powerfully, he treated this 'darker' current of Hellenism as something of a historical accident, caused when the Greeks were too weak to fend off an invading barbarism. He did not see the irrational as an elemental force which always demands an outlet.

Between Rohde and Dodds stood Freud. As heir to Freud's demonstration of the inexorable and, more importantly, universal power of the irrational element in man, Dodds saw in Dionysiac religion more of a concession to the human condition as such than a concession to a specific historical moment of weakness. Thus, although Dodds followed Rohde in the general line of his explanation, he gave religion a more important role in the economy of human behavior.

Dodds took several factors into account in describing religion's origin. On one level at least religion had evolved as a mental response to emotions and drives. Overwhelming psychological pressures had demanded some sort of causal explanation. The Greeks had used language of Divinity whenever confronted with a psychological or psychic 'intervention', in order to render this psychological event concrete and therefore easier to deal with. Since 'the Homeric poets were without the refinements of language which would have been needed to "put across" a purely psychological miracle',[4] they used the language of Divinity, which was 'the projection, the pictorial expression, of an inward monition'.[5]

This description is close to earlier genealogical accounts, yet Dodds also treated religion as a partially effective translation of genuine human states. The ideology of religion originated not only to satisfy man's curiosity but also to help stabilize psychological turbulence. Early man objectified emotions, drives, and the acts resulting from irrational impulses, ascribed to them an alien origin, and therefore projected them away from himself onto a supernatural realm.[6] By prescribing for themselves a regimen of ritual and ethical actions which were thought to please the gods of this projected realm, the Greeks were ostensibly guaranteeing their own freedom from divine assault. However, in modern parlance, they were really assuring their own emotional stability. Thus, to take a specific example, 'the Greeks believed in their Oracle, not because they were superstitious fools, but because they could not do without believing in it'.[7] Here Dodds has given a functionalist twist to his interpretation by describing religion in terms of the ways it operates to keep the culture going rather than in terms of its genesis.

Applying this analysis to Dionysos, Dodds saw the function of the Bacchic cult as primarily cathartic; it purged infectious irrational drives by allowing the individual to satisfy the impulse to reject responsibility.[8] Since man was ruled by more than rational motives, this emotional release was necessary; 'the "moral" of the *Bacchae* is that we ignore at our peril the demand of the human spirit for Dionysiac experience'.[9] Yet it was important to control this experience, and organized Dionysiac religion exercised this control by canalizing the emotional excess into well-bounded and relatively harmless outlets.[10]

Dodds explored other purposes of Dionysiac religion besides its cathartic function. He saw some Bacchic phenomena as utilitarian in intent. For example, the tearing and devouring of the sacrificial victim was homeopathic magic. In this rite the worshipper was incorporating the vital powers of the victim and, by extension, of the god who was represented by the victim.[11]

In addition to appropriating this external power, the worshipper also enjoyed intense religious experience through the cult.[12] Like Rohde before him, Dodds, even while disbelieving in the existence of the Divine,[13] gave credit to the intrinsic satisfactions of man's communion with his god. Also like Rohde, he saw religious ecstasy as one of the intended results of cultic activity rather than as an accidental off-shoot or as a miraculous divine gift.

Yet Dodds did not restrict himself to the alleged magical advantages and verifiable psychological benefits of Dionysiac religion but treated its expressive aspect as well. Here he seems to have adopted a considerable portion of Otto's analysis, divesting it of its supernaturalist content.[14] Dionysos expressed 'the elemental in one's own nature',[15] as opposed to the civilized. He testified to a domain of life which went beyond reason and morality.[16] In representing this elemental realm, Dionysos was an ambivalent god: the cause of madness, yet the deliverer from madness;[17] 'destroyer and liberator, master of the lightning and spirit of peace . . . "a god most dangerous to man, yet most gentle to him"'.[18] He embodied all the tragic contradictions of the primordial: 'joy and horror, insight and madness, innocent gaiety and dark cruelty'.[19]

Dodds also seconded Otto's portrayal of Dionysos' relationships with the natural world. Dionysos' domain was 'wet nature' (*hygra physis*): 'not only the liquid fire in the grape, but the sap thrusting in a young tree, the blood pounding in the veins of a young animal, all the mysterious and uncontrollable tides that ebb and flow in the life of nature'.[20] Dionysos represented nature's generative forces and, as the principle of animal life, could be represented either as the bull (*tauros*) in its unrestrained potency or as the hunter and devourer of the bull (*taurophagos*) seeking to assimilate its power.[21]

As Dodds portrayed it, this elemental world of creation and destruction was an aspect of natural reality which the Greeks respected and honored. Dodds did not follow Otto in postulating some primordial divine Form behind natural reality as the object of the Greeks' veneration. However, he did echo Otto's judgment that the elemental aspect of the universe which transcends reason and ethics had demanded and received from the Greeks its own particular acknowledgment. Operating out of a naturalistic perspective,

Dodds saw Dionysiac religion as representing verifiable phenomena, aspects of a violent dimension of existence which men met most poignantly in their own irrational impulses but which they also observed in other driving biological forces. He thus integrated one of Otto's helpful insights about the expressive function of Dionysiac religion into a hermeneutic of translation. By doing this he could reveal a level of meaning missed by most of the evolutionists while still treating the Dionysiac world-view as less adequate than modern scientific conceptions.

Dodds communicated a more modern tone than had the earlier evolutionists, largely because he seems to have confronted the problem of cultural relativism and discarded the evolutionists' arrogance about the inevitable 'rightness' of Western society. Acknowledging the limitations of Western Culture, Dodds qualified their confidence into a more cautious evolutionism. However, given this qualification, he still viewed modernity as the most authentic cultural option. If one could speak of the progress of civilization, it was not characterized by the elimination of the irrational (as it had been for some of the more superficial and optimistic evolutionists) but by the increase of knowledge. In the modern age man had begun to extend this knowledge into the irrational sphere, thereby bringing it under greater control.

Dodds seemed to acknowledge major limitations to man's knowledge and not to expect so confidently the kind of total explanation for which the earlier evolutionists had hoped. Nevertheless, in his view knowledge should be in the service of man and its extension should correspond to an extension of human freedom. Ultimately, to the degree that knowledge increased, the need for religion would decrease. In its day Dionysiac religion facilitated the objectification and expression of the Greeks' inner experience, but in the long run it was less satisfactory than modern techniques. The Greeks 'could describe what went on below the threshold of consciousness only in mythological or symbolic language; they had no instrument for understanding it, still less for controlling it. . . . '.[22] Thus, though Dodds integrated aspects from Otto's interpretation into his analysis and made it as sensitive to the values expressed in Dionysiac religion as any naturalistic interpretation is likely to be, his final stance toward Dionysiac religion was a calm exhortation to modern man to do better.

W. K. C. GUTHRIE AND THE STUDY OF DIONYSOS

Though he is best known for his monumental work on Greek philosophy, W. K. C. Guthrie[23] began his career with an intense concern for Greek religion. Like Nilsson, he confronted a multiplicity of explanatory methods; but, unlike Nilsson, he actually employed them all. Having been taught by Francis Cornford, one of the giants of the evolutionary method, Guthrie upheld many of the judgments that saw religion as growing out of undeveloped primitive thought. Yet he also saw religion as a legitimate mode of understanding and acting in the universe. The tension generated by the presence of these polar positions gives Guthrie's work an aura of breadth and, at the same time, a certain inconclusiveness.[24] In explaining Dionysos, Guthrie attempted to purge previous interpretations, both pro- and anti-religious, of dogmatic excesses and to combine them into a composite hermeneutic. As a result, his work, like that of Dodds, has a more balanced, less strident tone than the writings of earlier scholars who had been explicit in their attempts to discredit contrary interpretations. Yet his irenic approach made it difficult to tell which of the theories revealed the most about religion.

As is manifest from his brief history of the study of religion,[25] Guthrie saw many of the earlier arguments as sterile and wanted to return to issues which lent themselves better to demonstrable solutions. Thus, for example, he never speculated about the origins of religion and applauded the growing caution of other scholars in dealing with this issue.[26] In general, his work manifested 'a certain reaction from the anthropological and comparative point of view'.[27] He cited Wilamowitz' rejoinder 'The gods are there' as a necessary corrective to the evolutionists' assumption that religion began with no notion of deity. At the same time, he did not postulate another theory of religion's origin, as had Otto with his theory of *Ergriffenheit* ('seizure', primordial insight). Since Guthrie occasionally used evolutionist categories like vegetation magic to explain religious behavior, it is clear that his reluctance to hypothesize about the origin of religion did not stem from a total repudiation of evolutionism. In fact, he was quite pragmatic in his use of interpretive categories, applying those of evolutionism to some data, those of pro-religious hermeneutics to others.

Reacting against the earlier speculations, Guthrie focussed more on verifiable historical connections than had most of the other scholars examined here. This predisposition toward traditional history had a certain ascetic clarity in avoiding murky guesses and assumptions unconsciously disguised as 'raw data'. However, in some cases it necessitated explaining *ignotum per ignotius*, analyzing strange Greek beliefs and customs by tracing them to other cultures without explaining their meaning in their original context. To a degree, Guthrie's decision not to attempt the 'total' causal explanation for these phenomena came from a willingness to accept them as meaningful on their own terms rather than in terms of their genesis. Assuming an initial intelligibility in the data, Guthrie could concentrate on modifications which the Greeks had made.

Like other well integrated works, Guthrie's synoptic treatment of Greek religion, *The Greeks and their Gods,* focussed on a central issue: in this case, the relations between God and man. Guthrie took over the standard dichotomy between Olympian and chthonic religions and refined it by synthesizing and updating helpful aspects of the works of Rohde and Harrison. Like Harrison, he analyzed the different modes of worship in Olympian and chthonic religions; like Rohde, he explained the relation of each cult to conceptions of the afterlife. As Guthrie portrayed it, the primary difference between the two cults concerned the distance between deity and man: the Olympian religion demanded man's acknowledgement of his own inferior status and concomitant mortality; the chthonic religion exhorted man to transcend that which made him inferior, unite with the god, and thereby gain immortality.[28] The Olympian cult was 'virile, clear-cut and prosaic', while the chthonic was 'dark and orgiastic and in some ways far more primitive'.[29] As he developed the dichotomy, Guthrie portrayed Dionysos as the most striking embodiment of the chthonian *ethos.*

The duality of Olympian and chthonic cults was related to Guthrie's own dual concern in describing both the intellectual and the spiritual development of Hellenism. Whereas the evolutionists had portrayed Greek intellectual development as progressively undermining Greek religion to the point where the latter was no longer credible, Guthrie saw the relations between the two as a creative tension in which critical thought purified religion of naiveté but did not eliminate it altogether. Thus, he wanted to legitimate both philosophical-scientific and religious developments. This meant affirming aspects of conflicting hermeneutical positions and demanded greater balance than earlier scholars had chosen to muster. Guthrie was not entirely successful in his attempt to validate both the critical and traditional sides of Hellenism, but that he attempted it at all and with such a thorough understanding of both extreme positions is a sign of the moderation of recent scholarship.

For Guthrie it was a given that Hellenism had grown out of primitive culture. Here he accepted that the evolutionists had established their case; and, beyond that, he seemed, despite disclaimers to the contrary, to agree that in important dimensions primitive culture was intellectually deficient. His allegiance to Hellenism then led him to emphasize the ways Greek culture had 'become separated off' from its primitive background,[30] and to treat the results of this intellectual development as the paramount characteristics of Hellenism. Thus, he identified the Greeks as predominantly rational, always striving 'to exalt the conscious processes of the mind and suppress the unconscious or subconscious'.[31] In religion, the Greeks manifested this rationalism by developing the Olympian religion to a greater clarity than that enjoyed by cults of surrounding peoples. Even within Greek religion itself, the relation of the Olympian cult to the chthonic mirrored the relation of the Greek civilization to the barbarian: 'the intelligible, determinate, mensurable, as opposed to the fantastic, vague, and shapeless'.[32] Accepting the evolutionist tenet that the more vague chthonic ethos represented a form of early thought 'found all over the world at a certain stage of culture, with only minor differences',[33] Guthrie argued that the Greeks' preference for the determinate Olympian ethos led to their unique achievements. Thus, while not advocating the evolutionist argument that religion originated out of primitive stupidity, Guthrie agreed that the rationalization of Greek religion represented an intellectual advance.

In fact, in discussing the development of philosophy Guthrie seemed to accept the evolutionist argument. As he portrayed it, the earliest religion was an essentially naive state of mind where pre-critical men projected their own emotions on the world, explaining everything in terms of personal wills. Guthrie followed Cornford in seeing philosophy as a transformation of mythology, wherein the primitive personalism of mythology was replaced by

reason's attempt to discern an underlying order based on impersonal forces.[34] Between these two extremes, Homeric anthropomorphism, naive in its own way, was an advance 'both on
earlier popular notions of vague, uncanny power of the 'mana' type
(which certainly preceded it and have left unmistakable traces) and
on the monstrous forms which still haunt the *Theogony* of Hesiod'.[35]
Yet while Greek culture advanced, it was slow to throw off its earlier
heritage and consequently allowed primitive stages to persist as
survivals.[36]

This current of Guthrie's analysis paralleled standard evolutionary theory. What distinguished Guthrie from his predecessors
Cornford and Harrison was his concern to portray the ideological
content of Greek religion as an authentic human option for the
Greeks' self-understanding and definition of reality. The difference
between his analysis and theirs consisted as much in what he
refrained from doing as in what he did; his treatment was, in
comparison to theirs, almost entirely phenomenological. Whereas
he had discussed the origin of philosophy in terms of intellectual
progress, in discussing religion he consistently attempted to point to
its inner logic as representing an autonomous mode of thought and
behavior. Accordingly, he did not feel constrained to provide the
kind of external causal explanation of religion as had the evolutionists. He discussed historical antecedents of Greek cults at considerable length, but this was to show the modifications the cults had
undergone, not to unmask them as erroneous.

From the point of view of philosophy, the Olympian as opposed
to the chthonic cult had represented a greater freedom from
uncanny supernatural forces. However, from the spiritual point of
view, the survival and development of the chthonic cult allowed a
movement from the Homeric period's external, formalized and
often mechanical relationships between man and god to a more
profound kinship. For this reason Guthrie insisted that 'primitive'
was a meaningful description only as indicating 'chronologically
older'. In his view spiritual insight could be as deep in the earliest
stages of Greek religion as in the more 'developed', later stages.[37]

Although Guthrie generally agreed with Nilsson that the Olympian cult corresponded to the Indo-European racial group known as
the Achaeans and the chthonic to the Mediterranean pre-Achaean
stock, he did not share Nilsson's belief in the intellectual superiority

of the Indo-Europeans and saw the racial correspondences as only partially helpful in explaining the difference in ethos between the two religions. More important were the life situations and class distinctions of the different groups. The Homeric warrior-aristocrats naturally had different concerns and different hopes than did the peoples they had subdued. As conquerors, they had the leisure and the material resources to develop a cult of beauty and of martial prowess. Also, having migrated from their homeland, they were no longer in touch with either the spirits of fertility or their ancestors which they must have known earlier. The subjected peoples, on the other hand, had been reduced to tilling the soil in servitude. Their reliance on the land for their livelihood led them to the gods of fertility; the evils they suffered led them to cults promising a better afterlife.[38] Since this difference in basic concerns was more important for the Olympian/chthonic dichotomy than different racial characteristics, each *ethos*, in Guthrie's view, possessed its own spiritual authenticity. In an unusual passage on Empedocles Guthrie claimed that each ethos was essential to genuine Hellenism: the Appoline as Hellenism's 'classical' side, the Dionysiac as 'romantic'.[39]

Guthrie succeeded better than had previous scholars in celebrating the intellectual development involved in the emerging Greek philosophy while still upholding the legitimacy of Greek religious thought. However, between these two positions there was always a tension, albeit a generally creative one. This tension allowed him to point to various uses of religion from the most naive to the most sophisticated. It also allowed him to follow the dictates of common sense; he could present some religious phenomena as essentially superstitious while treating others as still metaphysically arguable. Consequently, he was not caught in Otto's bind of having to dismiss everything that smacked of utilitarian motives as degenerate; nor was he forced to see metaphysical dimensions of Greek religion as epiphenomena.

Guthrie never ranked the various purposes of religion into any hierarchy, but in one context or another he analyzed religious phenomena in terms of all available hypotheses, from the most utilitarian to the most philosophically expressive. On the instrumental side, he was like Nilsson in his recognition that religion corresponded to a people's needs, circumstances, and surroundings.[40]

Accordingly, he argued that where there was a need for fertility, the Greeks sometimes resorted to sympathetic magic. The *hieros gamos* between Dionysos and the wife of the Archon Basileus during the Athenian Anthesteria was an example of such vegetation magic.[41] Where there were difficult psychological pressures, religion provided a release, often in the form of excusing emotional outbursts as inadvertent results of external compulsion.[42] Like Rohde, Guthrie also saw man as having the independent religious need to be close to divinity; 'the purpose of its [Dionysiac religion's] orgiastic rites was to become *entheos*, filled with, and so at one with, the god'.[43] Religion also offered explanations for natural events[44] and, more important in Guthrie's analysis, preserved the memory of historical occurrences.[45]

In addition, Guthrie portrayed religion as expressing fundamental truths about the nature of reality. Especially through myth, religion identified the nature of the ultimate power behind the universe and thus defined man's status in the world and relation to Divinity.[46] Guthrie accepted the conclusions of non-evolutionist scholars who saw myth not as fairy tale but as 'the symbolic expression of some of the most universal and firmly held of human convictions',[47] Here he asserted that intellectual development entailed a transformation of myth but not its abolition. In the earliest period myth may be 'the only available means (and an effective one) of expressing profound and universal truths'.[48] At this stage of civilization many people would be content to accept such myths literally; however, for philosophy to progress, thinkers had to emancipate themselves from myth's personalism and seek impersonal causes. Yet reason and scientific investigation could progress only so far. At the culmination of reasoned argument great philosophers like Plato found themselves returning to myth as the only adequate expression for 'a region of truth, and that the highest, to which rational argument no longer supplied the key and the language of literal fact was no longer appropriate'.[49] Religious thought was, therefore, not a stage which had to be overcome, but it did require the constant purification given it by reflective and critical philosophy.[50]

There is a certain philosophical elitism which underlies Guthrie's work and gives it its distinction. On the one hand, the evolutionists never manifested the same kind of preference for philosophically 'purified' religious thought because they clearly did not take it as seriously as did Guthrie. Whereas he seemed to see it as the *telos* of the Greek religious impulse, they saw it as the most refined (and, in a way, best disguised) stage of an initial error. On the other side of the interpretive spectrum, Otto had seen religion fulfilling its role in a less intellectualized way than did Guthrie and so had not demanded such a high degree of self-conscious reflection as the price of authenticity. Since Otto was more of an artist than a philosopher, he accepted many religious rites and myths as legitimate even when an actual Greek participant might not have been able to verbalize their conceptual content. In his view the lived experience of universal reality undergone by the worshipper was more important than rigorous intellectual comprehension. To be sure, the ideological dimension was essential to religion, but it was appropriated in a totalistic fashion, with bodily action as well as reflective thought. Otto's position allowed him to validate more phenomena as religiously genuine than did Guthrie's, but at the same time it forced him to justify practically everything carried out in the name of religion. Guthrie's more critical position allowed him to classify some phenomena as undeveloped without implying that religion as a total phenomenon was illegitimate.

Consonant with his mediating position, Guthrie pointed to both positive and negative facets of the Dionysiac cult. His historical analysis of the entrance of Dionysos into Hellenism paralleled the standard evolutionist account, lacking only the theoretical superstructure which derived religion from primitive mentality. Although the presence of Dionysos in Mycenaean times is established by references on the Linear B tablets, originally, Guthrie argued, he entered Greece as a stranger to the established pantheon, coming probably from Anatolia and Thrace. Once there, he was recognized as identical with the Cretan Zeus (the chthonic form of Zeus) and thus brought into line with pre-Achaean religious forms.[51] Nevertheless, this identification with the often orgiastic, chthonic cults did little to gain for Dionysos acceptance in the Olympian pantheon. Since the predominant Greek characteristics at this time were 'sanity, self-consciousness and limit',[52] Dionysiac religion was resisted as a terrifying incursion. However, because it offered greater emotional satisfaction and the possibility of a new, closer relation to god, it eventually overcame the resistance of the 'calm and reasonable' Olympian religion.[53] Still, this victory was accompanied by profound modifications in the Bacchic cult. The orgiastic practices were restricted;[54] and the promise of immortality, so important in the Thracian cult,[55] was eliminated from the Hellenic version.[56] The Apolline cult forced most of the modifications which brought Dionysiac religion closer to the Hellenic ethos;[57] the reform movement of Orphism 'purified' other more primitive ideas.[58]

As much as Rohde, Guthrie treated the history of Dionysiac religion in Greece as the story of its taming by Hellenism's intrinsic moderation. Though Indo-European, it corresponded to the pre-Achaean chthonic cults and represented a minority view surpassed by Homeric rationalism. However, in terms of its internal structure, Guthrie did not follow Rohde's lead in attributing the ideological content of Dionysiac religion to animistic thought. Rather, he discussed it as equal in conceptual integrity to Olympian religion. While not, like Otto, espousing it as true, he treated its blend of emotional satisfaction and new conceptions of divine-human relations as a creative alternative to the dominant patterns. Whereas Rohde had suggested materialistic bases for mystical religion, Guthrie treated the cult purely descriptively, and the tone of his analysis seemed to leave open the possibility not only of mysticism's emotional validity (for which Harrison had argued) but of its cognitive validity as well. To a large extent this tone was established by his explaining the chthonic ethos more in terms of the 'pre-Achaean's' forced meditation on the problems of evil and of meaning than in terms of racial differences or primitive mentality.[59] Nilsson had also analyzed religion as a response to these problems, but by explicitly assuming that the universe was meaningless he reduced religion to the status of an anodyne. Guthrie, on the other hand, remained more phenomenological and accepted the world-view inherent in chthonic religion as an intelligible stance that did not need to be explained away.[60] In his view man's nature included some kind of structured relationship with the larger universe, and the traditional (and still serviceable) mode of this relationship was religion.

As a result he saw Dionysiac religion as referring to all layers of human experience. To a considerable extent he saw its function, like that of Greek religion in general, as explaining scientific and historical questions. Here he usually dealt with it in his historical account of the intellectual evolution from myth to critical reason, treating it as a function of pre-scientific limitations.[61] Dionysos as the typical 'year god' and the most famous Greek vegetation deity[62] offered a way to conceptualize the cycle of the seasons and the fate of biological life.[63] Dionysiac religion also conserved historical memories, as, for example, the resistance myths, which were best understood as transmuted accounts of Dionysos' violent incursion into Greece.[64] It also helped explain overmastering psychological impulses[65] and showed that men cannot submit to having his reason submerged beneath his animal elements without a struggle.[66]

Guthrie interpreted Dionysiac religion as referring also to a supernatural dimension. He treated Dionysiac conceptions of the soul not as pre-scientific but as reflecting a universal human concern.[67] In the same way he postulated Divinity as a referent of religion without explaining it as error or epiphenomenon. Here again his analysis was distinguished from that of the evolutionists not so much by the facts treated as by his willingness to let those facts stand as self-explanatory, trans-cultural human products. Thus, in his presentation, Dionysiac religion helped the Greeks define their own nature and their relation to Divinity. Furthermore, in the hands of religious and philosophical reformers, it served as a nucleus for authentic reflection which transcended the self-imposed limits of scientific and rational thought.

Both Dodds and Guthrie synthesized previous interpretations. Each, for example, saw in Dionysiac religion both utilitarian and expressive functions. Following the evolutionists, Dodds could see animistic and magical thought behind many of the practices and beliefs; following Freud, he could also see psychological impulses gaining expression (here more in the sense of catharsis or 'pressing out', than of 'testimony'). Guthrie also followed the evolutionists' lead to some degree in interpreting facets of Dionysiac religion as oriented towards improving man's material and psychological position, but in addition he saw man as by nature engaged in questions of meaning, post-mortem fate, and Divinity; and he therefore interpreted religion as the expression of a natural metaphysical concern. It is this acceptance of the metaphysical enterprise as a legitimate enterprise that separated Guthrie from Dodds. For Dodds Dionysos was the result of early man's striving to identify and come to terms with perceptible but ill-understood natural realities. For Guthrie the language of supernaturalism did not seem to be a function of conceptual inadequacy but of profound thought. However, because he never arranged his interpretations into an explicit hierarchy of importance, it is difficult to know which concern he thought more important, the material or the metaphysical.

CONCLUDING REMARKS

As can be seen from the works of Dodds and Guthrie, scholarship on Dionysiac religion, as on religion in general, has developed in the direction of moderation and synthesis. This partial *rapprochement* is due to the growing recognition that religion is practiced for both utilitarian and expressive reasons, that it is fueled by thought, emotions, and drives, and that it can be studied either diachronically or synchronically. To date, there is no hermeneutic which exhausts the nature of religious phenomena, nor is one likely. Therefore, even though eclecticism is a mark of scientific underdevelopment, the modern synthesizing approach has the merit of treating the multiple factors behind religion and avoiding unnecessary dichotomies. To say that each analysis we have examined reveals important facets of Dionysiac religion may sound lame, but the statement contains a measure of truth. Otto and Nilsson, mutually antagonistic, could have learned from one another. Otto was clearly the victim of wishful thinking in his belief that Greek religion was always disinterested, but Nilsson also erred in paying so little attention to the metaphysical needs of earliest man. Many of the other issues of disagreement would have been better elucidated had the two men, or, more generally, scholars with conflicting hermeneutics, been able to acknowledge the plausibility of alternative viewpoints.

Yet, ultimately there exist crucial presuppositions which mutually exclude one another, so that a thoroughgoing methodological synthesis is not really a possibility. Concerning Dionysiac religion, the most basic of these has been the question of the referent of Dionysos—no reality, natural reality misconstrued, or supernatural reality. The evolutionists argued for only the first two possibilities. In their view there was no reality addressed by religion which could not have been dealt with more effectively by science or expressed more accurately with a naturalistic vocabulary. 'Pro-religious' scholars held open the possibility that there was an aspect of reality which was not dealt with by natural-scientific, historical, psychological, and sociological knowledge but which was addressed by religion. Without necessarily believing in God themselves, they assumed that certain non- or meta-empirical issues demanded attention from man and that religion was one legitimate mode of attending to this extra-scientific dimension.

As we have noted, denying the possibility of such a dimension led one to see religion as the result of mental confusion. Thus, Rohde saw Dionysos as the emotionally charged precipitate of early man's fantastic logic, designed basically to explain biological phenomena. Harrison, in *Prolegomena*, saw him as an imaginary force expected to provide material benefits for man; in *Themis*, as the expression of genuine social effervescence. Nilsson had seen Dionysiac religion serving a complex network of human needs—material, emotional, and intellectual; but in the final analysis he saw Dionysos as a figment of a limited mind awed by uncomprehended natural phenomena. Finally, Dodds, like Rohde, saw Dionysos as a fantastic explanation of biological data but also as a partially effective expression of inevitable human drives and emotions.

When an extra-scientific dimension was considered a possibility or, at least, an arguable hypothesis, religion was seen as man's natural quest to perceive the fundamental basis of the world and to live in its superabundant reality. For Otto, Dionysos was the formed image of the universe revealed at its most primordial. Since the world was sanctified by the presence of the Divine, Dionysos was a crucial means through which the Greeks were able to transcend the profane dimension and participate in the deepest ontological layer of existence. Guthrie was much more value-free than Otto, but he too saw Dionysos as the focus for legimate human concerns centering on the nature of the human soul and of ultimate reality.

Inevitably, personal views about the nature of man and of existence condition whether an interpreter will see religion as meaningful on its own terms, including concepts of sacrality, supernaturalism, and the like. If he sees it as meaningful, then he will rearticulate religious data into a pattern of thoughts and practices with its own self-evident content. Then he will see Dionysos as one pole of man's relationship with what the Greeks and people of all cultures have considered to be transcendent reality. If he does not see religion as meaningful on its own terms, then he will either account for its errors through genealogy or translate it into some other frame of reference in which it has meaning. Then he will see Dionysos as a pseudo-explanatory concept, a pseudo-causal agent, or a projection of individual or social urges and emotions.

Ironically, deciding what religion refers to is usually the most private hermeneutical maneuver a scholar can make; yet it is the most consequential one for his understanding of Dionysos or any god. The varieties of important issues and of specific interpretive options seem almost numberless, but scholars arrange and explicate religious facts within a fundamental hermeneutical structure. Ultimately, they interpret Dionysos according to their assumptions about the 'real' data described by religious language, whether this be seen as the causal chain egregiously misunderstood, ordinary reality transmuted and projected, or genuine Being authentically perceived. In turn, interpreting Dionysos according to this basic hermeneutic, they help shape the contemporary view of the cosmos and of the possibilities of the human enterprise.

Notes

NOTES TO CHAPTER ONE

1. *American Anthropologist*, 66 (1964), 251–65.
2. *Patterns of Culture*, (Boston, 1934), pp. 79–80; cited in Smith, *ibid.*, p. 252.
3. *Man in the Primitive World* (New York, 1958), p. 647; cited in Smith, *ibid.*
4. *Cultural Anthropology* (New York, 1955), p. 339, cited in Smith, *ibid.*
5. *Cultural Anthropology* (New York, 1958), p. 157, cited in Smith, *ibid.*
6. *The Science of Man* (New York, 1954), p. 436, cited in Smith, *ibid.*
7. Smith, *ibid.*
8. Cf. Richard Arthur Firda, 'Wedekind, Nietzsche and the Dionysian experience,' *Modern Language Notes*, 87 (October 1972), 720–31.
9. Cf. *Life Against Death* (Middletown, Conn., 1959), pp. 156–76, esp. 174–76.
10. From *Götzendämmerung* (Werke, VIII, 172), quoted in O. Crusius, *Erwin Rohde. Ein biographischer Versuch* (Tübingen and Leipzig, 1902), p. 184.
11. *My Recollections*, trans. G. C. Richards (London, 1930), pp. 151f.
12. For an excellent account of these developments, see J. W. Burrow, *Evolution and Society* (Cambridge, 1968), esp. pp. 83–118. He argues convincingly against placing too much emphasis on Darwin's role as the mainspring of the evolutionary approach to social sciences by showing scientific currents already flowing in that direction independent of Darwin.
13. For a helpful discussion of this orientation in the context of social science, see Talcott Parsons, *The Structure of Social Action*, Vol. II (New York, 1968), 481–85.
14. Though Malinowski is the first systematic expositor of functionalism, the use of functionalist principles has been traced back to the nineteenth century just before Darwin's breakthrough. See Robert H. Lowie, *The History of Ethnological Theory* (New York, 1937), pp. 8, 40, 41, 43, 43, passim.
15. By 'natural' I mean 'theoretically explicable through scientific method' or, to use Danto's formulation, 'susceptible to explanation through methods which, although paradigmatically exemplified in the natural sciences, are continuous from domain to domain of objects and events' (Arthur C. Danto, 'Naturalism' *The Encyclopedia of Philosophy*, 1967, V, 448). The 'methodological monism' which Danto describes in this manner is held to account for cultural as well as natural facts. Cf. Durkheim's remark 'The social realm is a natural realm which differs from the others only by a greater complexity' (Emile Durkheim, *The Elementary Forms of the Religious Life*, trans. by Joseph Ward Swain [New York, 1965], p. 31).

NOTES TO CHAPTER TWO

1. For convenience, the pertinent works of each scholar will be listed in chronological order in the first footnote of each chapter.

   Since Rohde treated Greek religion systematically only in the last years of his life, there are essentially only two major works that need concern us here:

   Psyche. Seelencult und Unsterblichkeitsglaube der Griechen (Freidburg i. B. and Leipzig, 1894); 5th and 6th eds., 2 vols. (Tübingen, 1910). *Psyche* has been translated into English by W. B. Hillis; 2 vols., (New York, 1966).

   Die Religion der Griechen (Heidelberg, 1895), Rohde's much briefer Prorector's address at the University of Heidelberg.

   For a complete Rohde bibliography, see W. Schmid, 'Erwin Rohde,' *Jahresbericht über die Fortschritte der klassischen Altertumswissenschaft*, Index, XXVI (1899), 110–14.

2. Writing of the Greeks' understanding of madness as part of the explanation for the Dionysiac cult, E. R. Dodds initiated this tribute: 'In attempting to deal with [these questions] I shall of course be standing, as we all stand, on the shoulders of Rohde'. *The Greeks and the Irrational* (Berkeley, 1966), p. 65. W. K. C. Guthrie, in his Introduction to the 1966 reprint of the English translation of *Psyche*, p. xii, added that all modern classicists could echo Dodds' tribute.

3. Arthur Schopenhauer, *The World as Will and Idea*, trans. R. B. Haldane and J. Kemp (London, 1883), vol. 2, 359–60. Cf. 'Religion A Dialogue', in *Essays of Arthur Schopenhauer*, trans. T. Bailey Saunders, [New York, n.d.], pp. 218–19.

4. 'Religion, A Dialogue', p. 208. It is admittedly risky to identify Schopenhauer's own position with that of either of the interlocutors of the dialogue; it seems clear that by casting his ideas in the form of an argument, Schopenhauer was able to express the ambivalence of religion's role in human history. Demopheles, although convinced that religion falls short of philosophy, points to the intrinsic metaphysical satisfactions which it allows. Philalethes points to a different aspect of religion—its repressive and obscurantist character which must always be maintained so that 'revelation' never be compromised.

   It should be pointed out that what is at stake here is not whether Schopenhauer thought religion was true but what he thought religion was all about as a human behavior. The presence of a fully elaborated position relating religion to inevitable metaphysical needs links Schopenhauer to earlier Romantic interpretations of religion. He differed from most of the Romantics in that he felt that Kant's *Critique of Pure Reason* had closed off the possibility of knowing 'supernatural' reality and had thereby rendered metaphysics problematical as an adequate way to reach the truth. Nevertheless, epistemological concerns aside, from an anthropological viewpoint metaphysics seemed to be a constant human urge. Therefore, as Gardiner correctly notes, metaphysics was a problem to which he returned again and again; Patrick Gardiner, *Schopenhauer* (Baltimore, Md., 1963), p. 30.

   The essay 'Religion, A Dialogue' appeared in *Parerga and Paralipomena*, first published in 1851. From the Rohde-Nietzsche correspondence it seems clear that Rohde knew the work. In a letter to Rohde, November 3, 1867, written from his army post at Naumburg, Nietzsche speaks of reading the *Parerga* as recreation and seems to assume Rohde's familiarity with it; *Selected Letters of Friedrich Nietzsche*, ed. and trans. Christopher Middleton (Chicago, 1969), p. 27.

5. Talcott Parsons, *The Structure of Social Action*, I, 422. Cf. Clifford Geertz, 'Ethos, World-View, and the Analysis of Sacred Symbols', *Antioch Review*, 17 (1957), 436.

6. 'Religion, A Dialogue', p. 218. Over and over Schopenhauer returned to this point. Cf. p. 226: 'Man is a metaphysical animal—that is to say, he has paramount metaphysical necessities; accordingly he conceives life above all in its metaphysical significance and wishes to bring everything into line with that'. Demopheles' interlocutor, Philalethes, disagrees on almost every point but he agrees about man's metaphysical requirements; his complaint is that while religion may be practiced to satisfy those needs, it abuses them more than it satisfies them, p. 239.

7. 'Myth and allegory really form the proper element of religion; and under this indispensable condition, which is imposed by the intellectual limitation of the multitude, religion provides a sufficient satisfaction for those metaphysical requirements of mankind which are indestructible. It takes the place of that pure philosophical truth which is infinitely difficult and perhaps never attainable', 'Religion. A Dialogue', p. 217. Cf. p. 216: '. . . truth, which is inexpressible except by means of myth and allegory, is like water, which can be carried about only in vessels . . . Religion is truth allegorically and mythically expressed, and so rendered attainable and digestible by mankind in general'.

8. N. 21, Sunday, May 26, 1872, pp. 1–2. Reprinted in E. Rohde, *Kleine Schriften*, 2 vols. (Tübingen and Leipzig, 1901), II, 340–51.

9. Cogitatum 23, p. 228 in O. Crusius, *Erwin Rohde. Ein biographischer Versuch* (Tübingen and Leipzig, 1902). Cf. Cogitatum 86, p. 252. In his review of *The Birth of Tragedy*, Rohde even asserted that myth gave a more accurate picture of the world than did the clever but superficial views of his own day, *Kleine Schriften*, II, 346f.

10. *Ibid.*, Cogitatum 86, p. 252.

11. W. K. C. Guthrie, 'Introduction', in Erwin Rohde, *Psyche*, vol. I, ix–x.

12. Nietzsche was not the first to propose the oppostion between Apollo and Dionysos. Walter Kaufmann has drawn attention to this dichotomy in Schelling's *Philosophie der Offenbarung* (*Werke*, II, IV, 25). Cf. Kaufmann's *Nietzsche: Philosopher, Psychologist, Antichrist* (3rd ed.; New York, 1968), p. 128. Nevertheless, Nietzsche was the first professional philologian to apply this dichotomy systematically to a problem of classical scholarship.

13. Friedrich Nietzsche, *Die Geburt der Tragödie* (München: Wilhelm Goldmann Verlag, n.d.), pp. 22f; English translation by Walter Kaufmann, *The Birth of Tragedy and The Case of Wagner* (New York, 1967), p. 33. Except where noted, translations are the author's; references will be given to existing English translations, since these are often more accessible.

14. *Die Geburt der Tragödie*, p. 25 (Kaufmann tr., p. 35).

15. *Ibid.*

16. *Ibid.*, pp. 25f. (pp. 35f.).

17. '*Edle Einfalt, stille Grösse*', Johann Joachim Winckelmann, quoted in Kaufmann's 'Introduction' to his translation of *The Birth of Tragedy*, (p. 9). A more

complete and critical view of the Winckelmann description is found in Martin Vogel, *Apollinisch und Dionysisch. Geschichte eines genialen Irrtum* (Regensburg, 1966), pp. 42–45.

18. *Die Geburt der Tragödie*, p. 26 (Kaufmann tr., p. 36).
19. *Ibid.*, p. 27 (p. 37).
20. *Ibid.*, p. 28 (p. 38).
21. *Ibid.*, p. 30 (p. 39). Nietzsche did not specify what Apollo's taking the weapons from Dionysos entailed, but it seems to parallel Rohde's notion that Apollo took over mantic (god-inspired) prophecy from Dionysos.
22. *Ibid.*, pp. 14, 22 (pp. 22, 31f.).
23. *Ibid.*, pp. 46, 157, 14 (pp. 52, 141, 22).
24. While established classicists ignored the work, Nietzsche's younger contemporary, Ulrich von Wilamowitz-Möllendorff, who was later to become Germany's foremost classicist, vigorously attacked it. His polemic, *Zukunftsphilologie! Eine Erwiderung auf Friedrich Nietzsches, Ord. Professors der class. Philologie zu Basel, Geburt der Tragödie*, pointed out Nietzsche's historical errors to show that Nietzsche had misunderstood Hellenism. Rohde attempted to defend Nietzsche against Wilamowitz in his counterpolemic, *Afterphilologie. Zur Beleuchtung des von dem Dr. Phil. Ulrich von Wilamowitz-Möllendorff herausgegebenen Pamphlets*: '*Zukunftsphilologie!*' (Leipzig, 1872), by exposing historical errors on Wilamowitz' part. On this confrontation see J. H. Groth, 'Wilamowitz-Möllendorff on Nietzsche's Birth of Tragedy', *Journal of the History of Ideas*, 11 (1950), 179–90; Walter Kaufmann (tr.), *ibid.*, pp. 4–6; and Vogel, *Appolinisch und Dionysisch*, pp. 17–35. Vogel shows that German philologians have remained critical of Nietzsche's work and that the publication of *The Birth of Tragedy* was more disastrous for Nietzsche's pedagogical career than is allowed by Kaufmann, *ibid.*, pp. 7–9.
25. An entry of 1870 in Rohde's notebook presents an interesting parallel to Nietzsche's Apollo/Dionysos dichotomy; (Crusius, *ibid.*, p. 220). Here two years before the publication of *The Birth of Tragedy* Rohde divided religions and philosophies into two basic varieties: 'human' religions which emphasize the intellect and individual autonomy (parallel to Nietzsche's 'Apolline' and Schopenhauer's 'Idea' [*Vorstellung*]) and 'world' religions which bypass this individualization and emphasize the unconscious life, the total universe and its forceful will (parallel to Nietzsche's 'Dionysian' and Schopenhauer's *Wille*). The human religions are, in Rohde's view, often subjugated to the larger unconscious unity typical of 'world' religions, just as the sobriety of Apollinian religion was often swallowed up in Dionysian ecstasy.
26. Crusius, *Erwin Rohde*, p. 55. Crusius claimed this shows that Rohde met Nietzsche half-way in the development of ideas about Dionysos. Another of Rohde's biographers claims that the influence was one way, from Nietzsche; cf. Ernest A. A. L. Sellière, *Nietzsches Waffenbruder, Erwin Rohde* (Berlin, 1911), p. 24.
27. This verdict is shared by Nietzsche throughout *The Birth of Tragedy*, especially in his critique of 'Socratism' in sections 11 through 15 and is most forcefully expressed in section 4 of his later preface 'Attempt at a Self-Criticism', *ibid.*, pp. 13f. (pp. 21f): 'Could it be possible that, in spite of all "modern ideas" and the prejudices of a democratic taste, the triumph of *optimism*, the gradual prevalence of *rationality*, practical and theoretical *utilitarianism*, no less than

democracy itself which developed at the same time, might all have been symptoms of a decline of strength, of impending old age, and of physiological weariness'? (Kaufmann's translation).

28. Crusius, *ibid.*, p. 67, says that Cogitatum 55 (February 28, 1874) (*ibid.*, pp. 241f.) represents the turning point against Schopenhauer's philosophy: 'One cannot live with only the Schopenhauerian philosophy. Not merely because, taken seriously, it negates life and therefore contains in its negative conclusion an easily recognizable, fantastic inconceivability. Such a negative conclusion may perhaps be suitable for a religion, like Buddhism, according to whose premises, after all, this conclusion is not unthinkable, but not for a philosophical doctrine. Not only on that account. Rather, primarily because this doctrine directs its deeply piercing and persistent gaze at the uniformity (*auf das Einheitliche*) in the life of the world and, thus, even of mankind. According to its essence, this unity is always the same, absolutely invariable. With such thoughts, directed to an unalterable One, what sense would it make to continue living; that is, to act in life? Even more, why struggle for improvement and enhancement of life since, after all, that which man recognizes as essential, that which man in general acknowledges is totally incapable of change for the better or even for the worse? With this view (when it hides no fluttering veil of desire for life), all challenge toward acting in life ceases .... Indeed, what should a man do? Arbitrarily cloak himself in such a veil? Or rather should he be willing to follow the incessantly pressing call of man's duty without hesitation? Without doubt it should be the latter. This latter philosophical way of thinking is right a thousandfold, and it should sound out in the concert of human sentiments and acts like a deep bass, strictly harmonizing in the lower registers'.

Much the same moral commitment expressed here by Rohde motivated the work of Jane Harrison and Martin Nilsson who also focused on man's evolutionary advances. However, Walter F. Otto, Rohde's countryman, operated with a different conception of authentic humanity and therefore with a different moral commitment, and he argued that the repetition of a culture's central metaphysical insight did not negate man's interest in life but was, in fact, man's only living contact with reality. Part of Rohde's greatness lay in his ability to understand both types of commitment.

29. Crusius, *ibid.*, p. 66.
30. A remark about Mill and Tylor indicates a certain initial ambivalence about his shift in perspectives: 'With their ghastly commonsense style, these fellows often, I admit, bore one to death, but they understand excellently and without being obtrusive the difficult art of logical exposition', Crusius, *ibid.*
31. Sellière speaks of Rohde's shift from 'aesthetic appreciation' to 'historical reflection', Sellière, *ibid.*, p. 120.
32. Rohde never totally abandoned his earlier orientation and was able to draw on it in *Psyche*. The sophisticated combination of both approaches gave *Psyche* a breadth that even many later monographs lack.
33. Burrow, *Evolution and Society*, p. 263.
34. E. B. Tylor, *Primitive Culture*, Part II (*Religion in Primitive Culture*), (New York, 1958), p. 539.
35. Burrow, *ibid.*, pp. 108f.
36. *Ibid.*, p. 263.

37. *Ibid.*, pp. 98f.
38. *Ibid.*, pp. 93–95.
39. *Ibid.*
40. *Ibid.*, p. 53.
41. Tylor, *ibid.*, pp. 535–39.
42. In *Fortnightly Review* VI (1866), 86; cited in Burrow, *ibid.*, p. 248.
43. Tylor, *ibid.*, p. 84.
44. *Ibid.*, p. 12.
45. *Ibid.*
46. The concept of survivals was attacked vigorously by important twentieth century anthropologists, notably Franz Boas and Bronislaw Malinowski, and has lost most of its earlier luster. Margaret Hodgen's *The Doctrine of Survivals* (London, 1936) celebrates its demise. Other scholars have been more charitably disposed toward it as a useful tool. See Marvin Harris, *The Rise of Anthropological Theory* (New York, 1968), pp. 164–69, and p. 352, which reproduces an interesting remark by Robert Lowie that the attack on survivals harbored as much cant as had the doctrine itself.
47. Rohde's smaller *Die Religion der Griechen* covered the same ground as *Psyche* and will be used to supplement the analysis of the larger work.
48. This is a subject which had interested Rohde as early as 1874. See Cogitatum 53; Crusius, *ibid.*, pp. 240f. In 1882 Rohde addressed Tübingen's 'Tuesday Society' on this subject. Cf. W. Schmid, *ibid.*, p. 100.
49. In relying on Hellenic facts to make his analysis Rohde was resisting a genuine temptation to let anthropological theories determine the reconstruction of Greek religious history. The next chapter, on Jane Harrison, will detail the results of succumbing to such a temptation.
50. In the Preface to the First Edition Rohde proposed to trace the origin and development of post-mortem beliefs and practices. Classical testimony and evidence made the presentation of their development possible. Presentation of their origin (and the ultimate explanation) was possible only with the use of anthropological theory.
51. Crusius (*ibid.*, p. 188) errs in the claim that Rohde differed from Nietzsche in saying that Dionysis was not native to Greece. In his little-known *Der Gottesdienst der Griechen* (Vol. III of *Philologica. Unveröffentlichtes zur antiken Religion und Philosophie* [Leipzig, 1913], edited by Crusius himself along with Wilhem Nestle) p. 24, Nietzsche derived Dionysos from Thrace. Nietzsche and Rohde differed merely over the *role* of the once foreign deity.
52. Walter Kaufmann's commentary is helpful here. Nietzsche used the term 'Dionysian' in later works to stand for the world-affirming synthesis of Dionysos with Apollo as over and against 'Christian' as 'nay-saying'. (Kaufmann, tr. *The Birth of Tragedy*, p. 20, n. 5).
53. *Psyche* II, 4 (Eng. tr., p. 255).
54. *Psyche*, II, 9–10 (Eng. tr., p. 257); following Hillis translation.
55. *Psyche*, II, 18–20 (Eng. tr., pp. 259–60).
56. *Psyche*, II, 27–35 (Eng. tr., pp. 263–65).
57. *Psyche*, II, 1–55 (Eng. tr., pp. 253–89, 304–11).
58. Rohde nicely illustrated this movement from incredulity to a genealogical explanation using primitive parallels in *Psyche*, I, 6 (Eng. tr., p. 6) [following Hillis' translation]: 'Such and idea—that the psyche should dwell within the

living and fully conscious personality, like an alien and a stranger, a feebler double of the man, as his "other self"—this may well seem very strange to us. And yet this is what so-called "savage" peoples, all over the world, actually believe'. Rohde immediately went on to account for this belief in terms of the 'fantastic logic' of primitive man.

For Rohde's most programmatic statement identifying evolutionary anthropology as the key to understanding origins, see *Die Religion der Griechen*, p. 6.

59. *Die Religion der Griechen*, pp. 6–8.
60. *Ibid.*, pp. 8f.
61. The first paragraph of *Psyche* opened with Rohde's description of the astonishment man feels at seeing death and his growing wonderment about the nature of both life and death; *Psyche*, I, 1 (Eng. tr., p. 3).
62. *Psyche*, I, 6 (Eng. tr., pp. 6f.).
63. *Ibid.*
64. *Psyche*, I, 46 (Eng. tr., p. 30).
65. Rohde located the belief in the distinction between 'body' and 'soul' among 'all naive peoples and individuals'; *Psyche*, II, 34 (Eng. tr., p. 265).
66. *Psyche*, II, 11 (Eng. tr., pp. 257–58).
67. *Psyche*, II, 11–18 (Eng. tr., pp. 258–59). Cf. *Psyche*, II, 23–27 (Eng. tr., pp. 261–62).
68. *Psyche*, II, 18–20 (Eng. tr., p. 259).
69. This insight by Rohde preceded by many years the explicit 'ritual theory of myth' and, though limited to a single phenomenon, is considerably more convincing than the latter approach. In the perspective of the 'ritualists', myths had been invented for aetiological reasons, to explain rites whose existence needed justification. Attributing ideological development to demonstrable physiological disturbances instead of to forgetfulness and concomitant perplexity, Rohde was more forceful on this issue.
70. Both Crusius (*ibid.*, pp. 188f.) and Sellière (*ibid.*, p. 127) state that Rohde's mature view of Dionysos had become negative. Sellière waxes somewhat rhetorical on this point, claiming that in *Psyche* Dionysos is treated with aversion, even abhorrence. He makes the interesting speculation that this animosity was due to Rohde's horror at seeing Nietzsche's mental condition subsequent to the latter's collapse and his blaming Dionysos as the evil spirit who robbed his friend of his reason. (In the last stages of his deterioration Nietzsche did, in fact, refer to himself as Dionysos.) These personal events may have exacerbated Rohde's dislike, but the internal consistency of *Psyche* as a whole makes it appear that Rohde had fastened on Dionysos as a bane to world-affirming Hellenism well before Nietzsche's breakdown.
71. *Psyche*, II, 22 (Eng. tr., p. 260). Ostensibly, this characterization described how Dionysiac religion must have struck the Homeric Greeks, but it seems evident that Rohde meant it to refer also to the reaction which any enlightened modern man must have to the cult.
72. *Psyche*, II, 5 (Eng. tr., pp. 255–56).
73. Italics mine.
74. Rohde's assertion (Psyche II, 42 [Eng. tr., p. 283]) that even without external evidence we would expect the Greeks to greet the disorderly Thracian cult with antipathy speaks volumes about his presuppositions.

75. *Die Religion der Griechen*, p. 27: 'Mysticism was a drop of foreign blood in the veins of the Greeks'.
76. *Psyche*, II, 42 (Eng. tr., pp. 283–84, 305).
77. *Psyche*, II, 42–43 (Eng. tr., p. 284). Rohde's use of the 'epidemics' of the Middle Ages provides an interesting contrast with Nietzsche's in *The Birth of Tragedy*. For both, the same religious impulses lay behind the Greek and Medieval movements. For Rohde, this parallel helped interpret the Greek phenomenon because the obvious sickness of the Medieval events proved that such outbreaks were aberrations. As self-evidently sick, the phenomenon explained itself.

    For Nietzsche, on the other hand, the 'sickness' of both phenomena did nothing to discredit them. Both could be justified as violent, alternative ways of perceiving the universe. Though it might be condemned as sick by 'healthy-minded' Apollinian partisans, Dionysian experience transcended Apolline religion and negated the claims to health of the latter by its own higher and deeper insight. Since the two religions reflected conflicting visions of the world, their sickenss or health depended on one's perspective in judging. Each insight, in order to be understood, must be judged on its own level, as a viable perspective. Nietzsche attempted to evaluate both perspectives positively. For Rohde, Dionysiac religion, though a perspective to be sure, had its foundations in sickness and simply was not at the same level as healthier Hellenic phenomena. Ultimately Rohde's understanding of Dionysiac religion was always from the Apolline perspective.
78. This problem was addressed quite early in *Psyche* concerning Greek legends on bodily translation, which may have been borrowed from the Semites. Rohde dismissed the historical connections as relatively useless, important only for a mechanical explanation. The main question concerned the 'reason which led the Greek genius to wish to borrow this particular idea at this particular time from abroad', *Psyche*, I, 79 (Eng. tr., p. 60). The contrast between this procedure and the way Rohde analysed Dionysos is striking.
79. *Psyche*, II, 44 (Eng. tr., p. 284).
80. *Ibid*. (Eng. tr., pp. 284–85).
81. *Psyche*, II, 4I–47 (Eng. tr., pp. 284–86).
82. *Psyche*, II, 47–52 (Eng. tr., pp. 286–87).
83. *Psyche*, II, 52–55 (Eng. tr., pp. 287–89, 308–11).
84. *Psyche*, II, 56–61 (Eng. tr., pp. 289–91; 311–13). Rohde has been justifiably criticized for allowing his assumption of the antithesis between Apollo and Dionysos to lead him to attribute the irrational, emotional elements of Apolline worship to Dionysos. Guthrie, objecting to Rohde's thesis that inspired prophecy must have come from Dionysos, attributed Rohde's exaggerated antithesis to the influence of Nietzsche; Guthrie, *Psyche*, Eng. tr., p. x. Cf. also Guthrie, *The Greeks and Their Gods* (Boston: 1955), pp. 199–200; M. P. Nilsson, *A History of Greek Religion* (Oxford, 1925), p. 204.
85. *Psyche*, II, 62–69 (Eng. tr., pp. 291–93; 313–17).
86. *Psyche*, II, 69–80 (Eng. tr., pp. 294–97; 317–22).
87. *Psyche*, II, 80–89 (Eng. tr., pp. 297–99; 322–27).
88. *Psyche*, II, 89–102 (Eng. tr., pp. 299–303; 327–34). Since Rohde identified these figures and practices at least implicitly with the Dionysian impulse by placing them in the chapter on Dionysiac religion, it is interesting to note that

in Greek traditions these early philosopher-ascetics were nearly all associated with Apollo rather than with Dionysos. As in the case of Apolline mantic prophecy, Rohde seems to have carried too far his view that Apollo represented rationality; Dionysos, irrationality, superstition and world-denial.

89. *Psyche*, II, 115–31 (Eng. tr., pp. 340–55).
90. *Psyche*, II, 103–15 (Eng. tr., pp. 335–40, 348–52). Here again Rohde treated the Dionysiac phenomenon as at best ambiguous. It was only as it was transformed according to the demands of Greek thought that it became acceptable at all; and, even with the transformation, it still had not attained the level of philosophy.

   The difference between this evolutionary manner of analysing a religious movement and Rohde's earlier approach can be seen in the way *Psyche* treated the Orphic myth. Whereas before, Rohde had viewed myth as a specific mode of expression; different from, not propaedeutic to philosophy, in *Psyche* Rohde treated it as abortive philosophy: the concepts of Orphism strove to become pure abstractions, but they never totally succeeded in breaking through 'the veil of mythology'. *Psyche*, II, 115 (Eng. tr., p. 340).
91. Rohde's sensitivity to the intrinsic rewards of operative religious life also allowed him to take the expressive elements of the cult seriously and still, in contrast to Jane Harrison, give a non-Durkheimian interpretation of what was being expressed. For Rohde, as opposed to Harrison, Dionysos did not stand for the society itself but for an occult reality imagined by the worshippers to have independent, objective, but extra-empirical reality. They based their belief in this supernatural being on faulty logic, but they knew well enough what they were doing not to have mistaken Dionysos for the social group or its ideals.

Notes to Chapter Three

1. Since most of Harrison's published work dealt with Greek religion, her output was more voluminous than Rohde's. For a generally complete bibliography, marred by occasional faulty citations, see Jessie Stewart, *Jane Ellen Harrison: A Portrait from Letters* (London, 1959), pp. 203–8. Since Harrison frequently abandoned prior positions, the most important works for her mature interpretation can be limited to the following:

   Prolegomena to the Study of Greek Religion (Cambridge, 1903) [Citations will be from the 3rd edition (Cambridge, 1922) Cleveland and New York, 1959)], hereinafter cited as *Prolegomena*.

   'Mystica Vannus Iacchi', *Journal of Hellenic Studies*, XXIII, No. 2 (1903), 292–324; XXIV, No. 2 (1904), 241–54.

   The Religion of Ancient Greece (London, 1905).

   'The Kouretes and Zeus Kouros. A Study in Pre-historic Sociology', *Annual of the British School at Athens*, XV, (1908–09), 308–38.

   'The Influence of Darwinism on the Study of Religions', in *Darwin and Modern Science*, ed. by A. C. Seward (Cambridge, 1909), pp. 494–511, hereinafter cited as 'Darwinism.'

> *Themis. A Study of the Social Origins of Greek Religion* (Cambridge, 1912)
> [Citations will be from the 2nd edition (Cambridge, 1927). The texts of
> the two editions are identical; the second edition includes 'Addenda and
> Corrigenda', pp. xxxv–xxxvi].
> *Ancient Art and Ritual* (New York, 1913).
> *Alpha and Omega* (London, 1915).
> *Epilegomena to the Study of Greek Religion* (Cambridge, 1921).
> *Reminiscences of a Student's Life* (London, 1925).

2. *Alpha and Omega*, p. 206. The most surprising contradiction in Harrison's
   personal stance toward religion involves what seems to have been a religious
   conversion to a traditional belief in God. This conversion had no effect on her
   scholarship, where she continued to the end to present theistic belief as
   illegitimate. Personal letters cited in Jesse Stewart's biography of Harrison
   recount this change of heart, which followed profound personal turmoil. In
   September, 1912 (after writing *Themis*, her second mammoth interpretation
   of Greek religion) she wrote to Gilbert Murray the following:

   > Do you think a blasphemous Ker could be converted? Do you remember
   > contending with me on the cliffs and maintaining that there was more in
   > religion than the collective conscience? I think I know now at first hand that
   > there is . . . I can't describe it—the 'New Birth' is the best—it was what they
   > all try to describe, and it is what they mean by communion with God. Only
   > it seems senseless to me to give it a name and yet I do not wonder for it is so
   > personal.

   Stewart, *ibid.*, p. 113. In a letter of December, 1912 after the death of A. W.
   Verral she wrote Murray: 'I suppose I believe in God, worse luck, still for I
   know there is something I can't forgive for hitting him down and taking him
   away'. *Ibid.*, p. 136.

   There seems to be no way to reconcile these personal correspondences with
   her scholarship. Nine years later her *Epilegomena* was as reductionistic as
   Prolegomena and *Themis* which had both been written before this conversion.
   Then four years after the implicit attack on theism delivered in *Epilegomena*
   Harrison wrote in 1925 'I am inclined to make it up with old Zeus but not
   with Apollo, who remains as ever an ill-mannered prig', Stewart, *ibid.*, p. 194.
   I know of no explanation of this discrepancy. The religious thinker presented
   in *Alpha and Omega*, a collection of Harrison's non-specialist programmatic
   essays, and that of *Jane Ellen Harrison: A Portrait from Letters* seem to be two
   different persons. It should not be surprising that a thinker who could be so
   self-contradictory on matters of obvious personal concern would tend to slip
   into methodological inconsistency from time to time; and, as we will see, this
   was the case with Harrison more than with any other scholar examined here.

3. *Reminiscences of a Student's Life*, p. 83.

4. One catches a note of the liberation from the evils of theology which classical
   civilization worked on Harrison herself from her autobiography: 'To realise
   the release that Aristotle brought, you must have been reared as I was in a
   narrow school of Evangelicalism—reared with sin always present, with death
   and judgment before you, Hell and Heaven to either hand. It was like coming
   out of a madhouse into a quiet college quadrangle where all was liberty and
   sanity, and you became a law to yourself . . . . I remember walking up and
   down in the College garden, thinking could it possibly be true, were the chains

really broken and the prison doors open'. *Reminiscences of a Student's Life*, pp. 80f.

5. *Themis*, p. 531.
6. *Ibid.*
7. *Ibid.*, p. 533.
8. *Alpha and Omega*, pp. 206f.
9. She saw her work *Themis* standing in the same tradition as Frazer's *The Golden Bough*. Both were 'dangerous' books; both made freethinkers of the credulous. Not being an 'obscurantist' she was proud to have heard these things said of *Themis*; *Themis*, 'Preface to the Second Edition', p. viii.
10. 'Darwinism', pp. 497–98.
11. *Ibid.*, p. 510. Reflecting the tension that moved her to try to retain some residue of legitimacy for religion, she backpedaled a bit, saying that religion was not entirely a delusion and was an attempt to apprehend things of enormous importance, but she then reasserted religion's cognitive inaccuracy with the statement 'Every dogma religion has hitherto produced is probably false . . .'. *Ibid.*
12. *Alpha and Omega*, p. 179. In another article in the same volume of essays she noted that she shared with Bertrand Russell the sentiment that we must drop theology and keep religion, *Ibid.*, pp. 61–62. Also cf., *Ibid.*, p. 205.
13. Jessie Stewart recorded the significance for Harrison of a passage from Gilbert Murray's *Ancient Greek Literature* (p. 222) which expressed this 'residue': 'Reason is great, but it is not everything. There are in the world things, not of reason, but both below and above it, causes of emotion which we cannot express, which we tend to worship, which we feel perhaps to be the precious things in life. These things are God or forms of God, not fabulous immortal men, but "Things which Are", things utterly non-human and non-moral which bring man bliss or tear his life to shreds without a break in their own serenity', (*Prolegomena*, p. 657). Jane Harrison wrote to Murray, extolling his formulation, 'Do you mind my quoting you at the end? That sentence has been a sort of theological Alpha and Omega to me . . . in fact it really started the plot of my book four years ago'. Jessie Stewart, *ibid.*, p. 29.
14. Harrison spoke of her growing interest in preserving the legitimate kernel of religion in *Alpha and Omega* (1915), three years after the publication of *Themis*, her 'Durkheimian' work. She spoke of the 'magical' basis of religion and, though disagreeing with it theoretically, granted it more authenticity than before. What she thought was needed was not, however, a return to classical religion but a preserving of its underlying truth. 'Frankly, I am not concerned to keep up this or any other religious or magical *hocus-pocus*. What I am concerned with is the spirit that lies behind it—some element which I do believe to be essential to human progress and therefore a thing to be conserved'. *Alpha and Omega*, p. 183.
15. The clearest statement of this shift occurred in the Introduction to *Themis*, p. xii: 'Primitive religion was not, as I had drifted into thinking, a tissue of errors leading to mistaken conduct; rather it was a web of practices emphasizing particular parts of life, issuing necessarily in representations and ultimately dying out into abstract conceptions'.
16. Harrison argued that religion developed in a uniform and inevitable way, and she clearly drew on her overall genealogy as implicit background for

Dionysos. To spell out the origin and development of Dionysos involves a simple extrapolation from these general 'invariable' principles.

17. *Prolegomena*, pp. 425, 437, 443.

18. The indications of her debt to Frazer are numerous. In her autobiography she credited him with awakening classicists to the importance of anthropology: 'Tylor had written and spoken; Robertson Smith, exiled for heresy, had seen the Star in the East; in vain; we classical deaf-adders stopped our ears and closed our eyes; but at the mere sound of the magical words "Golden Bough" the scales fell—we heard and understood', *Reminiscences of a Student's Life*, p. 83. The similarity of Harrison's analysis to Frazer's is a second indication of this debt. As will be seen, her analysis in *Prolegomena* (1903) was quite different than her analysis prior to the publication of *The Golden Bough* and followed Frazer in postulating magic as the first stage of religion. On a more mechanical note, she referred to and used Frazer's work more than that of any other scholar (28 pages bear references to Frazer.)

19. The way in which Rohde and Harrison each attempted to document the origin of Dionysos from Thrace reveals as well as anything their differences as scholars. Rohde presented massive classical documentation suggesting that the original Thracian worship exactly paralleled that which occurred in Greece but which was later regulated. He also cited numerous classical sources which derived Dionysos from the north.

Harrison's discussion was much more impressionistic and drawn more from artistic and literary remains, with many fewer historical sources than used by Rohde. This in itself need not be a criticism; Harrison's early work had been in art and literature and these subjects form one whole support for classical studies. The problem was that as she used her sources, the evidence could just as well have led to the conclusion that Dionysos was a native Greek God. She admitted that Euripides portrays Dionysos as having been born in Thebes, stating lamely that the reason Euripides could do that was because he 'as poet can afford to contradict himself', (*Prolegomena*, p. 372). She admitted that the earliest artistic evidence showed Dionysos as a native Greek, and only in later works was he pictured as a Thracian or Oriental. Her way to explain this seemingly negative evidence was to call the earlier painter a 'simple vase painter', and claim that 'later the artist becomes more learned', (*Ibid.*, p. 373). She dismissed the absolute lack of hard evidence of a struggle between Dionysos and Apollo at Delphi as due to the Greeks' fastidiousness: 'over this past which was not for edification a decent veil was drawn', (*Ibid.*, p. 391). Finally and most startlingly she claimed that the Greeks portrayed Dionysos as Phrygian rather than Thracian because they had been ashamed to derive anything from Thrace. She gave no evidence of this shame. She then chided the Greeks for feeling this embarrassment, using Herodotus' comment that the Thracians were the greatest of all peoples after the Indians to show that such embarrassment was unnecessary (*Ibid.*, pp. 377–78). Herodotus' comment could just as easily be read as evidence that such embarrassment was not only unnecessary but non-existent, at least in Herodotus' circle. Analyses like this one have led scholars to evaluate her work as not always cogent. G. S. Kirk's judgment of her works is quite fair: 'lively, learned, yet unpedantic— and utterly uncontrolled by anything resembling careful logic'. G. S. Kirk, *Myth, Its Meaning and Functions in Ancient and Other Cultures* (Cambridge,

1970), p. 3.
20. *Prolegomena*, pp. 412, 424.
21. *Ibid.*, p. 424.
22. In the first edition of *Prolegomena* Harrison saw Dionysos' cult centering around a drink made first of fermented honey, then of fermented cereals, and only later of fermented grapes. *Prolegomena*, pp. 412–24. She based this succession on extremely ingenious but gratuitous etymological speculation. By the third edition she had given up this hypothesis and returned to a more orthodox position. Cf. *Ibid.*, p. 453, n. 1.
23. *Ibid.*, p. 425. Again note the contrast to Rohde's treatment. Both Rohde and Harrison felt that primitive logic compelled man to interpret states of exaltation as an infusion of divine life. Rohde, however, was considerably more conservative about what constituted this exaltation, seeing it as a driving, fairly violent religious experience for which wine served, at most, as an auxiliary stimulant. In Harrison's view the ordinary state of intoxication would have been strange enough to primitive man to lead him to attribute his feelings to a god.
24. In an earlier context Harrison described this intellectually limited primitive thinker as 'unable to conceive of any force except as resulting from some person or being or sprite, something a little like himself', *Ibid.*, p. 169.
25. *Ibid.*, p. 425.
26. *Ibid.*, p. 426.
27. *Ibid.*, p. 431.
28. *Ibid.*, pp. 428f.
29. *Ibid.*, p. 431.
30. *Ibid.*, p. 444. Cf. p. 431. Harrison's works preserve some of the finest gems ever written of the British evolutionary belief in the stupidity of primitive man. Harrison had an astonishing ability to create hypotheses which would render facts more amenable to the theory she was using, and the assumption of primitive ignorance served often to explain discrepancies between historical facts and what the evolutionary sequence was supposed to be. She ordinarily based her presentation of primitive logic on ethnologists' accounts, but she seems also, as in this case, to have supplied her own variations more or less on the rule that nothing was too stupid for primitive man to have believed. She never considered the possibility that phenomena such as totemism (as she will call this 'unity' in *Themis*) had symbolic or taxonomic value for the primitives and assumed that primitives literally believed that they themselves were plants and animals during such ritual and symbolic identifications. To say that Harrison's understanding of primitive mentality is different from that of most contemporary anthropologists is to put it mildly.
31. This camel was the famous though unfortunate dromedary whose death and consumption by his Bedouin owners was recorded by Nilus, a Christian saint, and interpreted by Robertson Smith as a totemistic sacrifice. Harrison gave no reasons why the Nilus account applied to the omophagia and seems to have presupposed the parallel as obvious from the similarity of the two rites.
    It now seems that even apart from the question of its relevance to the Greek materials, the utility of the Nilus report is highly questionable. Cf. Wilhelm Schmidt, *The Origin and Growth of Religion*, London, 1931), pp. 108–9 and Joseph Henninger, 'Ist der sogenannte Nilus-Bericht brauchbare

religionsgeschichtliche Quelle?' *Anthropos*, L, Fasc. 1–3 (1955), 81–148, eg. pp. 84–97.

32. *Prolegomena*, p. 486.

33. One reason it is crucial to point this out is that Harrison never clearly explained that her work involved such reconstruction of prehistory. Yet it is only as hypothetical reconstructions of Greek prehistory that both *Prolegomena* and *Themis* are defensible. In each of these works she isolated what she considered to be the most primitive phenomena in Greek religion and identified them as chronologically prior to other data. She ranged throughout Greek materials from Homer to Proculus with no regard for dates because her interest was not to trace the history of Greek religion after Homer but to show how the composite religion presented to us in the Homeric epics was the result of a long evolution already completed. Greek history could not inform us about this early development; only anthropology and sociology could do that. The data of Greek history were useful, however, as examples of earlier and later stages which, as survivals, could corroborate the stratification already established by anthropology.

As usual, the contrast with Rohde is instructive. He had uncovered a pre-Homeric and pre-historic concern with souls among the Greeks, but he had done this primarily through the use of Greek evidence. More important, what he attempted was a significant but essentially modest project: to demonstrate the existence of soul-beliefs before Homer. He did not try to reconstruct the entire history of pre-historic Greek religion; instead he dealt primarily with periods which provide historical documents. Harrison's entire history dealt with the period before documents were available and was open to neither proof nor disproof.

34. Where necessary she abandoned or ignored theories not compatible with her latest method but not always as ruthlessly as methodological purity might have dictated. In later years she tried to combine more or less incompatible methods in uneasy mélanges whose inconsistency blunted their intelligibility.

Harrison's enthusiasm for anthropology, sociology, and psychology as auxiliary tools for the classicist elicited divergent responses from fellow classicists. Francis Cornford, her close friend and colleague at Cambridge, not surprisingly applauded her openness to other disciplines; see his biographical note, 'Harrison, Jane Ellen (1850–1928)', *Dictionary of National Biography*. Fourth Supplement: 1922–30 (London, 1937), pp. 408–9. Campbell Bonner in his review of her *Themis* expressed what was probably the majority view of traditional classicists, saying that many critics would wish of this work 'as they have wished before, that her profound learning were less at the mercy of the venturesome theories of other writers', *Classical Journal*, 23 (November, 1927), 155. This reaction has continued to be voiced with each reprinting of her works. Cf. the comment of W. J. Verdenius: 'Her principle weakness was the susceptibility which induced her to adopt the latest fashion in philosophy, psychology and ethnology', 'Review. *Epilegomena and Themis*', *Mnemosyne*, 4th Series, 16, Fasc. 4 (1963), 434.

Harrison herself was not disturbed by her eclecticism and heavy borrowing from other theorists. As she put it in describing the Greeks, 'the most original and most artistic of peoples, as of individuals, borrow most', *The Religion of Ancient Greece*, p. 24; cf. p. 62.

35. Harrison's early works in which she followed Max Müller and then E. B. Tylor, dealt with art and literature rather than with religion. Competent in their own time, these books have little value today except for historical interest. In the present context they are illuminating because they demonstrate how radically Harrison's analysis was ruled by her presuppositions. We can see interpretations in these early works which diverged in major ways from conclusions in *Prolegomena* and *Themis* which she would later assert to be self-evident. The works in question are the following: *Myths of the Odyssey in Art and Literature* (London, 1882); *Introductory Studies in Greek Art* (London, 1885); and *Mythology and Monuments of Ancient Athens* (London, 1890).

In *Myths of the Odyssey in Art and Literature* Harrison combined several interpretations to explain the myths: (a) naturistic interpretations (the Cyclops as forces of nature, p. 28; Scylla and Charybdis likewise, pp. 194–204; the story of Odysseus' descent to Hades and return as based on the travels of the sun, p. 297), (b) soul-theory interpretations (longing for the dead as giving early man the certainty of post-mortem communications, p. 27; the sirens as based on evil funereal conceptions, p. 182), and (c) historicistic interpretations (the Cyclops as partly formed out of traveller's tales of Sicilian and African cannibalism, p. 30). Of the three, the nature-myth hypothesis was given most weight.

Certain themes Harrison would develop later occurred already in *Myths of the Odyssey*. First, she talked about the process of 'euphemism' in Greek culture (pp. 141, 177), a shift from deformed and monstrous mythological forms to those more humane and beautiful. This strong notion of progress marked Harrison's later works. Secondly, in her distinguishing between the 'Muses who dwell below' (the Sirens) and the 'heavenly Muses' (p. 182), she foreshadowed the dichotomy between chthonic and Olympic gods which she developed very fully in *Prolegomena*. Third, Dionysos, the most discussed deity of this work, was not treated as an incursion or as a primitive religious form but as an agent of the process of euphemism rendering the somber more joyous (p. 162) and the ugly more beautiful (p. 182).

In *Introductory Studies in Greek Art* Harrison saw nature worship and fetishism as the earliest forms of religion with animalism as an early by-product (pp. 23, 82).

In *Mythology and Monuments of Ancient Athens* she finally discarded the nature myth interpretation because of the successful attacks on Müller by Andrew Lang in the name of anthropology (p. iii). In this work she was much closer than before to the positivist interpretation and saw a practical purpose for religion rather than a poetic or philosophical one (p. iii).

The 1890 work contains one important hypothesis which the evolutionary school would see as a fruitful method of explanation: Harrison's ritual theory of myth ('the cult as the explanation of the legend', p. iii). 'In many, even in the large majority of cases *ritual practice misunderstood* explains the elaboration of myth' (p. iii). It is perhaps risky, given the intellectual activity and interchange of the time, to credit Harrison with the origin of this theory, but she thought it was original with her and at least one contemporary critic agreed. (See G. C. Richards, 'Review of *Mythology and Monuments of Ancient Athens*', *Journal of Hellenic Studies*, 11, No. 1 [1890], 218.) In her article 'Mythological Studies', (*Journal of Hellenic Studies*, 12, No. 2 [1891], 350–51) Harrison wrote, '. . . with considerable deference I offer for criticism a solution I believe to be wholly novel.

'The conviction has slowly grown in my mind that, in seeking for the significance of a mythological figure, the only fruitful method is to examine the cultus. Rites and ceremonies are the facts, and are of amazing permanence; myths are the professed explanations of these facts, and shift and vary with the development of generations of worshippers.'

The most important feature of *Mythology and Monuments of Ancient Athens* was Harrison's blending of interpretations explaining rituals as magic (pp. xxiv, xxxvi, xlii) with interpretations explaining them as offerings to deities (pp. lxxi, lxxii, 427). The magical explanation was new, but in this work Harrison did not propose magic as the earliest stage. She treated both ritual for magic and ritual for gods as belonging to the primitive stage of Greek religion. Consequently, in her discussion of Dionysos (pp. 241–60), a competent, conventional treatment, there was no suggestion that Dionysos had developed from something else out of some pre-deistic phase. Gods belonged to the origin of religion just as had simpler forms. By *Prolegomena* Harrison had changed her mind, and for the rest of her career she portrayed gods as midway stages in the evolution of religion.

36. Sir James George Frazer, *The Golden Bough*, 2nd ed. (London, 1900), Vol. I, p. 61.

37. *Ibid.*, pp. 10–60.

38. Harrison's argument is so labyrinthine as to defy adequate exposition in anything shorter than a small monograph. I will try to summarize and evaluate her thesis, but in all honesty I must admit that the more I read Harrison's works, the less sense they make. As was sometimes the case with Frazer, she often made her point so obliquely that it was closer to innuendo than explicit argument. She also frequently contradicted herself, and this makes representing her thought extremely precarious. The greatest difficulty with her argumentation was her habit of taking anything which agreed with her hypothesis and which she had shown to be remotely possible as established beyond doubt and then using it as a fact to support later argument. She certainly was not alone in this. A great amount of evolutionary social science in her time consisted of fitting random facts into a predetermined schema in total default of any empirical evidence, and she was merely following suit. Since she almost never presented anything resembling hard evidence, the only way to make sense out of her works is to recognize that she believed that the evolutionist paradigm was true and could be duplicated with Greek materials. If a Greek phenomenon resembled a primitive phenomenon, it must have originated at the level of Greek culture which corresponded to the level at which the primitive phenomenon was produced. In this manner, as long as there was a reliable stratification of primitive evolution, one could locate where in the development of Hellenism a Greek phenomenon originated, even though the present state of the evidence jumbled data from throughout prehistory. Once one loses faith in the evolutionist reconstruction of the stages of primitive culture, as most modern anthropologists have, the almost total lack of cogent argument in Harrison's work becomes glaring.

39. *Prolegomena*, pp. 1–31. She began by pointing out the difference between

Olympic and chthonic beings and their worship. the former were comparatively rational, cheerful and confident; the latter were more superstitious, gloomy, and fearful. Yet several festivals for Olympian gods had 'dark' and fearful elements. Rather than assume that the Greeks had not made a firm black and white dichotomy between chthonic and Olympian cults, she assumed that the dark cults must have originally been chthonic and only later taken over by the Olympians. Although she claimed that 'the conclusion is almost forced upon us' (p. 11), she never justified it with any evidence. It seems to have been based on the 'obvious' similarity between the superstitious chthonic religion and the superstitious religion of primitive man. Since, she felt, one can assume that what is primitive comes first, the chthonic stratum must have preceded the Olympian. The problem with this argument was that her assumption that the earliest primitive stratum had been gloomy and superstitious was questionable. Without this assumption, there was no reason to think that the gloomiest Greek cult was necessarily the first.

Harrison treated the chronological priority of the underworld cult and its absolute distinctness from the cult of more cheerful, this-worldly deities as self-evident in *Prolegomena*. That this judgment resulted from her choice of presuppositions rather than from its intrinsic obviousness can be seen from the fact that she had argued the opposite case in earlier works. For example, in *Prolegomena* (p. 34), she stated that the Bacchic festival of the Anthesteria could not be explained 'as evidence of the fact that Dionysos had a "chthonic side" and was "Lord of Souls"' but must have been the result of Dionysos' adding his cult to an earlier, more primitive ghost ritual. Yet twenty-one years earlier, in *Myths of the Odyssey in Art and Literature* (p. 160) she had interpreted the connection between Dionysos and the dead as evidence of conceptual richness rather than of cultic mixing due to evolutionary development: 'The Greek mind, in its early freshness at least, was little troubled by the dualism of this world and the next . . . . No doubt this close connection of Bacchus and Aphrodite with the dreadful gods of Hades had a deep mystic significance, of which much is lost to us, only the lighter aspect remaining'.

40. Harrison's insistence that the earliest magical stage had been concerned primarily with the expulsion of evil was not really paralleled in Frazer's *Golden Bough* and seems to have been derived from Herbert Spencer. Spencer had asserted that primitive man thought of ghosts 'chiefly as the causes of evils' rather than as beneficent agents (*Principles of Sociology*, Vol. I, Part I [New York, 1896], 281; cf., p. 437). Harrison conflated Spencer's ghost theory, somewhat fuzzily, with Frazer's magic theory and presented the initial stage of religion sometimes as the driving away of physical evils by magic and sometimes as the placation of angry ghosts. Generally she argued for magical aversion; cf. *Prolegomena*, p. 9: 'The gods of Aversion by the time of Pausanias, and probably long before, were regarded as gods who presided over the aversion of evil; there is little doubt that to begin with these gods were the very evil men sought to avert'.

The most crucial portion of her thesis, that a purely magical stage preceded the belief in gods reduces essentially to a presupposition embellished with dubious and unverifiable etymological speculations and anthropological parallels, masquerading as an argument. Even had she established that the chthonic cult was chronologically prior to the Olympian cult, the chthonic worship was directed to a well-populated hierarchy of gods and spirits. She offered no substantive evidence that impersonal magic preceded veneration of these gods and spirits. For example, her analysis of the pharmakos rite during the Thargelia, in which a man was sacrificed to restore Athens to a state of normalcy, relied entirely on parallels of dubious relevance to prove that the ceremony had been purely magical before it was dedicated to a god or ghost (*Prolegomena*, pp. 95–108). The classical texts themselves speak of the sacrifice being made to Apollo, as had Harrison herself in *Mythology and Monuments of Ancient Athens* (p. lxxii). Similarly, some of the harvest festivals Harrison analysed in *Prolegomena* (pp. 79–82) as magical ceremonies of first fruits had been analysed in *Mythology and Monuments of Ancient Athens* (pp. cxxxv–cxxxvii) in terms of gods and the Theseus legend. The existence of hypothetical magical forerunners of the religious cults was not, to use one of Harrison's typical phrases, 'abundantly clear'; it was speculation without evidence.

41. Harrison's own reading of the nature of the earliest, underworld cult tended to be elastic—now it was evil, now ambiguous, now sending blessings. For example, at the beginning of *Prolegomena* (p. 9) when she was trying to establish that the allegedly earliest mythical stratum (chthonic deities and heroes) was concerned with apotropaic magic she stated that 'it remains, broadly speaking, true that dead men and the powers of the underworld were the objects of fear rather than love, their cult was of "aversion" rather than "tendance".' From such a negative cult one may well wonder how the relatively cheerful Olympian religion originated. Harrison derived the Olympian cult primarily from the underworld cult but only after reversing herself about the nature of chthonic religion: 'The cult of heroes had in it more of human "tendance" than of demonic "aversion"', *ibid.*, p. 340.

42. *Ibid.*, p. 161.

43. *Ibid.*, p. 162; cf. pp. 240, 257, 321. Harrison was inconsistent as to when personification took place in the development of primitive thought. She explained its existence as the result of original intellectual limitations ('primitive man seems unable to conceive of any force except as resulting from some person or being or sprite, something a little like himself', p. 169) and seems to have classified it as part of the original primitive legacy. However, in her analyses of specific mythical figures she claimed that they had been natural, material forces before they became personified (e.g., the Keres as Telchines, [originally 'bad influences',] p. 172; the Harpies [originally 'winds'], p. 178; the Gorgon [originally a ritual mask], p. 187). The view that personification was a later development accorded more easily with the theory that the first stage was one of impersonal magic. However, once again Harrison presented no substantive evidence to show that the mythical figures she analyzed had been impersonal forces before they took on the personal traits by which the Greeks recognized them.

44. *Ibid.*, p. 124.

45. *Ibid.*, p. 256.

46. *Ibid.*, p. 363.

47. Cf., *ibid.*, p. 164.

48. *Ibid.*, pp. 402–3. She seems to have based her assertion of an original matriarchal stage on E. B. Tylor's 'The Matriarchal Family System',

Nineteenth Century (July, 1896); cf. *Prolegomena*, p. 261, n. 3.

49. *Ibid.*, pp. 411–12; cf., pp. 560–61.
50. *Ibid.*, pp. 379–400, 498–500.
51. *Ibid.*, pp. 363–64.
52. *Ibid.*, p. 444. Interestingly, Harrison respectfully derived the conception of Dionysos as the breaker of barriers from Nietzsche's *The Birth of Tragedy*: cf. *Prolegomena*, p. 445, n. 4.
53. *Ibid.*, p. 364.
54. *Ibid.*, p. 654.
55. *Ibid.*, p. 657.
56. Given Harrison's treatment of the evolution of gods from chthonic sprites and bogeys, Dionysos himself did not fit easily with the pictured evolution. Though Harrison tried to link him with other chthonic beings, the connection was purely mechanical and unconvincing. She portrayed the chthonic cult as the first mythical stage, fundamentally demonic in character; as soon as a chthonic being had become somewhat gracious it was on the way to becoming an Olympian. Dionysos violated this progression; he was both extremely close to the earth and to his worshippers (hence of chthonic nature) and very genial and beneficent (hence of Olympian nature). Harrison's portrayal of his beneficent character is impossible to reconcile with her presentation of the earliest stages of religion as apotropaic magic. Later, in *Themis*, when she saw religion originating in man's socialization instead of magic, she linked him to religion's earliest stages in a more logical manner.
57. It was Gilbert Murray's lectures on Euripides' *Bacchae* which led Harrison to write more about Dionysos in *Prolegomena*. As a result the focus shifted from the origin of religion out of magic (the evolution from *Ker* to god) to Dionysos and Orphic religion. 'It's rather dreadful, the whole center of gravity of the book has shifted. It began as a treatise on Keres with a supplementary notice of Dionysos. It is ending as a screed on Dionysos with an introductory talk about Keres', Stewart, *ibid.*, p. 25.
58. Again it is interesting to note how different presuppositions and different foci of interest shape results in such radically divergent ways. In Rohde's analysis Dionysiac and Orphic religion had been the main causes of a rejection of life; for Harrison, they symbolized 'life itself in its supreme mysteries of ecstasy and love'. (*Ibid.*, p. 657). Largely this difference resulted from different estimations of the uses of the Dionysiac ecstasy. Rohde saw it as driving man away from ordinary life into fantasy; Harrison saw it as unveiling an aspect of life otherwise hidden.
59. The *liknon* was a container used as a winnowing fan, a basket for first fruits, and a cradle. Both in *Prolegomena* (pp. 518–34) and, more explicitly, in her 1903 article 'Mystica Vannus Iacchi', Harrison identified the Liknophoria, a Bacchic rite involving the carrying of the liknon, as a magical purification and promotion of fertility. See, 'Mystica Vannus Iacchi', pp. 314, 317.
60. Harrison used her ritual theory of myth in *Prolegomena* but not systematically. In *Themis* it served as a basic explanation for the invention of gods.
61. Between 1903 and 1912 Harrison produced three substantial works: *The Religion of Ancient Greece* (1905), 'The Influence of Darwinism on the Study of Religions', (1909), and 'The Kouretes and Zeus Kouros' (1909). The first of these works presented nothing remarkably different from *Prolegomena*

except that it attempted to connect Olympian religion with Northern invaders and the chthonic stratum with indigenous southerners Harrison calls Pelasgians. (W. K. C. Guthrie would argue this theory in a more sober and consistent fashion in his *Orpheus and Greek Religion* and *The Greeks and their Gods* several decades later).

The 1909 article on Darwinism showed the influence of Durkheim. In it Harrison derived the conceptual part of religion from individual intellectual processes and the ritual from social processes based on will and emotions.

The article 'The Kouretes and Zeus Kouros' (subtitled 'A Study in Prehistoric Sociology') reflects the total victory of the Durkheimian perspective:

> This is not the place to discuss the question how far religious conceptions are the outcome of collective representation and as such are socially induced. But I should like here to record my conviction that so far as Greek religion goes the theories of MM. Durkheim and Hubert and Mauss are supported by the fact that Orphic ritual and religion clearly takes its rise socially in tribal initiation rites. In the light of these new sociological investigations the phenomena of early Greek religion as well as early Greek philosophy will have to be entirely reconsidered.

(*Ibid.*, p. 326, n. 3)

62. It should be noted that the new approach was restricted in England primarily to sympathetic members of the 'Cambridge school'. At the same time that Harrison was applying the sociological approach to Greek religion, her close friend and colleague Francis Cornford was applying it to Greek philosophy in his *From Religion to Philosophy*.

In particular, Harrison's ritual theory of myth had a signficant impact on contemporary scholarship, even beyond the boundaries of classicism. Due to this theory *Themis* has enjoyed considerable repute in literary critical circles. Stanley Edgar Hyman, a consistent supporter of the myth and ritual school, went so far as to say of *Themis*, 'there are times when I think it is the most revolutionary book of the 20th century', (quoted in Joseph Fontenrose, *The Ritual Theory of Myth* [Berkeley, 1966], p. 26. Fontenrose himself is considerably less ecstatic about the myth and ritual approach, and his work offers a more balanced picture of its contemporary status than does Hymen's 'The Ritual View of Myth and the Mythic', in Thomas A. Sebeok, ed., *Myth, A Symposium* [Bloomington, Indiana, 1958], pp. 89–94.) The myth and ritual approach was also applied to Ancient Near Eastern and Old Testament studies, most notably in three works edited by S. H. Hooke, *Myth and Ritual* (London, 1933); *The Labyrinth* (New York, 1935); and *Myth, Ritual and Kingship* (Oxford, 1958) and in Theodore H. Gaster's *Thespis* (New York, 1950).

Professional classicists have generally been skeptical of *Themis*. Since it was thoroughly grounded in a speculative sociological theory which they were reluctant to accept, it has had little noticeable impact on their published work. On another side it is interesting to note that *Themis* was reviewed with considerable reserve in *L'Année Sociologique*, the house organ of the Durkheimian school. M. David, the reviewer, criticized Harrison for ascribing to the Greeks a sociological theory of their own religion and for drawing overhasty comparisons. See *L'Année Sociologique*, 12 (1909–12), 254–60, esp. 259f.

63. Emile Durkheim, 'Sociologie religieuse et théorie de la connaissance', *Revue de Métaphysique et de Morale* (November, 1909), p. 751. Durkheim used this article as the Introduction to his *The Elementary Forms of the Religious Life.* This passage can be found on p. 29 of the English translation, which I follow here.

64. Durkheim, 'Sociologie religieuse', pp. 734–35 (*Elementary Forms,* pp. 14–15).

65. *Themis,* p. 47.

66. Harrison did not explicitly distinguish between 'chronological' and 'logical' order, but some such distinction clearly functioned in her work, based on the assumption that phenomena representing the earliest stages may have been removed from the historical record for centuries, surfacing only later as 'survivals'. If this were the case, simply reconstructing Greek history chronologically from the available evidence would mislead scholars about the 'real' development of Hellenism which had occurred before written sources and which could be deciphered only by means of something more trustworthy than the scant classical data available today, i.e., the universal evolutionary series discovered by anthropology.

67. *Themis,* 'Preface to the Second Edition', p. vii.

68. In *Prolegomena* 'the haze of the primitive "one"' (p. 164) was invoked to explain why the primitive produced mythology rather than clear analytical thought. In this state of intellectual non-differentiation, he did not distinguish himself from the rest of nature, because he had not evolved to a high intellectual plane.

69. This haze stood at the beginning not only of religion but of philosophy as well: 'the whole history of epistemology is the history of the evolution of clear, individual, rational thought, out of the haze of collective and sometimes contradictory representations', (p. xiii). In both religion and philosophy it was due to the 'herd' character of early society.

70. *Themis,* pp. 42–43. This passage owes as much to Marett as to Durkheim. Cf. Marett's idea that 'primitive religion is not so much thought out, as danced out'.

71. *Themis,* pp. 63–64. For Harrison as for other scholars sensitive to the ambiguous quality of religion, the awe experienced before sacred things included wonder as well as fear, attraction as well as repulsion (p. 64). It is interesting to see Harrison reflecting Marett's characterization ('a certain religious sense . . . whereof the component "moments" are fear, admiration, wonder and the like', *The Threshold of Religion,* [1899], p. 10), and using it in an almost antithetical way to the way Rudolf Otto would use it in *Das Heilige* in 1917.

72. *Themis,* p. 64.

73. *Themis,* p. 475.

74. *Themis,* p. 66.

75. *Themis,* p. 122, cf., p. 131.

76. *Ibid.,* pp. 126–27. It should be noted that, although she still asserted that magic had been prior to religion, (conceived of as worship of supernatural beings) as she had while influenced by Frazer, she disagreed with his intellectualist explanation and explained it instead as a result of an over-

zealous will; *ibid.*, p. 84.

77. By the time of *Themis* it was impossible to say what the basis of her presentation of evolutionary theory was. She relied heavily on Durkheim but also changed his argument when it suited her purpose. The influence of many evolutionary theorists is apparent. She combined several contradictory evolutionary models into her own analysis and then presented this analysis as the consensus of scholarly opinion. From *Themis*, even more than from *Prolegomena*, one gets the impression of reading indisputable fact whereas what Harrison presented was an extremely personal synthesis of the arguments of an evolutionary camp rather seriously at odds with itself.

78. *Themis*, pp. 46–47.

79. *Themis*, p. 48.

80. Harrison's method of argumentation or her lack of one is typified by her justification for interpreting a section of Euripides' *The Bacchae* as proof of an initiation ceremony underlying the myth: 'Once the suggestion made, it is surely evident that we have in the song the reflection, the presentation, of rites of initiation seen or heard by Euripides among the Bacchants of Macedonia', *Themis*, p. 33. All one can say is that the truth of the assertion is *not* evident and is even less so if one does not use Murray's translation. Harrison herself is forced to use a different translation on pp. 34–35 in order to make sense out of the passage.

81. *Themis*, p. 34. She mentioned some interesting uses of fire in Greece, which may have had initiatory significance, but she gave no other reason to interpret this passage in that manner.

82. *Themis*, pp. 35–38. A wild potpourri of facts implied to be parallels, reminiscent of Frazer at his most confusing, was the only 'proof' for this assertion.

83. Her explanation for the broken pattern was the weakest form of the argument from silence: 'Literature, even hieratic literature, tends to expurgate savage material', *Themis*, p. 15. Her argument was that the cult of the Olympians was no longer associated with the dramatic stories of separation, dismemberment, and revivification or with groups of guardian figures because religion had evolved away from the primitive interest in initiation. The argument is, of course, circular, since it is the existence of such original initiatory patterns that needs to be proved.

84. *Themis*, p. 38.

85. *Themis*, pp. 38–41. Here Harrison suggested that the Maenads had been conceived of as mothers. This was by no means the case. Specifically in Euripides' *Bacchae*, *all* of the women of Thebes rage on Cithaeron in honor of Dionysos, not just mothers. Some myths speak of the *nurses* of Dionysos, but Harrison's identification of the two as equivalent was forced: 'only a decadent civilization separates the figures of mother and nurse', *Themis*, p. 39.

86. *Themis*, p. 38.

87. *Themis*, p. 133.

88. *Themis*, p. 139.

89. *Ibid.*, p. 148.

90. *Themis*, p. 16. She hedged a bit even in this formulation in saying 'they *probably* arose together'. Italics mine. For other general statements stressing

the interdependence of myth and ritual, see pp. 328 and 486.

91. Harrison had held this view from the time of *Mythology and Monuments of Ancient Athens* (see above, p. 213), but only in *Themis* did the postulation of ritual as the origin of myth serve as a fundamental part of her analysis. She seems to have received encouragement for this view from Durkheim's 'De la Definition des phénomènes religieux', esp. pp. 14–16.

92. Specific examples of this analysis can be found on the following pages in *Themis*: 28, 42–46, 83, 136, 148, 156–57, 260 and 413. In each case she explained some mythical figure as the projection of participants in a ritual.

93. Harrison made up the term from the Greek *eniautos*, 'year' and more specifically 'a *period* in the etymological sense, a cycle of waxing and waning' and *daimōn*, (*Themis*, p. xvii). She admitted that the phrase does not occur in Greek. Cf. Fontenrose, *ibid.*, p. 34.

It should be noted that Dionysos also serves as the prototype for the 'mystery god' and the 'Agathos Daimōn', these terms being roughly synonomous for Harrison.

94. *Alpha and Omega*, p. 195.

95. *Ibid.*, p. 204.

96. *Ibid.*, pp. 200–2.

97. *Ibid.*, p. 205.

98. Harrison clearly conceived of this force as a naturalistic version of Bergson's *élan vital*, though she never used Bergson's formulation.

99. *Themis*, p. xii.

100. *Alpha and Omega*, p. 50.

101. *Ibid.*, p. 65.

102. *Ibid.*, p. 79.

103. Harrison's clearest statement of this occurred in *Alpha and Omega* rather than in either of the two major works: 'In the development of religion, it is now an accepted law that things begin with the imagination of beings of whom you cannot in any fair sense of the word predicate divinity. Perhaps the greatest advance made in the study of Greek religion of late has been to show that the Greek *gods*, Zeus, Apollo, and the rest, are a temporary phase, an outcome of particular social activities and social structure, which inevitably causes anthropomorphism, or as I prefer to call it, anthropophuism—the making of gods with human natures—and the anthropopathic action of the worshipper', *Alpha and Omega*, p. 198.

104. After *Themis* Harrison wrote two substantial works: *Ancient Art and Ritual* (1913) and *Epilegomena to the Study of Greek Religion* (1921). In both she tried with only partial success to meld different, sometimes discordant methods. *Ancient Art and Ritual* mixed the Durkheimian model with a revived Frazerian approach stressing magic. As in *Themis*, she explained Dionysos as resulting from ritual. *Epilegomena* was even more internally discordant. In this work she conflated the methods of Frazer, Durkheim, and Freud, jumping from one to another as she saw fit. Using her new knowledge of Freud, Harrison explained gods as images of desire rather than of social emotions. In *Epilegomena* she had moved away from seeing religion as self-transcendence to seeing it as useful only in preventing suppression of conflict through fantasy. In effect, *Epilegomena* represented something of a return to genealogy.

105. Joseph William Hewitt, 'Review: *Themis*', *Classical Weekly* 7 (January 10, 1914), 88.
106. Cf. W. H. D. Rouse's statement, 'The importance of the "lower religion", if the phrase may be allowed, is for the first time brought out in something like its true force...' 'Miss Harrison's *Greek Religion*', *Classical Review*, 18 (December, 1904), 469.

NOTES TO CHAPTER FOUR

1. Nilsson's output of published work on Greek religion was staggering. The bibliography of his works (including references to reviews of his works by other scholars) runs to 109 pages, most of it on Greek religion. See Erik J. Knudtson, 'Beiträge zu einer Bibliographie Martin P. Nilsson 1897–1939', *Kungl. Humanistiska Vetenskapssamfundet i Lund. Scripta Minora 1967–1968* (Lund, 1968), pp. 29–116; Christian Callmer, 'The Published Writings of Professor Martin P. Nilsson 1939–1967', *ibid.*, pp. 117–39. The following list, obviously not exhaustive, represents the most important works relative to his interpretation of Dionysos:
    Studia de Dionysiis atticis (Lund, 1900).
    Griechische Feste von religiöser Bedeutung mit Ausschluss der attischen (Leipzig, 1906).
    Primitive Religion (Tübingen, 1911).
    Primitive Time Reckoning (Lund, 1920).
    A History of Greek Religion, trans. by F. J. Fielden (Oxford, 1925).
    The Minoan-Mycenaean Religion and its Survival in Greek Religion (Lund, 1927); second revised edition (Lund, 1950). Except where otherwise noted, references will be to the second edition.
    'Early Orphism and Kindred Religious Movements', *Harvard Theological Review*, XXVIII (July, 1935), 181–230.
    Greek Popular Religion (New York, 1940); also entitled *Greek Folk Religion* (New York, 1961).
    Geschichte der griechischen Religion, Vol. I: *Die Religion Griechenlands bis auf die griechische Weltherrschaft* (Munich, 1941); third edition (Munich, 1967), hereinafter cited as *Geschichte*, I. Except where otherwise noted, references will be to the third edition.
    Greek Piety, trans. by H. J. Rose (Oxford, 1948).
    'Letter to Prof. A. D. Nock on Some Fundamental Concepts in the Science of Religion', *Harvard Theological Review*, XLII (April, 1949), 71–107.
    Geschichte der griechischen Religion, Vol. II: *Die hellenistische und römische Zeit* (Munich, 1950).
    'Second Letter to Professor Nock on Positive Gains in the Science of Greek Religion', *Harvard Theological Review*, XLIV (October, 1951), 143–51.
    'Religion as Man's Protest against the Meaninglessness of Events', *Kungl. Humanistiska Vetenskapssamfundet i Lund. Årsberättelse 1954*, pp. 25–92.
    The Dionysiac Mysteries of the Hellenistic and Roman Age (Lund, 1957).
    Opuscula Selecta (3 vols.; Lund, 1951–1960).

2. Nilsson respected Rohde's analysis in *Psyche* as the first adequate treatment of the ecstatic cult (cf. *Griechische Feste*, p. 258), but he felt that Rohde had not sufficiently treated the Lydian-Phrygian stream of Dionysiac religion (cf. *Geschichte* I, 578). In fact, Rohde had used Phrygian materials to some extent (cf. *Psyche*, II, 9) but had not distinguished between Phrygian and Thracian cults, as Nilsson was to do.

3. Nilsson never accused Harrison of irresponsible scholarship, but he criticized as inadmissible several of the ideas with which she associated herself. For example, he felt that the 'discovery' of totemism in Greek religion was merely the result of overzealous *a priori* expectation (*Geschichte*, I, 215–216; cf. *ibid.*, p. 37; *A History of Greek Religion*, p. 78). Harrison's own explanation of the Hymn of the Kouretes from savage group thought was due to her telescoping the millenia (*The Minoan-Mycenaean Religion*, p. 549), and her entire theory deriving Greek religious practices from age grade initiations represented 'an inadmissible "foreshortening" of the historical perspective', (*A History of Greek Religion*, p. 78). In *Greek Folk Religion*, p. 3, Nilsson stated that Harrison's tendency 'to represent Greek religion as essentially primitive' was misleading. To be sure, these are not devastating critiques. Nilsson was not concerned to chastise any particular scholar, but in more general statements he did warn against the kind of *a priori* reconstructions to which Harrison was so prone.

4. His first enunciation of two distinct tasks in the study of religion occurred in his early *Primitive Religion*, p. 3. Within the category of *Religionswissenschaft* he distinguished between the historical and psychological aspects. The psychological constants discovered by investigations of primitive people explained facts left unexplained by lack of historical evidence. By 1941, when Nilsson wrote the *Geschichte*, (cf. *ibid.*, p. 37) the use of 'psychological stages' to recapture evolutionary sequences was somewhat suspect, so he identified the extra-historical aspect as entailing a 'logical' succession. However, his actual use of this analysis remained basically the same as it had been in *Primitive Religion*.

5. *A History of Greek Religion*, pp. 3, 9; *Greek Folk Religion*, p. 3; 'Second Letter to Professor Nock on Positive Gains in the Science of Greek Religion', pp. 143–44.

6. In this manner he dismissed Malinowski's structural-functionalist approach (*Geschichte*, I, 13, n. 1) and Preuss' and Malinowski's treatment of myth as an 'archetype' or 'charter' for religious belief and practice ((*Ibid.*, p. 55). The same indifference held for Dumézil's interpretation of the structure of Indo-European ideology (*Ibid.*, p. 5, n. 4). He made the statement, repeated even in the third edition, that after the discovery of the primacy of the cult over the myth for understanding religion no new methods had emerged except the problematic one of Walter F. Otto (*Ibid.*, p. 10). This claim is surprising, since not only had the work of Pettazzoni, Eliade, Dumézil, Kerenyi and others assumed importance, but Nilsson even cited Eliade's *Traité d'histoire des religions* as the best overview of the modern science of religion (*Ibid.*, p. 36, n. 1). Many of these scholars resembled Otto in that they took myth and cult to be serious expressions of religious ideology, but Nilsson never dealt with their specific ideas.

7. *Geschichte*, I, 746.

8. In his review of Walter F. Otto's *Dionysos*. *Mythos und Kultus* (*Gnomon* 11 [April, 1935], 178) Nilsson asserted that *Kausalitätsbedürfnis*, the need for a causal explanation, was the correct ground of science. Nilsson's rather specific understanding of causal understanding underlay his critique of Otto's unwillingness to attribute utilitarian motives to religious actors: 'Den zweiten Grundfehler, an dem die Religionsforschung krankt, sieht der Verf. darin, dass sie dem Nützlichkeitsprinzip folgt; es wäre gerechter zu sagen, dass sie irgendeinen Zweck für die religiösen Handlungen und einen Grund für den Glauben sucht'. Nilsson misrepresented Otto's objection. Otto did, in fact, look for the purpose of religious actions and the reason for beliefs; he simply denied that these were utilitarian. As will be seen, Otto analyzed religion as man's expression of deeply held values and beliefs about the nature of being. In its own way this was a 'causal' explanation, but Nilsson seemed to assume that an explanation was causal only if it imputed *to the actor* the conscious attempt to engage in causal behavior, i.e., to manipulate his environment.

9. The *Durchschnittsmensch* of the *Geschichte* (pp. 844, 847). The *Durchschnittsmensch* was the individual equivalent of *das Volk* on the collective level. Nilsson used the concept of *das Volk* both to account for the persistence of the low mentality which sustained religion and to justify his comparing primitive phenomena with folk customs. (Cf. *Greek Folk Religion*, pp. 34, 102, 139; 'The Psychological Background of Late Greek Paganism', pp. 124–25; 'Ueber die Glaubwürdigkeit der Volksüberlieferung mit besonderem Bezug auf die alte Geschichte', *Scientia*, 48, No. 223 [1930], 319–28, esp. pp. 321–33; 'Der Ursprung der Tragödie', p. 673; *Geschichte*, I, 11; *Ibid*., pp. 614, 746). The mentalities of the *Durchschnittsmensch* and of *das Volk* were both essential elements in the causal explanation of religion.

10. *Greek Piety*, p. 21.

11. *Griechische Feste* (1906), p. 262–63; *Primitive Religion*, (1911), pp. 76–77. In *A History of Greek Religion* (1925), pp. 95, 206, Nilsson stated that the omophagy was later transformed into a means for mystical elevation but that originally the rite's purpose was to arouse the fertility of nature. As will be seen (cf. below, p. 115), he more or less abandoned this explanation in later works.

12. 'Die Anthesterien und die Aiora', *Eranos*, 15 (1915), 198–200; *Greek Folk Religion* (1940, 61), p. 33.

13. 'Die Anthesterien und die Aiora', pp. 198–200; *Geschichte*, I, 583.

14. *Geschichte*, I, 584, 585.

15. *Studia de Dionysiis atticis* (1900), pp. 90–109, esp. 95, 102, 109; *Griechische Feste* (1906), pp. 261–65, 'Die Prozessionstypen im griechischen Kult. Mit einem Anhang über die dionysischen Prozessionen in Athen', *Archäologisches Jahrbuch*, 31 (1916), 322; *A History of Greek Religion* (1925), p. 205; *Geschichte*, I, 119, *Greek Folk Religion*, pp. 35–36.

16. *Studia de Dionysiis atticis*, pp. 117–21; *Greek Folk Religion*, p. 34; *Geschichte*, I, 121, 583–84.

17. *Geschichte*, I, 232.

18. 'Die eleusinischen Gottheiten', *Archiv für Religionswissenschaft*, 32 (1935), 99–100. In this case Mannhardt's conception 'Kind und Korn' rather than Frazer's magic theory was Nilsson's interpretive model, but the interpretation of the rite as instrumental activity to compel fertility remained the same.

19. Dionysos as bull: *Griechische Feste*, p. 261; as snake: *The Minoan-Mycenaean Religion*, pp. 574–75.
20. *Geschichte*, I, 583–84.
21. 'Der Ursprung der Tragödie', *Neue Jahrbücher für das klassische Altertum, Geschichte und deutsche Literatur und für Pädagogik*, 27, No. 10 (1911), 674–75. Reprinted in *Opuscula Selecta*, I, 112–14.
22. *Geschichte*, I, 578.
23. Nilsson credited Harrison for inventing the useful category *eniautos daimon* (*Geschichte*, I, 11) and generally agreed with her estimation of the great importance of fertility magic in Greece. However, he thought that the orgia (the ritual acts associated with the ecstatic cult) were not related to vegetation and, though not mentioning Harrison by name, vigorously denied that they were connected with wine (*Geschichte*, I, 585, 586).
24. The distinction which Nilsson would draw forcefully in *The Minoan-Mycenaean Religion* was incipient in *A History of Greek Religion*, where Nilsson treated the different types of Dionysiac religion separately, the Divine Child motif on pp. 32–33 and the ecstatic cult on pp. 205–10. However, he included material related to the fertility cult in his discussion of the ecstatic cult, whereas in the fully elaborated dichotomy of 1927 he would locate fertility associations exclusively with the Divine child motif.
25. *Geschichte*, I, 568–59. Nilsson continued and broadened Rohde's evidence that the original home of Dionysos was Thrace, adding for example the fact that theophoric personal names involving Dionysos occurred much more frequently in Thrace and Macedonia than in Greece and that those involving his mother Semele occurred only there. Nilsson believed that the most probable source of the influence was possible Thracian settlements in Greece, in Phokis and Boeotia, made in the beginning of the first millenium. Even if the transmission had not taken place in this manner, the Ionic Greeks would have encountered Dionysos among the Phrygians after their settlement in Asia Minor around 1200 B.C.; *Geschichte*, I, 565–68.

   One problem which surfaced well into Nilsson's career was the discovery of the name Dionysos on the Linear B tablets (cf. *Geschichte*, I, 343, n. 3) which Nilsson dated as Later Minoan II. This dating would make Greek knowledge of Dionysos earlier than the hypothetical Thracian settlements in Greece and even than the Thracian migration to Phrygia. In addition, given Nilsson's schema (cf. *Geschichte*, I, 582), it is doubtful that contact between Ionic Greeks and Phrygians would have led to an ecstatic Bacchic cult in Greece since the Dionysiac cult familiar to the Ionians was oriented primarily toward vegetation and was mild, not orgiastic, in tone. Nilsson never satisfactorily resolved this problem.
26. See pp. 109f.
27. *Geschichte*, I, 570–71. As Nilsson grew older, his certainty about this interpretation waned. In *Greek Piety*, p. 22, he wrote that even if the taking of the god and his power into the worshippers 'was the original significance of the rite, it is far from certain that Dionysos' worshippers in Greece were conscious of it'. In a later article, 'Nähe zu und Distanz von der Gottheit', published only in the third volume of his *Opuscula*, Nilsson stated this in even stronger terms, saying that such a belief, if once entertained, had disappeared and left no trace; *ibid*., p. 16.

28. *Geschichte*, I, 571–72.
29. *Geschichte*, I, 572–76.
30. The four interpretations were as follows: (1) the eating of Dionysos incarnated in the animal was done perhaps to gain the power of this vegetation deity and help promote fertility (so Frazer). (2) The orgia could represent a means to a sacramental union with the god (so Robertson Smith). (3) The actions of the maenads could be compared to Central European agricultural rites with their ideas of spirits of the dead, ragamuffins, and torch processions to help the fertility of the crops (so Mannhardt) (4) the ecstatic religion is its own end and corresponds to a deep religious need in many people (so Rohde, though Nilsson did not name him.) *Geschichte*, I, 576–78.
31. *Greek Piety*, pp. 21–22.
32. Nilsson had used the 'mana' theory before; however, in his early interpretations he had explained the Greeks' interest in this supernatural power as part of an attempt to increase fertility. Once he discarded this utilitarian interpretation, he analyzed the purpose of this power in vaguer terms. Nevertheless, from 1906 to the end of his career he persistently used the mana theory as an explanation. Cf. *Griechische Feste*, p. 262; *Primitive Religion*, p. 6; *A History of Greek Religion*, pp. 93–95; *The Minoan-Mycenaean Religion* (1st ed.), pp. 492–93; (2nd ed.), pp. 564–65; *Geschichte*, I, 45; *Greek Piety*, pp. 21–22.
33. *Greek Piety*, p. 22. In this regard, Nilsson agreed with Harrison (and Rohde to a lesser extent) that the cult was more fundamental than any particular religious ideas. This treatment of religious concepts as secondary was common to most evolutionists.
34. *A History of Greek Religion*, p. 209.
35. *Geschichte*, I, 577.
36. So Jane Harrison in *Prolegomena* and Raffaele Pettazzoni in *La religione nella Grecia antica fino ad Alessandro* (Turin, 1925); French tr., *La Religion dans la Grèce antique* (Paris, 1953).
37. *The Minoan-Mycenaean Religion* (2nd ed.), p. 32.
38. *Ibid.*, p. 555.
39. *Ibid.*, pp. 572–73.
40. *Ibid.*, p. 572.
41. *Ibid.*, p. 579. Nilsson stated that the same lack of Dionysiac cult occurred also in, of all places, Phrygia itself and accounted for this in much the same way: Sabazios already filled the niche Dionysos would have occupied. Nilsson argued around the additional startling fact that the Phrygians themselves rejected the identification between Dionysos and Sabazios; *ibid.*, pp. 579–80.
42. *A History of Greek Religion*, p. 31. Both the Divine Child and the Eniautos Daimon represented the dying and rising pattern proposed by Frazer to explain the origin and function of religion as basically vegetative magic. The primary difference between the two was that their sequences were staggered. Harrison began with the child alive, and therefore included his *re*birth as the last act of the cycle. Since Nilsson began with the yearly *birth* of the god he could present the last act of the drama as the god's death. In both versions the complete cycle—birth, death, rebirth—is implicit.
43. *Geschichte*, I, 579. It should be noted that none of these sources was earlier than the second century A.D., which is rather late considering Nilsson was trying to demonstrate something about Phrygian religion in prehistoric

times.
44. *Geschichte*, I, 566–67, 579–80. Cf. *Greek Folk Religion*, p. 93.
45. *The Minoan-Mycenaean Religion* (1st ed.) p. 493; (2nd ed.). pp. 564–65; *Geschichte* (1st ed.), I, 547–58.
46. *The Minoan-Mycenaean Religion* (2nd ed.), pp. 564–67.
47. *Geschichte*, I, 580–81.
48. *Geschichte*, I, 581. Cf. 'The Bacchic Mysteries of the Roman Age', *Harvard Theological Review*, 46 (October, 1953), 181.
49. *Geschichte*, I, 581–82. As he said of another of the prototypes for the Divine Child mythologem, 'The old gods, who were born and died, met with a variety of treatment in the Greek age, to which this idea was not familiar; they were thus adapted to suit later conceptions in various manners', *The Minoan-Mycenaean Religion* (1st ed.), p. 492; (2nd ed.), p. 564.
50. *The Minoan-Mycenaean Religion*, p. 567. Italics mine. Cf. *A History of Greek Religion*, p. 33.
51. 'Dionysos Liknites', *Bull. Soc. des Lettres de Lund* (1951–52), pp. 1–18; cf. *The Dionysiac Mysteries of the Hellenistic and Roman Age*, pp. 40–41.
52. Trieteric rites occurred every other year, not every third year. As the Greeks reckoned time, such a term included the festival year at the beginning of the reckoning and again at the end. Therefore, only one year would intervene between the two festival years.
53. Cf. *Geschichte*, I, 580.
54. Nilsson again argued for this connection deductively: 'The child Dionysos as a spirit of vegetation must be born annually and so must die annually', *The Minoan-Mycenaean Religion* (1st ed.), p. 495; (2nd ed), p. 566.
55. *The Minoan-Mycenaean Religion* (2nd ed.), pp. 568–69.
56. *Ibid.*; *Geschichte*, I, 579: Μητρὶ ʽΙπτα καὶ Διεὶ Σα[βαζίῳ]ʼ, 'To Mother Hipta and Zeus Sa[bazios]'. Since Sabazios was here identified with Zeus, as he usually was by the Phrygians, it was gratuitous to assert that this inscription tells us anything about Dionysos. Nilsson adduced other references to show that Sabazios himself was regarded as a child in the care of Hipta (*Geschichte*, I, 579–80), but again the identity of Sabazios with Dionysos was not sufficiently established to be the sole early proof for the existence of the Dionysos child in Asia Minor.

The problem of the identity of Sabazios is genuinely vexatious. Rohde had identified Sabazios with Dionysos in deriving the latter from Thrace and Phrygia (cf. *Psyche*, II, 7–8), but his testimonies were mixed, some identifying Sabazios with Dionysos, some with Zeus, and one with Helios. Nilsson stated flatly (*Geschichte*, I, 566–67, 580) that the identity between the two gods is obvious and commonly admitted. Yet in other contexts he states that the Phrygians rejected the identification with Dionysos and instead identified their god with Zeus (*The Minoan-Mycenaean Religion*, pp. 579–80) while the Greeks for their part perceived Sabazios as a foreign god and not as the equivalent of Dionysos. As Nilsson stated in another context, 'of course Sabazios is akin to Dionysos but his cult was foreign and despised', *The Dionysiac Mysteries*, p. 23; cf. *Geschichte*, I, 836. Nilsson had creditable evidence for his position, but equally compelling evidence existed against it as well. The problem is that many ancient writers thought that there was an 'obvious' identity between Sabazios and a Greek god, but they never agreed which Greek god.

57. *Geschichte*, I, 579; *The Minoan-Mycenaean Religion*, p. 570. Again a vexing problem. The quote from Plutarch ('Isis and Osiris', 378F) is as follows: 'The Phrygians, believing that the god is asleep in the winter and awake in the summer, sing lullabies for him in the winter and in the summer chants to arouse him, after the manner of bacchic worshippers [βακχεύοντεσ]. The Paphlagonians assert that in winter he is bound fast and imprisoned but that in the spring he bestirs himself and sets himself free again', *Plutarch's Moralia*, trans. Frank Cole Babbitt (Cambridge, Mass., 1962), Vol. V, 160–61.

The presence of the participle βακχεύοντεσ has been taken by many to prove that 'the god' refers to Dionysos. It need not. The verb βακχεύω has a more general meaning of 'to speak or act like one frenzy-stricken, to be frantic or fanatic', as well as the specific 'to keep the feast of Bacchus', and in this case it probably means the former. Given that Plutarch was discussing conceptions related to seasonal changes from many locations, to the west of Greece as well as in Anatolia, and that he explicitly mentioned other gods in this connection such as Cronus, Aphrodite and Persephone, the fact that he did not name Dionysos means that his reference to 'the god' can hardly be used by itself to reconstruct a pattern for Dionysiac religion in Phrygia.

58. This can be a legitimate way in which to discover past patterns which have become disarticulated. The irony is that Nilsson was so scathing in his criticism of the 'patternists' of the myth and ritual and of the High God schools who were following essentially the same strategy he had employed for the Divine Child: 'The ritual pattern is found whole nowhere, it is pieced together from parts, found at various places, because they enter into a logically coherent connection. The pattern is in fact always found "disintegrated". The ritual pattern is consequently a logical construction whose existence is not proved in the world of realities', 'Letter to Prof. A. D. Nock on Some Fundamental Concepts in the Science of Religion', p. 105.

59. *Geschichte*, I, 570, 585; 'Eine neue schwarzfigurige Anthesterienvase', *Kungl. Humanistiska Vetenskapsamfundet i Lund. Årsberättelse*, 1933, 46–47 (reprinted in *Opuscula* II, 460–61). In his earlier *Griechische Feste*, p. 260, he, like Harrison, had seen wine as one of the more important means used to attain the ecstasy.

60. *Geschichte*, I, 572.

61. In *The Minoan-Mycenaean Religion* (pp. 574–75) Nilsson had interpreted Dionysos as 'the spirit of the fruit of the fields', based on the god's association with the liknon. Cf. *Greek Folk Religion*, p. 35. In the *Geschichte* (p. 585), he had come to believe that as we can know Dionysos he had nothing to do with agrarian fertility.

62. *The Dionysiac Mysteries*, p. 42, n. 20.

63. *Primitive Religion*, pp. 94–95.

64. *Geschichte*, I, 612; *A History of Greek Religion*, p. 206.

65. *Geschichte*, I, 18, 20, 371; *A History of Greek Religion*, pp. 49, 52, 173.

66. *A History of Greek Religion*, p. 73.

67. *Primitive Religion*, p. 95; *Geschichte*, I, 160, 373; *Greek Piety*, p. 25; *A History of Greek Religion*, pp. 73–75, 178.

68. Cf. *A History of Greek Religion*, p. 180.

69. *The Minoan-Mycenaean Religion*, pp. 575–76, 577, 583.
70. *A History of Greek Religion*, p. 206; *Greek Piety*, p. 21.
71. *Griechische Feste*, pp. 259, 296–97; *Geschichte*, I, 496, 499.
72. Given the fact that Nilsson stated that Artemis was the most popular goddess of Greece (*A History of Greek Religion*, p. 287) and that such orgiastic elements belonged to her cult, one might well wonder why Dionysiac religion represented such a radical departure from 'ordinary' Greek religion. Nilsson could reply that her ecstatic cult was foreign to the male Homeric nobility who knew Artemis primarily as a sender of quick death (cf. *Geschichte*, I, 482–83) and as a goddess of the hunt (*ibid.*, 498–99).
73. *Geschichte*, I, 324, 610–11, 845.
74. 'The Race Problem of the Roman Empire', *Hereditas*, 2 (December, 1921), 384; also in *Opuscula*, II, 958–59. In this thoroughly racist essay Nilsson accounted for the deterioration of the Roman empire largely in terms of the 'bastardizing' (sic) of the races through intermarriage ('Race Problem', p. 385; *Opuscula*, II, 960). It should be noted that in 1939 when the issue was more crucial, Nilsson wrote another article 'Über Genetik und Geschichte', *Hereditas*, 25 (June, 1939), 211–23 (reprinted in *Opuscula*, II, 964–79) in which, because of the misuse of the word race, he substituted the word 'variant'. Though he still asserted that different 'variants' were of different values, he tried to show that civilized races resulted from race mixtures.
75. *Greek Piety*, p. 21; cf. *Greek Folk Religion*, p. 96; *A History of Greek Religion*, p. 206.
76. *A History of Greek Religion*, p. 180.
77. *Ibid.*, p. 181; cf. *Geschichte*, I, 610.
78. *Greek Piety*, p. 20.
79. *Greek Folk Religion*, p. 95; *Geschichte*, I, 578, 845.
80. *Greek Piety*, p. 22.
81. *Geschichte*, I, 614; cf. 570.
82. *A History of Greek Religion*, p. 206.
83. *Ibid.*, p. 205; *Greek Piety*, p. 22. Nilsson liked the terminology of epidemic and infection so much that he used it to account for numerous phenomena: prophets and seers such as Aristeas, Abaris, etc. (*A History of Greek Religion*, p. 205); unbelief and blasphemy in the classical period (*Ibid.*, p. 288); a superstitious backlash against unbelief and blasphemy (*ibid.*); a disposition for occultism and theosophy (*Greek Piety*, p. 138); and for superstition in general (*Ibid.*, p. 192; 'The Psychological Background of Late Greek Paganism', *Review of Religion*, 11 [January, 1947], 124).
84. *A History of Greek Religion*, p. 207.
85. *Greek Piety*, p. 22; cf. *Geschichte*, I, 611.
86. *Geschichte*, I, 614; *A History of Greek Religion*, p. 208; *Greek Piety*, pp. 22, 41.
87. *Geschichte*, I, 586.
88. *Ibid.*, 588-89.
89. *A History of Greek Religion*, p. 295; *Geschichte*, II, 348.
90. *Geschichte*, I, 590.
91. *Geschichte*, II, 345.
92. *Greek Folk Religion*, p. 36.
93. *Ibid.*, 'Der Ursprung der Tragödie', pp. 674–76.

94. *Ibid.*
95. *Ibid.*, pp. 687–88.
96. *Griechische Feste*, p. 259; *A History of Greek Religion*, p. 210; *Geschichte*, I, 594–601.
97. *A History of Greek Religion*, pp. 209–10.
98. *Greek Piety*, p. 22; *The Dionysiac Mysteries*, p. 118.
99. *The Minoan-Mycenaean Religion*, p. 576.
100. *Griechische Feste*, pp. 267, 272.
101. *Geschichte*, I, 596.
102. *Griechische Feste*, p. 273; *Geschichte*, I, 597.
103. *Geschichte*, I, 598.
104. *Ibid.*
105. *Greek Folk Religion*, p. 48.
106. *The Dionysiac Mysteries*, pp. 131; 118–23. Nilsson noted the interesting point that in the later years of the Dionysiac cult there was no trace of Dionysos' role as a vegetation god, since interest had shifted so decidedly to the issue of post-mortem existence; *ibid.*, p. 44.
107. *Geschichte*, I, 685–86.
108. 'Early Orphism', pp. 203, 221–22.
109. *A History of Greek Religion*, p. 217; *The Minoan-Mycenaean Religion*, p. 582.
110. *Geschichte*, I, 37.
111. Nilsson's early theoretical work *Primitive Religion* (p. 3) opposed 'psychological' to historical explanation. In the *Geschichte*, (I, 37) he spoke of a 'logical' as opposed to a historical succession. The intent of both oppositions is basically the same: to distinguish from the flux of historical circumstance a deeper level where relatively permanent habits and thought processes lead to non-rational behavior.
112. *Primitive Religion*, p. 5. 'Das Gebiet der Religionswissenschaft sind die nicht vernunftmässig zu erklärenden Reste in der Vorstellungswelt der Menschen und die daraus hervorgehenden Handlungen'.
113. *Ibid.*
114. One could compile an extensive litany of quotes like the following from Nilsson's entire oeuvre: 'The cult and the gods are created from the practical needs of men', *Primitive Religion*, p. 50. Cf. *ibid.*, pp. 67, 120; *A History of Greek Religion*, pp. 112, 118–19, 206; *Greek Folk Religion*, pp. 17–21; *Geschichte*, I, 389, 391.
115. *Geschichte*, I, 118.
116. 'When distress knocks on the door and man cannot help, the belief in the gods wakes up', 'Kult und Glaube in der altgriechischen Religion', *Opuscula Selecta*, III, 8. Cf. *Primitive Religion*, p. 6; *Greek Piety*, p. 115.
117. Even in relatively enlightened times man turned to religion to explain events for which he could not account naturalistically. 'The concept of cause does not suffice even in our own day, and still less could it satisfy antiquity', *A History of Greek Religion*, p. 282. In the same vein, curiosity about the existence of the world led early men to the aetiological maneuver of inventing a creator god, though this was rather late in the process, cf. *Primitive Religion*, p. 120; *Geschichte*, I, 33–34.
118. *A History of Greek Religion*, p. 260; *Geschichte*, I, 828.

119. *A History of Greek Religion*, p. 181; *Geschichte*, I, 845.
120. Most especially in his *Primitive Religion*; 'Existe-t-il une conception primitive de l'âme'? *Revue d'Histoire et de Philosophie religieuse*, 10 (March–April, 1930); the introduction and first section of the *Geschichte*; and 'Letter to Prof. A. D. Nock on Some Fundamental Concepts in the Science of Religion'.
121. *Primitive Religion*, p. 6.
122. In *Primitive Religion* (pp. 6f.) and *A History of Greek Religion* (p. 166) Nilsson said the idea of power had been the first seed-ground of religion, apparently intending this as a historical statement. By the time of the *Geschichte* (cf. I, 48) he claimed that it was psychologically rather than historically older. Still as he developed his analysis he consistently described other 'stages' as later and traced them back to an origin in mana, cf. *Geschichte*, I, 59, 68, 199, 845.
123. *Geschichte*, I, 69: cf. *A History of Greek Religion*, p. 97.
124. 'Existe-t-il une conception primitive de l'âme'? p. 114; *Geschichte*, I, 37–38. Among other things, Lévy-Bruhl had attempted to show that primitive logic had other concerns than our own and therefore was not just an ineffective travesty of scientific thought. In his redefinitions of Lévy-Bruhl's terminology, Nilsson blunted the differences Lévy-Bruhl had drawn between pre-logical and logical mentality and, in effect, presented the former as an inept version of the latter. This was necessary if he was to portray religion as pseudo-instrumental behavior.
125. *Primitive Time Reckoning*, p. 90.
126. *Primitive Religion*, p. 22.
127. *Ibid.*, p. 80.
128. *Ibid.*, p. 87.
129. *Ibid.*, pp. 31, 11–12; cf. *Geschichte*, I, 57.
130. *Geschichte*, I, 40–41; cf. 'Letter', pp. 84–89.
131. *Geschichte*, I, 52–53.
132. *Ibid.*, pp. 95–96.
133. *Ibid.*, pp. 43–44, 50, 216; *Primitive Religion*, pp. 12, 22; 'Letter', p. 100.
134. Though Nilsson sometimes hedged on the chronological priority of magic over gods, the overwhelming weight of his work affirmed this priority, either directly (*A History of Greek Religion*, p. 89, *Geschichte*, I, 51, *Primitive Religion*, p. 4, 'Religion as Man's Protest against the Meaninglessness of Events', pp. 60–61) or indirectly ([a] predeistic rites, by definition prior to belief in gods, lose their magical character only as gods enter: *A History of Greek Religion*, pp. 98, 99; *Greek Folk Religion*, pp. 28, 29, 35; 'Die Prozessionstypen im griechischen Kult', p. 318; *Geschichte*, I, 52, 139–40, 459; [b] the lower on the cultural ladder, the more a people practice magic: *Primitive Religion*, pp. 39, 84; 'Der Ursprung der Tragödie', p. 673; *Geschichte*, I, 52; [c] magicians are earlier than priests: *Geschichte*, I, 54; *Primitive Religion*, p. 10).
135. Thus, Nilsson believed, man's first commerce with vegetation spirits was not reverential worship but manipulation of the images of these spirits to make their power magically available for his use, *A History of Greek Religion*, p. 107.
136. *Primitive Religion*, p. 58; cf. *ibid.*, 112; *Geschichte*, I, 32; *A History of Greek Religion*, p. 166.

137. *Primitive Religion*, p. 38; *A History of Greek Religion*, p. 112; *Greek Folk Religion*, p. 16; *The Minoan-Mycenaean Religion*, p. 548; *Geschichte*, I, 297, 388, 499.

138. So, Hermes (*A History of Greek Religion*, p. 109); the house goddess (*Geschichte* I, 348), Ploutos and Zeus (*ibid.*, p. 323), Paieon (*ibid.*, p. 540). In 'Letter to Prof. A. D. Nock' (p. 100) Nilsson explained a number of Greek gods as personifications of drives or natural forces—Aphrodite, Ares, Zeus, Artemis, Demeter. This personification itself was one of the fundamental errors of primitive mentality, resulting from a mistaken analogy between the human and the non-human.

139. *Geschichte*, I, 579.

140. In *A History of Greek Religion* (p. 118), Nilsson asserted 'the proposition that man's needs create the gods and that beginning with the gods of Nature he rises to those which are an expression of the highest functions of his life. This implies that divine personalities cannot be taken as unities, as is generally done, but must be split up into their different component parts'. Cf. *Geschichte*, I, 386.

141. *A History of Greek Religion*, p. 293; *Greek Folk Religion*, p. 90, 101, 121; *Geschichte*, I, 388; *Greek Piety*, pp. 68, 71–72.

142. *Greek Piety*, p. 20.

143. *A History of Greek Religion*, p. 205; *Geschichte*, I, 571–78; *Greek Piety*, p. 142.

144. *Griechische Feste*, p. 263; *Greek Folk Religion*, p. 95; *Geschichte*, I, 577–78; *Greek Piety*, p. 22.

145. The article itself appeared in the *Kungl. Humanistiska Vetenskapssamfundet i Lund. Årsberättelse* (*Bull. Soc. des Lettres de Lund*), pp. 25–92, in 1954. Nilsson had first enunciated the main idea in 1947 in *Greek Piety* (pp. 114–15): 'Religion is man's protest against the meaninglessness of events, which is contained in mechanical causality'. He mentioned it again in 1950 in the second volume of the *Geschichte*, (pp. 700–1) and in 1952 in 'Universal Religion' (*Review of Religion*, 17, No. 1 [1952], 5–10). Though the article is remarkably erudite, drawing from all areas of the science of religion, and extremely thought-provoking, Nilsson never integrated it into his analysis of Greek religion.

146. 'Religion as Man's Protest', p. 25.

147. *Ibid.*, p. 61.

148. His argument was almost entirely restricted to refuting the 'High-God' school. He never really dealt with other alternatives to evolutionism such as the structural-functional approach or phenomenology.

149. 'Letter', p. 72.

150. What seems to have happened is that, consciously or unconsciously, to make this argument, Nilsson drew on the ambiguity of the German word *Entwicklung*, which could mean either 'evolution' or 'development'. In the German this ambiguity is easy to use: 'Sie [die Hochgott Schule] führt einen erbitterten Kampf gegen den *Evolutionismus*. Aber es ist vergeblich, eine *Entwicklung* der Religion zu leugnen', (*Geschichte*, I, 61. Italics mine). In an English treatment of the same issue there is no ambiguity, and Nilsson's argument is considerably more transparent: 'The battle against evolutionism is in part a tilting against windmills. *There is always a development, always an*

evolution. That it is lacking among primitive peoples is an illusion due to the fact that we know but a brief space of their existence'. 'Letter', *ibid.* Italics mine. Cf. also 'Second Letter to Professor Nock on Positive Gains in the Science of Greek Religion', *Harvard Theological Review*, 44 (October, 1951), 146.

151. 'Letter to Prof. A. D. Nock', p. 72.
152. *Ibid.*
153. *Ibid.*, p. 73. Nilsson issued the same caveat against confusing the logical succession for an historical one in the *Geschichte*, I, 37.
154. 'Letter', p. 73.
155. Nilsson worded his reliance on primitive parallels provided by evolutionary anthropology quite cautiously: 'A comparison of the religion of the Greeks with those of primitive people and with primitive customs and beliefs enlarges our understanding of Greek religion, in general, but only in general, for it is a mistake to think that such a comparison can help to reconstruct phenomena in Greek religion in detail, as at times has been attempted', 'Second Letter to Professor Nock', pp. 143–44. In *A History of Greek Religion*, pp. 78–79 Nilsson justified identifying many beliefs and practices as primitive legacies because of their universality, which he attributed to the common psychic capacity of man in the lower state of development (*Geschichte*, I, 36, 844; *Primitive Religion*, p. 4; 'Der Ursprung der Tragödie', p. 613).
156. *Geschichte*, I, 58.

NOTES TO CHAPTER FIVE

1. While Otto's publications were not as numerous as Nilsson's, his productivity was still impressive. The most complete published bibliography of his writings is in his *Das Wort der Antike*, pp. 383–86. Because many of his shorter articles are most readily available in collected works published towards the end of Otto's life, they are cited as they appear in these collections. The following works are the most important for understanding Otto's position:

'Religio und Superstitio', *Archiv für Religionswissenschaft*, (1909), 533–54; XIV (1911), 406–27.

Die Manen oder von den Urformen des Totenglaubens (Bonn, 1923), hereinafter cited as *Die Manen.*

Der Geist der Antike und die christliche Welt (Bonn, 1923).

Die altgriechische Gottesidee (Berlin, 1926).

Die Götter Griechenlands. Das Bild des Göttlichen im Spiegel des griechischen Geistes (Bonn, 1929). English translation by Moses Hadas: *The Homeric Gods. The Spiritual Significance of Greek Religion* (Boston, 1964).

Der europäische Geist und die Weisheit des Ostens. Gedanken über das Erbe Homers (Frankfurt am Main, 1931).

Dionysos, Mythos und Cultus (Frankfurt am Main, 1933), hereinafter cited as *Dionysos.* English translation by Robert B. Palmer: *Dionysus. Myth and Cult* (Bloomington, Indiana, 1965), hereinafter cited as Eng. tr.

'Der Durchbruch zum antiken Mythos im 19. Jahrhundert', *Vom Schicksal des deutschen Geistes*, ed. by Wolfgang Frommel (Berlin, 1934), pp. 35–46, hereinafter cited as 'Durchbruch'.

Der junge Nietzsche (Frankfurt am Main, 1936).
Der Dichter und die alten Götter (Frankfurt am Main, 1942).
Das Vorbild der Griechen (Tübingen und Stuttgart, 1949).
Gesetz, Urbild und Mythos (Stuttgart, 1951).
Die Gestalt und das Sein. Gesammelte Abhandlungen über den Mythos und seine Bedeutung für die Menschheit (Düsseldorf-Köln, 1955).
Die Musen und der göttliche Ursprung des Singens und Sagens (Düsseldorf-Köln, 1955).
Theophania. Der Geist der altgriechischen Religion (Hamburg, 1956).
Die Wirklichkeit der Götter. Von der Unzerstörbarkeit griechischer Weltsicht (N.p.: Rowohlt, 1963).
Das Wort der Antike (Stuttgart, 1962).
Mythos und Welt (Stuttgart, 1962).

2. *Die Götter Griechenlands*, pp. 3f. (*The Homeric Gods*, pp. 3f.); *Theophania*, p. 8.
3. *Die Götter Griechenlands*, pp. 86f. (*The Homeric Gods*, p. 68); *Die Manen*, pp. 50, 52.
4. *Die Manen*, p. 50; *Die Götter Griechenlands*, pp. 86f. (*The Homeric Gods*, p. 68).
5. 'Der Mythos und das Wort', in *Das Wort der Antike*, pp. 360f.
6. *Ibid.*; cf. *Gesetz, Urbild und Mythos*, p. 63.
7. *Die altgriechische Gottesidee*, p. 4. Though unnamed, Otto's antagonist at this point seems to have been Rudolf Otto.
8. *Die Götter Griechenlands*, pp. 179f. (*The Homeric Gods*, p. 140).
9. *Die altgriechische Gottesidee*, p. 5. Cf. *Theophania*, p. 9, where Otto asserted that Divinity has appeared to each culture and given form to each culture's being.

It should be noted that while Otto did not postulate a single, generally valid religious experience common to all mankind and affirmed the multiplicity of the types of divine manifestations, he consistently used the words 'Divinity' (*die Gottheit*), or 'the Divine' (*das Göttliche*) to describe the object of religion as though this category had absolute cross cultural validity. Otto was never explicit on this point but the Divine seems to be characterized by its being eternal and/or superhuman. In Otto's view, because there was Divinity which was manifested to all cultures, interpretation was a *possibility*; because Divinity was perceived in different forms, interpretation was a *task*.

10. *Der junge Nietzsche*, p. 7; *Das Vorbild der Griechen*, pp. 28f.
11. *Das Vorbild der Griechen*, p. 29.
12. In *Der Geist der Antike und die christliche Welt*, pp. 58f., Otto proposed why, since we could not go back to the past, we should study the Greeks: 'We look to the present but from the point of view of the eternally human. What took form in heathen antiquity are timeless ideas and ideals of that humanity for which we fight with all our strength...'.
13. Of course for the evolutionists history had also been existentially relevant but not in a way that satisfied Otto. By demonstrating the error of the base of religion, one showed that religion was untenable in the contemporary period. One showed the past to be no longer usable; but in doing this, the evolutionists obviously felt they were contributing to man's self understanding. Furthermore, it would have been fair for the evolutionists to use Otto's

demands against him, since he wanted the Greek *religious* past to communicate itself to the present but made no effort to mediate the truths discovered by *irreligious* Greek thinkers to his contemporary readers.

14. 'Der griechische Mensch und die Nachwelt', *Die Gestalt und das Sein*, p. 162.
15. *Ibid.*
16. *Ibid.*, p. 170; *Der europäische Geist und die Weisheit des Ostens*, p. 8; *Das Vorbild der Griechen*, p. 29; 'Das Weltgefühl des klassischen Heidentums', *Mythos und Welt*, p. 36; *Die Götter der Griechen*, pp. 13f. (*The Homeric Gods*, p. 11).
17. *Der junge Nietzsche*, p. 9.
18. *Dionysos*, p. 14 (Eng. tr., p. 11); 'Hölderlin', *Mythos und Welt*, p. 119.
19. *Theophania*, p. 12.
20. 'Der griechische Göttermythos bei Goethe und Hölderlin', *Die Gestalt und das Sein*, p. 183. Otto drew on a relatively limited coterie of thinkers, mostly German-speaking, to provide insights into the 'real' meaning of Greek culture and religion. In the first rank were Hölderlin, Goethe, Nietzsche, and Frobenius. Of lesser importance were Schelling, Hegel, and Schiller. Certain historian of religions such as C. G. Heyne, J. J. Görres, C. O. Müller, J. J. Bachofen and philosophers such as Cassirer and Lévy-Bruhl provided ancillary insights. He never justified his choice of these figures or of the specific judgments which he selected out of their writings, perhaps because intuition played such a heavy role in his work.
21. *Dionysos*, pp. 45f. (Eng. tr., p. 46.) Cf. *Theophania*, p. 12.
22. For this reason the entire first section of *Dionysos. Mythos und Cultus* is devoted to methodology.
23. *Dionysos*, pp. 23f. (Eng. tr., p. 21).
24. *Dionysos*, p. 27 (Eng. tr., p. 25).
25. *Dionysos*, pp. 44f. (Eng. tr., p. 45). Many classicists who had been disturbed by the uses made of primitive parallels had dismissed the primitives as irrelevant for interpreting Greek religion. In general, Otto did not share their skepticism and used ethnological materials rather frequently. Cf. *Die Manen*, p. 46; 'Ein griechischer Kultmythos von Ursprung der Pflugkultur', *Das Wort der Antike*, pp. 140–61; 'Der ursprüngliche Mythos im Lichte der Sympathie von Mensch und Welt', *Mythos und Welt*, p. 240. What Otto felt made primitive parallels admissible was the recognition by many scholars at the beginning of this century that 'primitive' peoples had a form of thought which was not bungling but as valid as our own; 'Durchbruch', pp. 43f. Thus he hoped to use the primitives as a weapon against the evolutionists.
26. 'Tragödie', *Das Wort der Antike*, pp. 221.
27. 'Der Mythos und das Wort', *Das Wort der Antike*, p. 354.
28. *Die Manen*, p. 50. Cf. 'Der Mythos und das Wort', *Das Wort der Antike*, pp. 354f.; 'Der Ursprung von Mythos und Kultus, Zu Hölderlins Empedokles', *Die Gestalt und das Sein*, p. 256.
29. *Dionysos*, p. 39 (Eng. tr., p. 39), quoting Nilsson's *Griechische Feste*, p. 112.
30. *Ibid.*
31. *Ibid.*, pp. 40f. (Eng. tr., pp. 40f). Otto used Frobenius' notion of semantic depletion as an indication that utilitarian concerns were not original. Arguing that creative expressions become increasingly utilitarian as times passes, he asserted that more expressive and less instrumental phenomena must be more

original. One then recovers the creative beginning state primarily by excising the utilitarian aspects as later accretions. This argument is, of course, circular and rests as much on debatable presuppositions as had the evolutionist reconstruction.

32. 'Die Menschengestalt und der Tanz', *Die Gestalt und das Sein*, pp. 402f.
33. *Die Götter Griechenlands*, pp. 11f. (*The Homeric Gods*, pp. 9f.)
34. Otto's understanding of biological evolution seems to have been weak. He believed that biologists always implied the existence of self-established organisms when they discussed evolution, and he argued that only that which was alive was capable of developing (*Dionysos*, p. 12; Eng. tr., pp. 8f.) Here the same problem with the German word *Entwicklung* is operative as had occurred with Nilsson. Otto applied the word in its sense of 'development' but not in its more radical sense of 'evolution'. A thoroughgoing evolutionary explanation of biological life need not, in fact, presuppose life at the beginning.
35. 'Apollon', *Das Wort der Antike*, p. 60. In his review of Otto's *Dionysos*, Nilsson called attention to the similarity of Otto's view about revelation and the theology of Karl Barth; *Gnomon* 11 (April, 1935), 179.
36. A Greek word meaning 'lesson' or 'that which is taught'.
37. 'Leo Frobenius', *Mythos und Welt*, p. 213. The language employed here has affinities to A. L. Kroeber's category of 'the superorganic', but whereas Kroeber used this concept to deny the importance of individuals relative to the total cultural process, Frobenius and Otto applied the category to demonstrate the determinative importance of the creative geniuses who established the content of each specific *paideuma*.
38. 'Apollon', *Das Wort der Antike*, p. 85. While Otto's language reifies abstractions from reality, it can be reformulated so as to be no less legitimate than Durkheimian sociology. Behind the homiletical tone was the simple and justifiable claim that cultural facts are externalized in the world; take on a certain reality because they are publicly shared; and, because they are transmitted as part of society's accepted reality, shape the individuals in that society. Otto clearly believed that an objective *Geist* was manifesting itself through cultural configurations, but his analysis can be useful even to those restricting themselves to observable human behavior.
39. *Ibid.*, p. 86.
40. *Ibid.*, pp. 86f.
41. *Die altgriechische Gottesidee*, p. 5.
42. *Dionysos*, pp. 27f. (Eng. tr., pp. 25f.)
43. *Ibid.*, p. 31 (Eng. tr., p. 28).
44. *Ibid.*, pp. 29f. (Eng. tr., pp. 27f.)
45. *Theophania*, p. 9. Cf. 'Epikur', *Das Wort der Antike*, p. 322.
46. 'Der Mythos', *Mythos und Welt*, p. 270.
47. 'Der Ursprung von Mythos und Kultus. Zu Hölderlins Empedokles', *Die Gestalt und das Sein*, p. 280.
48. 'Tragödie', *Das Wort der Antike*, p. 201.
49. 'Apollon', *Das Wort der Antike*, p. 88; *Die Götter Griechenlands*, pp. 127, 153, and especially 206–11 (*The Homeric Gods*, pp. 100, 120, 160–164).
50. *Die altgriechische Gottesidee*, p. 19.
51. Cf. *Das Vorbild der Griechen*, p. 16: 'The being of things which discloses itself

in the Truth is totally other than that which is so well known to everyday examination and to the practical utilitarian traffic with things'.

52. From the evolutionist viewpoint, of course, such talk about different 'levels' would be a form of obscurantism or mystification.

53. 'Rom und Griechenland', *Das Wort der Antike*, p. 344. Italics mine. Otto's acceptance of Goethe's ontology also indicated his view that the earthly manifestation of Divinity did not exhaust its reality. According to this ontology, the 'primal phenomena' of being are revealed to man on earth; *behind these* stand the gods, 'Der Mensch als göttliche und religiöse Persönlichkeit in Antike und Neuzeit', *Mythos und Welt*, p. 41.

54. 'Rom und Griechenland', *Das Wort der Antike*, p. 336.

55. *Der Geist der Antike und die christliche Welt*, pp. 13, 43.

56. 'Religio und Superstitio', p. 544. This assertion is a not particularly instructive use of the ad hominem argument, but it does illustrate how strongly Otto felt about the existence of God. (Or perhaps how weakly he felt about justifying this belief; he never attempted another proof.)

57. 'Everything absolutely old is imperishable', (*Alles Älteste ist unvergänglich*), 'Durchbruch', p. 45. Cf. 'Der griechische Mensch und die Nachwelt', *Die Gestalt und das Sein*, p. 171; *Dionysos*, p. 129 (Eng. tr., p. 139); *Die Götter Griechenlands*, p. 183 (*The Homeric Gods*, p. 142); 'Die Frage der geistigen Überlieferung', *Die Wirklichkeit der Götter*, p. 47; *Die Manen*, pp. 82, 104.

58. 'Durchbruch', p. 45.

59. *Dionysos*, p. 40 (Eng. tr., p. 40). Otto's analogy in this passage comes from art, but in other passages he also explained this cathartic function using the more appropriate model of tragedy.

60. 'Durchbruch', p. 46; *Dionysos*, p. 31, (Eng. tr., p. 30).

61. Wilamowitz, the foremost German classicist of the first third of this century, in his massive *Der Glaube der Hellenen* (2 vols.; Berlin, 1931–32), rejected the interpretation of evolutionary anthropologists. He demanded that one wishing to understand Greek religion acknowledge that for the Greeks themselves the gods were a real part of the world. As he put it pungently: '*Die Götter sind da*', ('The gods are there'.) *Glaube*, I: 17, 41, cf. p. 9. Like Otto, Wilamowitz believed that the knowledge of God has been a fact of human life from the start and that only those who are able to experience the presence of a god are able to understand Divinity; *Glaube*, I, 9; cf. also a personal credo in his autobiography, *My Recollections: 1848–1914*, trans. G. C. Richards (London, 1930), p. 60. Yet though Wilamowitz assumed the knowledge of gods on the part of the Greeks and retained the language of supernaturalism as a meaningful way to interpret Greek religion, he dismissed mythology as non-religious. In his view myths were the inventions of the poets and merely obscured the genuine religious faith. Hence, when Otto wished to analyze myth as primary religious language, he had to dispute Wilamowitz along with the evolutionists. See *Dionysos*, pp. 11–13 (Eng. tr., pp. 7–9). From Otto's perspective the problem with Wilamowitz' attempt to remove the 'husk' of mythology to get at the 'kernel' of religion was that it discarded the most basic source of knowledge about the gods and left the interpreter (and any worshipper) with only vague surmises about the nature of Divinity. Ultimately this is a problem for any program of dymythologization.

62. *Dionysos*, pp. 18–19, 33–34 (Eng. tr., pp. 15, 16, 32); 'Der Mythos', *Mythos*

und Welt, pp. 271–72. In 'Der ursprüngliche Mythos im Lichte der Sympathie von Mensch und Welt', *Mythos und Welt*, p. 233, he went so far as to assert that even mystical experience presupposes a myth. This assertion, of course, puts the problem of the original religious experience which gave form to the myth in a very confused state, to say the least.

63. 'Der Mythos und das Wort', *Das Wort der Antike*, p. 359.
64. 'Allgemeine Würdigung des Phänomens der griechische Tragödie', *Das Wort der Antike*, pp. 238f.
65. 'Durchbruch', pp. 44f.
66. *Ibid.*, p. 44; cf. 'Der Mythos', *Mythos und Welt*, pp. 269f.
67. 'Der Mythos und das Wort', *Das Wort der Antike*, p. 349.
68. *Ibid.*, p. 358.
69. 'Allgemeine Würdigung des Phänomens der griechische Tragödie', *Das Wort der Antike*, pp. 238f.
70. 'Die Menschengestalt und der Tanz', *Die Gestalt und das Sein*, p. 408.
71. *Gesetz, Urbild und Mythos*, p. 81.
72. 'Der Mythos und das Wort', *Das Wort der Antike*, p. 363.
73. 'Der ursprüngliche Mythos im Lichte der Sympathie von Mensch und Welt', *Mythos und Welt*, p. 237.
74. *Ibid.*, p. 266.
75. *Dionysos*, pp. 19f. (Eng. tr., pp. 17f.).
76. *Dionysos*, p. 25 (Eng. tr., p. 23): myth is generally a better witness for meaning than cult since cult forms are not so well known or are often obscure and since myth is more distinct. However, as he stated in 'Der Durchbruch zum antiken Mythos im 19. Jahrhundert', p. 45, sometimes myth is mysterious and cult helps interpret it.
77. Cult presupposes a myth even if that myth is only latent (*Dionysos*, p. 19 [Eng. tr., p. 16]), while genuine myth demands cult ('Der Mythos und das Wort', *Das Wort der Antike*, p. 364).
78. Otto frequently employed the term *Ergriffenheit* ('seizure') coined by Frobenius to identify this moment when man was gripped by the universe in a particular mode of being and given the equivalent of a revelation. One of the few weaknesses of Palmer's English translation of *Dionysos* is its failure to acknowledge the semi-technical nature of the term. Thus, from p. 40 of the German text, the words *Ergriffenheit, ergriffen*, and *ergreift* are translated 'Emotion', 'affected', and 'affected' respectively (Eng. tr., p. 40). While not wrong, this translation loses much of the force of the original.
79. On at least three occasions ('Der Mythos und das Wort', *Das Wort der Antike*, pp. 365–68; *Theophania*, pp. 24–27; and 'Der Mythos', *Mythos und Welt*, pp. 273f.), Otto portrayed a spectrum of religious responses. On one level the presence of the Divine or *das Ungeheuer* (the 'Colossal', the 'Terrible') caused man to assume certain bodily postures and gestures (e.g., lifting his hands to heaven, bowing, kneeling) which themselves manifested something about man's bearing in the universe. On another level man acted out his religious experience by participating in ritual and by constructing physical objects (temples, statues, etc.) which testified to the nature of Divinity. On yet a third level, the primal religious experience gave birth to myth in the strict sense, the verbal presentation of the Divine. These three levels of behavior were all natural and autonomous responses and should not be ranked in any

order of priority.
80. 'Das Offenbarwerden des heiligen Seins der Gottheit', *Theophania*, p. 25.
81. He was really the first modern historian of religions to argue this. Scholars antagonistic to religion had argued that gods were later developments, that myths were themselves secondary, and that cults were originally not designed to serve deities. Scholars favoring religion had disputed the evolutionists but had not asserted that god, myth, and cult were all inseparable elements in religion's original state. Schmidt and Lang, for example, had argued that the High God had been the most primitive religious form but that myth represented a degeneration. Schmidt even allowed himself the peculiar position of denying the mythical character of the cosmogony. Rudolf Otto and Gerardus van der Leeuw both argued 'for' religion but without seeing its origin as containing gods. Walter Otto broke with these views and showed the interdependence of god, myth, and cult well before the mature work of both Raffaele Pettazzoni and Mircea Eliade. Yet 'pro-religious', 'anti-evolutionist' scholarship has not accorded him the same stature as these other scholars.
82. Though Otto rarely referred to Greek historical development in interpretations of Greek gods, he did, on occasion, discuss the role of specific cultural and social movements in the formation of the Greek *Geist*. In his view, the Greeks had been formed by the mixture of Indo-European and Mediterranean strata. Greek-speaking Indo-Europeans migrated to the Balkan peninsula in waves until the end of the second millenium B.C. and there confronted the indigenous Mediterranean peoples. Each side influenced the other so that what we recognize as Hellenism was born out of the melding of the victorious Indo-European culture with the subjugated indigenous culture. ('Die Herkunft des griechischen Menschen, die Geburt der griechischen Welt', *Das Wort der Antike*, pp. 15–17). The formation of Hellenism, however, was not merely the result of a racial fusion. It came from a fundamental religious creation which defined reality in a new way and therefore shaped Greek man as a unique type of humanity. The discovery of the 'new' Olympian gods in their specific Hellenic guise gave birth to the Greek *Weltanschauung* and provided a model on which to base the Greek spirit. (*Die altgriechische Gottesidee*, p. 13).

What distinguished this analysis from the evolutionists' presentation was Otto's insistence that the formation of the Hellenic *Geist* had represented a break with the past and a new creation. Thus Otto was uninterested in the 'origin' of the Olympian gods. He claimed that as found in Homer they were neither gods of the Mediterranean nor of the north. He argued that their names (e.g. Apollo, Artemis, Hera, Hermes, Athena, Dionysos) were pre-Greek and assumed that the Greeks must have met, admired, and accepted them on entering Greece. Indisputably, however, the Indo-Europeans brought the worship of Zeus; and, Otto argued, under the aegis of Zeus, they transformed the great gods of the pre-Greek culture into the authentic Hellenic divinities familiar to classicists. ('Die Herkunft des griechischen Menschen', pp. 14, 18, 19.) Only after this transformation did the Greek gods assume their specifically Hellenic nature. Therefore, proper interpretation involved investigating them as *formed* phenomena, not as they were *becoming formed*.
83. *Geschichte der griechischen Religion*, I, 564–65, n. 1.

84. *Die Götter Griechenlands*, p. 20 (*The Homeric Gods*, p. 16); *Dionysos*, pp. 31f. (Eng. tr., p. 30); *Die altgriechische Gottesidee*, pp. 15f.
85. Otto's discussion of pre-Homeric religion is confined primarily to the section on 'Religion and Myth of Antiquity' in *Die Götter Griechenlands*, esp. pp. 21–33 (*The Homeric Gods*, pp. 17–26), but see also 'Die Herkunft des griechischen Menschen', *Das Wort der Antike*, p. 38.
86. Otto's clearest presentation of the post-Homeric ethos occurs in his anti-Christian polemic, *Der Geist der Antike und die christliche Welt*, esp. pp. 47f. Disdaining salvation as a selfish religious motive, he classed such major phenomena as the mysteries as 'post-Homeric' and, by implication, not really authentically Hellenic. Cf. 'Tragödie', *Das Wort der Antike*, p. 220.
87. *Die Götter Griechenlands*, p. 211 (*The Homeric Gods*, p. 164).
88. *Ibid.*, p. 37 (p. 29).
89. *Ibid.*, p. 28 (p. 22).
90. *Ibid.*, pp. 21f. (p. 17). Here the limitations of Otto's selectivity are particularly striking. His general contrast suggested that the Homeric gods had no concern with nature or death; yet as even he portrayed the individual deities, each had *some* connection with death (Athena; pp. 56–58 [pp. 44f.]; Apollo and Artemis: pp. 95–96 [p. 75]; Aphrodite: p. 128 [p. 100]; Hermes, p. 144 [p. 113]) and each was connected to the natural sphere in some way. The difference appears to be a matter of the style of involvement in these realms rather than of the involvement itself.
91. *Ibid.*, p. 101 (p. 79).
92. *Ibid.*, p. 47 (p. 37).
93. *Der Geist der Antike und die christliche Welt*, p. 47.
94. *Die Götter Griechenlands*, p. 13 (*The Homeric Gods*, p. 11); cf. *Dionysos*, p. 193 (Eng. tr., p. 208).
95. *Der Geist der Antike und die christliche Welt*, p. 224.
96. 'Der Mensch als göttliche und religiöse Persönlichkeit in Antike und Neuzeit', *Mythos und Welt*, p. 49; cf. *Das Vorbild der Griechen*, p. 43.
97. 'Zeit und Antike', *Mythos und Welt*, p. 15.
98. *Die altgriechische Gottesidee*, p. 8.
99. *Theophania*, p. 58.
100. *Die Götter Griechenlands*, p. 218 (*The Homeric Gods*, p. 170).
101. *Ibid.*, p. 210 (p. 163).
102. *Ibid.*, p. 207 (p. 161).
103. *Der Geist der Antike und die christliche Welt*, pp. 22f.
104. *Ibid.* Cf. 'Zeit und Antike', *Mythos und Welt*, pp. 13f.
105. *Der Geist der Antike und die christliche Welt*, p. 132.
106. *Theophania*, p. 67; cf. *Der europäische Geist und die Weisheit des Ostens*, p. 9.
107. *Ibid.*, p. 23.
108. 'Tragödie', *Das Wort der Antike*, pp. 197–9.
109. 'Die Herkunft des griechischen Menschen', *Das Wort der Antike*, p. 22; cf. *Der Dichter und die alten Götter*, p. 33; 'Der griechische Göttermythos bei Goethe und Hölderlin', *Die Gestalt und das Sein*, p. 195.
110. *Der Geist der Antike und die christliche Welt*, p. 96; *Die Götter Griechenlands*, p. 99 (*The Homeric Gods*, p. 78).
111. 'Hölderlin', *Mythos und Welt*, p. 129; *Die Götter Griechenlands*, p. 198 (*The Homeric Gods*, p. 154).

112. *Die Götter Griechenlands*, p. 205 (*The Homeric Gods*, p. 159).
113. *Theophania*, p. 114.
114. 'Zeit und Antike', *Mythos und Welt*, p. 13; *Die Götter Griechenlands*, p. 309 (*The Homeric Gods*, p. 241).
115. 'Goethe und die Antike', *Mythos und Welt*, p. 73.
116. See 'Der ursprüngliche Mythos im Lichte der Sympathie von Mensch und Welt', *Mythos und Welt*, p. 238.
117. *Die Geburt der Tragödie*, pp. 36f., 42 (Kaufmann translation, pp. 45f., 49f.)
118. Even though Goethe and Nietzsche were hardly compatible in their religious views, Otto amalgamated aspects of their thought to construct his interpretation of Greek religion and his own closely related theological position. He defined his position negatively through Nietzsche's anti-Christian polemic (which itself had been influenced by Goethe) and positively through Goethe's proclaimed 'paganism'.
119. Guthrie's comment that Otto's *Dionysos* is both a contribution to religious history and itself a document of the Dionysiac cult (*The Greeks and their Gods*, p. 146) is fair, but it obscures the fact that Otto thought that the only adequate history was one which revealed the experienced reality of the religion and therefore which of necessity was a kind of modern-day cultic document. Of course, the real dispute is not over the desirability of knowing the subjective experience of the Greeks. Direct experience of the cult's lived reality would help interpretation immeasurably, but more cautious scholars, like Guthrie, can be legitimately skeptical about the *possibility* of evoking in twentieth century readers the experience of classical Greeks and of verifying the similarity of the two subjective experiences.
120. *Theophania*, p. 115.
121. *Dionysos*, pp. 89, 127 (Eng. tr., pp. 95, 136).
122. *Ibid.*, pp. 89–95 (pp. 95–106).
123. *Ibid.*, pp. 103–5 (pp. 110–13).
124. *Ibid.*, pp. 113 (p. 121).
125. *Ibid.*, p. 126 (pp. 135f.)
126. *Ibid.*, pp. 132, 175–76 (pp. 142, 189–90).
127. *Die Geburt der Tragödie*, p. 36 (Kaufmann translation, pp. 46f.).
128. *Ibid.*, p. 55 (p. 59).
129. *Ibid.*, pp. 110f. (pp. 104f.).
130. *Ibid.*, p. 72 (p. 73).
131. *Ibid.*, pp. 46, 157 (pp. 52, 141).
132. As with Nietzsche, it was in his treatment of tragedy that Otto discussed how existence can be justified. Cf. the following articles in *Das Wort der Antike*: 'Ursprung der Tragödie, Aischylos' (pp. 162–89), 'Tragödie' (pp. 190–222), 'Allgemeine Würdigung des Phänomens der griechischen Tragödie', (pp. 223–49), and 'Die antiken Grundlagen des abendländischen Theaters' (pp. 250–73). He argued convincingly that at least an important segment of the Greeks were able to accept existence with all its horrors because they believed that the gods existed in and behind the world and that everything was therefore due to divine action.
133. 'Der griechische Göttermythos bei Goethe und Hölderlin', *Die Gestalt und das Sein*, p. 187.
134. 'Tragödie', *Das Wort der Antike*, pp, 192, n. 2; 201–2.

135. *Dionysos*, pp. 52–56 (Eng. tr., pp. 54–58). Otto assumed that all of the passages referring to Dionysos came from the earliest strata of Homer. It should be noted that other scholars have disagreed with this assumption.
136. *Ibid.*, p. 56 (p. 58). This evidence has also been contested, since many argued that Dionysos was a later addition to the Anthesteria.
137. *Ibid.*, pp. 56–62 (pp. 58–64).
138. On the Pylos fragment XaO6 the name occurs in the genitive as di-wo-nu-so-jo. Cf. Michael Ventris and John Chadwick, *Documents in Mycenaean Greek* (Cambridge, 1956), p. 126; John Chadwick, *The Decipherment of Linear B* (Cambridge, 1967), p. 124. The name was subsequently discovered on another Pylos table (Xb1419) and restored on a Knossos table (X 1501). Cf. T. B. L. Webster, *From Mycenae to Homer*, 2d. ed. (New York, 1964), p. 319.
139. *Theophania*, p. 113.
140. Semele, daughter of Cadmos, King of Thebes, had been impregnated by Zeus and carried Dionysos in her womb. Tricked by Hera, Semele demanded that Zeus honor his pledge to grant any request and appear to her in his true form. Bound by his promise, Zeus reluctantly assumed his godly and overpowering form as a thunderbolt and destroyed the mortal Semele. Zeus then saved his son Dionysos by carrying him to term in his own thigh. Thus, Dionysos was born twice, once of a mortal mother and again of the greatest god.
141. *Dionysos*, pp. 62–70 (Eng. tr., pp. 65–73).
142. In fact, all three scholars more or less acknowledged that these myths were the only 'evidence' of the Greeks' resistance to the Dionysian cult. Cf. *Psyche*, II, 41–43 (Eng. tr., pp. 283f.); *Prolegomena*, p. 366; *Geschichte der griechischen Religion*, I, 612.
143. *Dionysos*, pp. 71–75 (Eng. tr., pp. 74–78). Though Otto portrayed Dionysos as suffering and dying, nowhere in this chapter did he present a myth of the god's death.
144. *Ibid.*, pp. 75–81 (pp. 79–85).
145. *Ibid.*, pp. 81–86 (pp. 86–91). Perhaps here better than anywhere else one can see the potential weakness of Otto's approach. If one assumes that every aspect of a religion is conceptually significant, one is tempted to levels of inflated overinterpretation which are avoided by more sober, sometimes less imaginative interpreters. Otto's analysis of the duality of the mask is clearly not related to Greek conceptions of the time and, depending on one's sympathy with his general endeavor, evokes discomfiture, embarrassment, or scornful hilarity. In this vein, scholars rejecting Otto's perspective would see most of his interpretations, not just that concerned with the mask, as gratuitous. The problem is that in the conflict of interpretations not everyone draws the line between sensitive interpretation and free association in the same place.
146. *Ibid.*, pp. 86–88 (pp. 92–94).
147. *Ibid.*, pp. 89–93 (pp. 95–101).
148. *Ibid.*, pp. 96–112 (pp. 103–114).
149. *Ibid.*, pp. 113–24 (pp. 121–33).
150. *Ibid.*, pp. 118, 125f. (pp. 127, 134f.).
151. Since Otto argued that duality was the essential nature of Dionysos from the beginning, he felt compelled to argue that wine was originally associated with the Dionysiac cult. (As we have seen, other scholars have argued that wine

was a later addition). Otto's argument for the original association was rather weak, but he also justified the association, even if it had been later, by saying that wine would have deepened the worshippers' understanding of Dionysos, *Ibid.*, pp. 135–37 (pp. 145–48). If he had pursued this approach to the development of Dionysiac religion, arguing that changes represented new discoveries of complementary facets of the Dionysiac world rather than random accretions, he could have dealt more satisfactorily with history. Instead, he insisted that the original insight of Dionysiac reality had carried with it all the basic elements of the cult.

152. *Ibid.*, pp. 137–41 (pp. 147–51).
153. *Ibid.*, p. 148 (p. 159).
154. *Ibid.*, pp. 141–48 (pp. 152–59).
155. *Ibid.*, p. 149 (p. 161).
156. *Ibid.*, pp. 150–52 (pp. 162–64).
157. *ibid.*, pp. 152–58 (pp. 164–70).
158. *Ibid.*, pp. 159–75 (pp. 171–88).
159. *Ibid.*, p. 182 (p. 196).
160. *Ibid.*, pp. 175–87 (pp. 189–201).
161. *Ibid.*, pp. 187–93 (pp. 202–8).
162. In fairness to Otto it might be pointed out that the evolutionists had imposed their own monolithic structure on Greek religion, interpreting it through the category of 'primitive mentality' which had been abstracted only after a considerable flattening of primitive thought and behavior.

NOTES TO CHAPTER SIX

1. The most relevant works for Dodds' interpretation of Dionysos are as follows:
   'Maenadism and the *Bacchae*', *Harvard Theological Review*, XXXIII (July, 1940), 155–76.
   Euripides *Bacchae*, ed. E. R. Dodds (Oxford, 1944), (2nd ed., 1960), especially his insightful 'Introduction' (pp. ix–lv in the first edition, pp. xi–lix in the second) and his painstaking 'Commentary' (pp. 59–228 in the first edition, pp. 61–242 in the second). Citations will refer to the second edition.
   The Greeks and the Irrational, (Berkeley and Los Angeles, 1966).
2. *The Greeks and the Irrational*, p. vii.
3. Dodds drew on Karl R. Popper's discussion in the latter's *The Open Society and Its Enemies*; cf. *The Greeks and the Irrational*, pp. 237, 254 n. 1, passim.
4. *The Greeks and the Irrational*, p. 14. This quotation exemplifies the centrality of the issue of language for understanding the meaning of religion. Scholars sympathetic to religion, like Otto, asserted that ordinary (naturalistic) language was insufficient for understanding either religion or the totality of reality and argued that language must therefore be pushed beyond its ordinary usage in order to be open to truth. Naturalistically-oriented scholars like Dodds argued that the nature of reality was better 'put across' by refining scientific language rather than by deforming it into a supernaturalistic framework.
5. *Ibid.*
6. *Ibid.*, pp. 16–17.

7. *Ibid.*, p. 75.
8. *Ibid.*, pp. 76f. Cf. Euripides *Bacchae*, p. xx.
9. Euripides *Bacchae*, p. xlv.
10. *The Greeks and the Irrational*, p. 272.
11. Euripides *Bacchae*, pp. xvii–xviii. Here Dodds seems to have followed Nilsson's interpretation. Like Nilsson, he saw the biennial character of the mountaintop *orgia* as discounting a yearly nature-magic interpretation.
12. *Ibid.*, p. xiv.
13. In *Pagan and Christian in an Age of Anxiety* (Cambridge, 1965), p. 5, Dodds characterized himself as an agnostic.
14. This judgment is made on the basis of striking similarities in parts of the two men's work. Dodds cited Otto's work along with others, adding the reasonable caveat that it should be used with caution; Euripides *Bacchae*, p. xii.
15. *The Greeks and the Irrational*, p. 273.
16. *Ibid.*, p. 187.
17. *Ibid.*, p. 273; Euripides *Bacchae*, p. xvi.
18. Euripides *Bacchae*, p. 183.
19. *Ibid.*, p. xliv.
20. *Ibid.*, p. xii.
21. *Ibid.*, p. xx.
22. *The Greeks and the Irrational*, p. 254.
23. The following works are the most relevant for Guthrie's interpretation of Dionysos:
    > *Orpheus and Greek Religion. A Study of the Orphic Movement* (London, 1935). References will come from the American printing of the second, revised edition (New York, 1966).
    > 'The Resistance Motif in Dionysiac Mythology', Xerox copy from author. Resumé in *Proceedings of the Cambridge Philological Society*. CLXXIX (1946–47), 14–15.
    > *The Greeks and their Gods*. References from the American printing (Boston, 1955).
    > *In the Beginning. Some Greek Views on the Origins of Life and the Early State of Man* (Ithaca, New York, 1957).
    > 'The Legacy of Greek Thought', *Journal of the Australasian Universities Language and Literature Association*, VIII (May, 1958), 3–17.
    > 'Early Greek Religion in the Light of the Decipherment of Linear B', *Bulletin of the Institute of Classical Studies*, VI (1959), 35–46.
    > *A History of Greek Philosophy*, 4 vols. to date (Cambridge, 1962–75).
    > *The Religion and Mythology of the Greeks* (Cambridge, 1964).
24. Guthrie's ability to respect both interpretive options derived from his belief that the basic religious question of the possible existence of God and His relation to the universe had not been settled. The evolutionists had treated God as self-evidently non-existent; theists like Otto or Wilamowitz had assumed God to be self-evidently existent. Because he balanced both metaphysical arguments, Guthrie could argue that each hermeneutic revealed important aspects about religion.

Guthrie's argument for moderation reflects the modern period's acknowledgment of the inevitable existence of different presuppositions and deserves to be quoted in full: 'behind all the detail lies the perennial clash of philosophies, the two irreconcilable answers to a question that is as pertinent to our life as it was to that of ancient Greece: is nature the product of mind, or is mind only one among the many products of nature?

'Today in our Western world the conviction lives on that there is a purpose in history, that nature is not self-subsistent but owes its being to a transcendent First Cause whose mind is reflected, however feebly, in the thoughts and wills of men—in other words that men are sons of the God who created the world. It is the conviction of the Christian religion. On the other side are ranged not only the materialistic determinism of the Marxist but a variety of philosophies of a positivist or humanist tendency. To choose between the fundamental alternatives carries one beyond the findings of science and the niceties of logic. For most of us, the decision is made at a deeper level of the human psyche, and that is why it is so difficult for one side to persuade the other by an appeal to facts or argument. Men of equal intelligence, education, and honesty may hold to either conviction with a sense that they can no other. Where this is so, what matters is that each should recognize the sincerity of his fellow and practice the virtue of tolerance, and this becomes easier when we know that it is not merely a conflict of our time but one which has divided the human mind in every civilized age', *In the Beginning*, pp. 109–10. Cf. *The Greek Philosophers from Thales to Aristotle* (New York, 1960), p. 19–21.

25. *The Greeks and their Gods*, pp. 1–26.
26. *Ibid.*, p. 8.
27. *Ibid.*, p. 23.
28. Guthrie's clearest statement of the dichotomy occurs in his *Religion and Mythology of the Greeks*, p. 5. Cf. also *The Greeks and their Gods*, pp. 114–15, 143, 206, 213, 214, 256, 294.
29. *Ibid.*, p. 42.
30. *Ibid.*, pp. xii, xiv, 214.
31. 'The Legacy of Greek Thought', pp. 6, 11.
32. *Ibid.*, pp. 4, 6; *The Greeks and their Gods*, pp. 152f., 183, 193; *A History of Greek Philosophy*, I, 205. The quote originally comes from E. Fraenkel's *Rome and Greek Culture* (Oxford, 1935).
33. 'Legacy', p. 6.
34. *A History of Greek Philosophy*, I, 26. Cf. *Ibid.*, pp. 28, 29; *In the Beginning*, p. 15.
35. *Religion and Mythology of the Greeks*, p. 40.
36. *Ibid.*, pp. 34, 36; *The Greeks and their Gods*, pp. 18, 28, 31. Cf. *The Greek Philosophers from Thales to Aristotle*, pp. 12–16.
37. *The Greeks and their Gods*, pp. 33–35.
38. *Ibid.*, pp. 35, 301–4.
39. 'Indeed it is here above all, in the union of rational thought with mystical exaltation, that Empedockles sums up and personifies the spirit of his age and race. Apollo was Greek and Dionysos was Greek. It was Greek to say with Pindar, Herodotus and the tragedians that man must know himself mortal and not seek to vie with the gods; and it was Greek to say of a dead man "God shalt thou be instead of mortal". We have perhaps been too long accustomed to equating "Greek" with "classical". In admiring the exact proportions, the pure, formal beauty of the Parthenon (which we see without the garish colours that once adorned it), we think of its builders as the people of "Nothing too

much"; forgetting perhaps that the very place where these words were written up was also the scene of the noctural *orgia* of Bacchus where all restraint was abandoned in the emotional purgation of *ekstasis* and *enthusiasmos*—"outside oneself" and "god in us". The Hellenic mind has its romantic as well as its classical aspect, and both reach a climax without incongruity in the genius of this remarkable Sicilian,' *A History of Greek Philosophy*, II, 125f.

40. *Religion and Mythology of the Greeks*, p. 8; *The Greeks and their Gods*, p. 16.
41. *Ibid.*, p. 56. It should be noted that Guthrie infrequently explained religion in terms of magic.
42. *A History of Greek Philosophy*, I, 27. Guthrie continued, 'In our own age the impersonal factors (repression, complex, trauma, and the like), which have replaced Aphrodite or Dionysos, are sometimes put to the same use'.
43. *Ibid.*, p. 372; cf. p. 231.
44. For example, the myth of the fire god's creating life from a mixture of water and earth helped explain the generative nature of heat, *In the Beginning*, p. 41. As in the case of the magic theory, Guthrie interpreted very few myths as explanations of natural phenomena.
45. The myths of resistance to Dionysos reflected the opposition of the Greeks to the incoming Bacchic cult, 'The Resistance Motif in Dionysiac Mythology'; *The Greeks and their Gods*, pp. 159–74. Some myths commemorated earlier rituals which had been suppressed because of their savagery: for example, myths of the devouring of the infant Dionysos, *Orpheus and Greek Religion*, p. 132.
46. The theme of man's relationship to deity forms the core of both *Orpheus and Greek Religion* and *The Greeks and their Gods*.
47. *Socrates and Plato* (Brisbane, 1958), p. 23.
48. *A History of Greek Philosophy*, I, 2.
49. *Socrates and Plato*, p. 23.
50. As the 'culmination of reasoned argument', myth is 'genuine myth and its validity and importance are uncontested', *A History of Greek Philosophy*, I, 2.
51. *The Greeks and their Gods*, pp. 56, 153–74; *Orpheus and Greek Religion*, p. 55; *Religion and Mythology of the Greeks*, p. 28; 'Early Greek Religion in the Light of the Decipherment of Linear B', pp. 40f.
52. *The Greeks and their Gods*, p. 173.
53. *Ibid.*, p. 201; *Orpheus and Greek Religion*, pp. 113, 117f.
54. *The Greeks and their Gods*, pp. 176–78.
55. The evidence cited by Guthrie for the Thracian belief in immortality refers to the god Zalmoxis, rather than to Dionysos. Guthrie linked the two by calling Zalmoxis Dionysos' 'Brother god', *The Greeks and their Gods*, p. 176.
56. *Ibid.*, p. 174.
57. *Ibid.*, pp. 199–202. Unlike Rohde, Guthrie presented Apollo as already possessing a non-rational side *before* the conciliation with Dionysos and therefore did not attribute the non-rational side of Greek religion to a Dionysiac contamination.
58. *Orpheus and Greek Religion*, pp. 44, 48, 199f., 207.
59. *The Greeks and their Gods*, p. 303.
60. Ultimately the chthonic world view is equivalent to the modern Christian

viewpoint 'that men are sons of the God who created the world' (see note 24), a position which Guthrie asserted was still an arguable alternative to materialism, though he did not identify himself with either side.

61. See his general remarks in *A History of Greek Philosophy*, I, 26, 28 and *In the Beginning*, pp. 15, 17.
62. *The Greeks and their Gods*, p. 61.
63. Guthrie shared Otto's and Dodds' position, based on Plutarch, that Dionysos stood for 'the whole wet element' in nature; *ibid.*, p. 156; *A History of Greek Philosophy*, I, 372.
64. *The Greeks and their Gods*, pp. 165–74; *Orpheus and Greek Religion*, p. 55. Guthrie also explained the myths as testifying to recurring features of the cult; but, unlike Otto, who interpreted both myth and cult as expressing the nature of the god (for example, as the 'mad god'), he saw the myths as aetiological, as mere projections of the cult. Cf. 'The Resistance Motif in Dionysiac Mythology', pp. 10–12.
65. *A History of Greek Philosophy*, I, 26.
66. *The Greeks and their Gods*, p. 172.
67. Cf. *ibid.*, pp. 180, 280f.

Selected Bibliography

Beattie, John. *Other Cultures*: *Aims, Methods and Achievements in Social Anthropology*. New York, 1964.

Bonner, Campbell. 'Review. Jane Harrison, *Themis*'. *Classical Journal*, XXIII (November, 1927), 154–55.

Brown, Norman O. *Life Against Death*. Middletown, Conn., 1959.

Burrow, J. W. *Evolution and Society*. Cambridge, 1968.

Callmer, Christian. 'The Published Writings of Professor Martin P. Nilsson 1939–1967'. *Kungl. Humanistiska Vetenskapssamfundet i Lund. Scripta Minora 1967–1968*. Lund, 1968, pp. 117–139.

Cornford, Francis M. 'Harrison, Jane Ellen (1850–1928)'. *Dictionary of National Biography*. Fourth Supplement, 1922–1930. London, 1937.

Crusius, Otto. *Erwin Rohde*. *Ein biographischer Versuch*. Tübingen and Leipzig, 1902.

Dodds, E. R. *Euripides Bacchae*. Oxford, 1944.

——, *Euripides Bacchae*. 2nd ed. Oxford, 1960.

——, *The Greeks and the Irrational*. Berkeley, 1966.

——, 'Maenadism and the *Bacchae*'. *Harvard Theological Review*, XXXIII (July, 1940), 155–76.

Douglas, Mary. *Purity and Danger*. *An Analysis of Concepts of Pollution and Taboo*. Baltimore, Md., 1970.

Durkheim, Emile. *The Elementary Forms of the Religious Life*. Translated by Joseph Ward Swain. New York, 1965.

——, 'Sociologie religieuse et theorie de la connaissance'. *Revue de Metaphysique et de Morale*, (November, 1909), 733–58.

Ehnmark, Erland. *The Idea of God in Homer*. Uppsala, 1935.

Eliade, Mircea. *Cosmos and History*. *The Myth of the Eternal Return*. Translated by Willard R. Trask. New York, 1959.

——, *Patterns in Comparative Religion*. Translated by Rosemary Sheed. Cleveland and New York, 1963.

——, *The Quest*: *History and Meaning in Religion*. Chicago, 1969.

——, *The Sacred and the Profane*. *The Nature of Religion*. Translated by Willard R. Trask. New York, 1961.

Evans-Pritchard, E. E. *Social Anthropology and Other Essays*. New York, 1964.

——, *Theories of Primitive Religion*. Oxford, 1965.

Firda, Richard Arthur. 'Wedekind, Nietzsche and the Dionysian experience'. *Modern Language Notes*, 87 (October, 1972), 720–31.

Fontenrose, Joseph Eddy. *The Ritual Theory of Myth*. Berkeley, 1966.

Frazer, James George. *The Golden Bough*. Second Edition. Three Volumes. London, 1900.

Gjerstad, Einar. 'Martin P. Nilsson in Memoriam'. *Kungl. Humanistiska Vetenskapssamfundet i Lund. Scripta Minora 1966–1967*. Lund, 1967, pp. 17–28.

Grant, Frederick C. 'Professor Nilsson's Contribution to the History of Religions'. *The Review of Religion*, XVIII, No. 1 (1953), 5–17.

Groth, J. H. 'Wilamowitz-Möllendorf on Nietzsche's *Birth of Tragedy'. Journal of the History of Ideas*, XI (April, 1950), 179–90.

Guthrie, W. K. C. 'Early Greek Religion in the Light of the Decipherment of Linear B'. *Bulletin of the Institute of Classical Studies*, VI (1959), 35–46.

——, *The Greek Philosophers from Thales to Aristotle*. New York, 1960.

——, *The Greeks and their Gods*. Boston, 1955.

——, *A History of Greek Philosophy*. 4 vols. to date. Cambridge, 1962–75.

——, *In The Beginning. Some Greek Views on the Origins of Life and the Early State of Man*. Ithaca, New York, 1957.

——, 'The Legacy of Greek Thought'. *Journal of the Australasian Universities Language and Literature Association*, VIII (May, 1958), 3–17.

——, *Orpheus and Greek Religion. A Study of the Orphic Movement*. 2nd ed., rev. New York, 1966.

——, *The Religion and Mythology of the Greeks*. Cambridge, 1964.

——, 'The Resistance Motif in Dionysiac Mythology'. Xerox copy from author. Resumé in *Proceedings of the Cambridge Philological Society*, CLXXIX (1946–47), 14–15.

——, *Socrates and Plato*. Brisbane, 1958.

Harris, Marvin. *The Rise of Anthropological Theory*. New York, 1968.

Harrison, Jane E. *Alpha and Omega*. London, 1915.

——, *Ancient Art and Ritual*. New York, 1913.

——, 'Bird and Pillar Worship in Connexion with Ouranian Deities'. *Transactions of the Third International Congress for the History of Religions*. Vol. II. Oxford, 1908.

——, *Epilegomena to the Study of Greek Religion*. Cambridge, 1921.

——, 'The Influence of Darwinism on the Study of Religions'. *Darwin and Modern Science*. Edited by A. C. Seward. Cambridge, 1909.

——, *Introductory Studies in Greek Art*. London, 1885.

——, 'The Kouretes and Zeus Kouros. A Study in Pre-historic Sociology'. *The Annual of the British School at Athens*, XV (1908–09), 308–38.

——, 'Mystica Vannus Iacchi'. *Journal of Hellenic Studies*, XXIII, No. 2 (1903), 292–324; XXIV, No. 2 (1904), 241–54.

——, 'Mythological Studies'. *Journal of Hellenic Studies*, XII (1891), 350–55.

——, *Mythology*. Boston, 1924.

——, *Mythology & Monuments of Ancient Athens*. Being a translation of a portion of the 'Attica' of Pausanias by Margaret de G. Verrall with introductory essay and archaeological commentary by Jane E. Harrison. London, 1890.

——, *Myths of the Odyssey in Art and Literature*. London, 1882.

——, *Prolegomena to the Study of Greek Religion*. Cambridge, 1903.

——, *Prolegomena to the Study of Greek Religion*. 3rd ed., rev. Cambridge, 1922.

——, *The Religion of Ancient Greece*. London, 1905.

——, *Reminiscences of a Student's Life*. London, 1925.

——, *Themis. A Study of the Social Origins of Greek Religion*. Cambridge, 1912.

Harrison, Jane E. *Themis. A Study of the Social Origins of Greek Religion.* 2nd ed., rev. Cambridge, 1927.

Helfer, James S., ed. *On Method in the History of Religions. History and Theory, Studies in the Philosophy of History.* Beiheft 8. Middleton, Connecticut, 1968.

Henninger, Joseph. 'Ist der sogenannte Nilus-Bericht brauchbare religionsge-schichtliche Quelle?' *Anthropos*, L, Fasc. 1–3 (1955), 81–148.

Henrichs, Norbert. *Bibliographie der Hermeneutik und ihrer Anwendungsbereiche seit Schleiermacher.* Düsseldorf, 1968.

Hewitt, Joseph William. 'Review: *Themis*'. *Classical Weekly*, VII (January 10, 1914), 86–88.

Hirsch, E. D., Jr. *Validity in Interpretation.* New Haven and London, 1967.

Hodgen, Margaret Trabue. *The Doctrine of Survivals, A Chapter in the History of Scientific Method in the Study of Man.* London, 1936.

Hughes, H. Stuart. *Consciousness and Society. The Reorientation of European Social Thought 1890–1930.* New York, 1958.

Hyman, Stanley Edgar. 'The Ritual View of Myth and the Mythic'. *Myth, A Symposium.* Edited by Thomas A. Sebeok. Bloomington, Indiana, 1958.

——, *The Tangled Bank: Darwin, Marx, Frazer and Freud as Imaginative Writers.* New York, 1966.

Jensen, Adolf E. *Myth and Cult among Primitive Peoples.* Translated by Marianna Tax Choldin and Wolfgang Weissleder. Chicago, 1963.

Kaufmann, Walter. *Nietzsche: Philosopher, Psychologist, Antichrist.* 3rd ed. New York, 1968.

Kimpel, Ben. 'Contradictions in Malinowski on Ritual'. *Journal for the Scientific Study of Religion*, VII, No. 2 (1968), 259–71.

Knudtson, Erik J. 'Beiträge zu einer Bibliographie Martin P. Nilsson 1897–1939'. *Kungl. Humanistiska Vetenskapssamfundet i Lund. Scripta Minora 1967–1968.* Lund, 1968, pp. 29–116.

Lang, Andrew. *The Making of Religion.* London, 1898.

Leeuw, Gerardus van der. *Religion in Essence and Manifestation.* Translated by J. E. Turner. 2 vols. New York, 1963.

Lessa, William A. and Vogt, Evon Z. *Reader in Comparative Religion. An Anthropological Approach.* 2nd ed. New York, 1965.

Lévi-Straus, Claude. 'Introduction à l'oeuvre de Marcel Mauss'. *Marcel Mauss. Sociologie et Anthropologie.* Paris, 1950.

——, *Structural Anthropology.* Translated by Claire Jacobson and Brooke Grund-fest Schoepf. Garden City, New York, 1967.

Lienhardt, Godfrey. *Social Anthropology.* 2nd ed. London, 1966.

Lowie, Robert H. *The History of Ethnological Theory.* New York, 1937.

Marett, Robert Ranulph. *The Threshold of Religion.* New York, 1914.

Nietzsche, Friedrich. *The Birth of Tragedy* and *The Case of Wagner.* Translated by Walter Kaufmann. New York, 1967.

——, *Die Geburt der Tragödie.* München: Wilhelm Goldman Verlag, n.d.

——, *Der Gottesdienst der Griechen.* Vol. III of *Philologica. Univeröffentlichtes zur antiken Religion und Philosophie.* Edited by Otto Crusius and Wilhelm Nestle. 3 vols. Leipzig, 1913.

——, *Selected Letters of Friedrich Nietzsche.* Edited and translated by Christopher Middleton. Chicago, 1969.

Nilsson, Martin Persson. 'Die Anthesterien und die Aiora'. *Eranos*, XV (1915), 181–200.
——, 'The Bacchic Mysteries of the Roman Age'. *Harvard Theological Review*, XLVI (October, 1953), 175–202.
——, *Cults, Myths, Oracles, and Politics in Ancient Greece*. Lund, 1951.
——, *The Dionysiac Mysteries of the Hellenistic and Roman Age*. Lund, 1957.
——, 'Dionysos im Schiff'. *Archiv für Religionswissenschaft*. XI (1908), 399–402.
——, 'Early Orphism and Kindred Religious Movements'. *Harvard Theological Review*, XXVIII (July, 1935), 181–230.
——, 'Eine Anthesterien Vase in München'. *Sitzungsberichte der Bayerischen Akademie der Wissenschaften*, Philosophisch-historische Abteilung, 1930, Heft 4. Munich, 1930. Reprinted in *Opuscula Selecta*, Vol. I, pp. 414–28.
——, 'Eine neue schwarzfigurige Anthesterienvase', *Kungl. Humanistiska Vetenskapssamfundet i Lund. Årsberättelse. 1933*. Reprinted in *Opuscula Selecta*, Vol. II, pp. 457–62.
——, 'Die eleusinischen Gottheiten'. *Archiv für Religionswissenschaft*, XXXII (1935), 79–141.
——, 'En marge de la grande inscription bacchique du Metropolitan Museum'. *Studi e materiali di storia delle religioni*, X, No. 1 (1934), 1–18.
——, 'Erwin Rohde'. *Encyclopedia of the Social Sciences*. 1934, Vol. XIII.
——, 'Exist-t-il une conception primitive de l'âme'? *Revue d'Histoire et de Philosophie religieuses*, X (March–April, 1930), 115–25.
——, *Geschichte der griechischen Religion*. Vol. I: *Die Religion Griechenlands bis auf die griechische Weltherrschaft*. Munich, 1941.
——, *Geschichte der griechischen Religion*. Vol. I: *Die Religion Griechenlands bis auf die griechische Weltherrschaft*. 3rd ed. rev. Munich, 1967.
——, *Geschichte der griechischen Religion*. Vol. II: *Die hellenistische und römische Zeit*. Munich, 1950.
——, 'Götter und Psychologie bei Homer'. *Archiv für Religionswissenschaft*, XXII, No. 2, (1923/24), 363–90.
——, *Greek Folk Religion*. New York, 1961. (Reprinting of *Greek Popular Religion*.)
——, *Greek Piety*. Translated by Herbert Jennings Rose. Oxford, 1948.
——, *Greek Popular Religion*. New York, 1940.
——, *Griechische Feste von religiöser Bedeutung mit ausschluss der attischen*. Leipzig, 1906.
——, *A History of Greek Religion*. Translated by F. J. Fielden, Oxford, 1925.
——, 'The Immortality of the Soul in Greek Religion'. *Eranos*, XXXIX (1941), 1–16.
——, 'Kult und Glaube in der altgriechischen Religion'. *Opuscula Selecta*, Vol. III, pp. 3–10.
——, 'Letter to Professor Arthur D. Nock on Some Fundamental Concepts in the Science of Religion'. *Harvard Theological Review*, XLII (April, 1949), 71–107.
——, *The Minoan-Mycenaean Religion and its Survival in Greek Religion*. Lund, 1927.
——, *The Minoan-Mycenaean Religion and its Survival in Greek Religion*. 2nd ed. revised and enlarged. Lund, 1950.
——, *The Mycenaean Origin of Greek Mythology*. Cambridge, 1932.

Nilsson, Martin Persson. 'Nähe zu und Distanz von der Gottheit'. *Opuscula Selecta*. Vol. III, pp. 11–26.

——, *Opuscula Selecta*. 3 vols. Lund: C. W. K. Gleerup, 1951–60. In *Skrifter Utgivna avv Svenska Institutet i Athen*. Acta Instituti Atheniensis Regni Sueciae 8°, II: 1–3.

——, *Primitive Religion*. Tübingen, 1911.

——, *Primitive Time Reckoning*. Lund, 1920.

——, 'Die Prozessionstypen im griechischen Kult. Mit einem Anhang über die dionysischen Prozessionen in Athen'. *Archäologisches Jahrbuch*, XXXI (1916), 309–39.

——, 'The Psychological Background of Late Greek Paganism'. *Review of Religion*, XI (January, 1947), 115–25.

——, 'The Race Problem of the Roman Empire'. *Hereditas*, II (December, 1921), 370–90.

——, 'Religion as Man's Protest against the Meaninglessness of Events'. *Kungl. Humanistiska Vetenskapsammfundet i Lund Årsberättelse 1954*, pp. 29–92.

——, Review of 'H. J. Rose, *Primitive Culture in Greece*'. *Litteris*, III (April, 1926), 12–16.

——, Review of Jane Ellen Harrison, *Themis*. *Gnomon*, IV (June, 1928), 456.

——, Review of W. F. Otto, *Die Götter Griechenlands*. *Deutsche Literaturzeitung*, L (July 13, 1929), cols. 1334–1337.

——, Review of Walter F. Otto, *Dionysos. Mythos und Kultus*. *Gnomon*, XI (April, 1935), 177–81.

——, 'Second Letter to Professor Nock on Positive Gains in the Science of Greek Religion'. *Harvard Theological Review*, XLIV (October, 1951), 143–51.

——, *Studia de Dionysiis atticis*. Lund, 1900.

——, 'Über Genetik und Geschichte', *Hereditas*, XXV (June, 1939), 211–23.

——, 'Universal Religion'. *The Review of Religion*, XVII, No. 1 (1952), 5–10.

——, 'Der Ursprung der Tragödie'. *Neue Jahrbücher für das klassische Altertum, Geschichte und deutsche Literatur und für Pädagogik*, XXVII, No. 9 (1911), 609–42; No. 10, 673–96.

——, 'Ueber die Glaubwürdigkeit der Volksüberlieferung mit besonderem Bezug auf die alte Geschichte'. *Scientia*, XLVIII, No. 223 (1930), 319–28.

Otto, Rudolph. *The Idea of the Holy*. Translated by John W. Harvey. New York, 1958.

Otto, Walter Friedrich. *Die altgriechische Gottesidee*. Berlin, 1926.

——, *Der Dichter und die alten Götter*. Frankfurt am Main, 1942.

——, *Dionysos. Mythos und Kultus*. Frankfurter Studien zur Religion und Kultur der Antike, Vol. IV. Frankfurt am Main, 1933.

——, *Dionysus. Myth and Cult*. Translated by Robert B. Palmer. Bloomington, Indiana, 1965.

——, 'Der Durchbruch zum antiken Mythos im 19. Jahrhundert'. *Vom Schicksal des deutschen Geistes*. Edited by Wolfgang Frommel. Berlin, 1934.

——, *Der europäische Geist und die Weisheit des Ostens. Gedanken über das Erbe Homers*. Frankfurt am Main, 1931.

——, *Der Geist der Antike und die christliche Welt*. Bonn, 1923.

——, *Gesetz, Urbild und Mythos*. Stuttgart, 1951.

——, *Die Gestalt und das Sein. Gesammelte Abhandlungen über den Mythos und seine Bedeutung für die Menschheit*. Düsseldorf-Köln, 1955.

Otto, Walter Friedrich. *Die Götter Griechenlands. Das Bild des Göttlichen im Spiegel des griechischen Geistes.* Bonn, 1929.
——, *The Homeric Gods. The Spiritual Significance of Greek Religion.* Translated by Moses Hadas. Boston, 1964.
——, *Der junge Nietzsche.* Frankfurt am Main, 1936.
——, *Die Manen oder von den Urformen des Totenglaubens. Eine Untersuchung zur Religion der Griechen, Römer und Semiten und zum Volksglauben überhaupt.* Bonn, 1923.
——, *Die Musen und der göttliche Ursprung des Singens und Sagens.* Düsseldorf-Köln, 1955.
——, *Mythos und Welt.* Stuttgart, 1962.
——, 'Religio und Superstitio'. *Archiv für Religionswissenschaft*, XII (1909), 533–54; XIV (1911), 406–27.
——, *Theophania. Der Geist der altgriechischen Religion.* Hamburg, 1956.
——, *Das Vorbild der Griechen.* Tübingen und Stuttgart, 1949.
——, *Die Wirklichkeit der Götter. Von der Unzerstörbarkeit griechischer Weltsicht.* N.p.: Rowohlt, 1963.
——, *Das Wort der Antike.* Stuttgart, 1962.
Parsons, Talcott. *The Structure of Social Action.* 2 vols. New York, 1968.
Penner, Hans, and Yonan, Edward. 'Is a Science of Religion Possible'? *Journal of Religion*, LI (April, 1972), 107–33.
Pettazzoni, Raffaele. *Essays on the History of Religions.* Translated by H. J. Rose. Leiden, 1967.
——, *La Religion dans la Grèce antique.* Paris, 1953.
Pinard de la Boullaye, H. *L'Etude comparée des religions.* Vol. I: *Son histoire dans le monde occidental.* 2nd ed. Paris, 1925.
Richards, G. C. 'Review. *Mythology and Monuments of Ancient Athens*, by Margaret de G. Verrall and Jane Harrison', *Journal of Hellenic Studies*, XI, no. 1 (1890), 218–20.
Ricoeur, Paul. *The Symbolism of Evil.* Translated by Emerson Buchanan. New York, 1967.
Rohde, Erwin. *Kleine Schriften.* 2 vols. Tübingen and Leipzig, 1901.
——, *Psyche. The Cult of Souls and Belief in Immortality among the Greeks.* Translated by W. B. Hillis. 2 vols. New York, 1966.
——, *Psyche. Seelencult and Unsterblichkeitsglaube der Griechen.* Freiburg i.B. and Leipzig, 1894.
——, *Psyche. Seelencult and Unsterblichkeitsglaube der Griechen.* 5th and 6th eds. 2 vols. Tübingen, 1910.
——, *Die Religion der Griechen, Rede zum Geburstfeste des höchstseligen Grossherzogs Karl Friedrich und zur akademischen Preisvertheilung.* Heidelberg, 1895.
Rouse, W. H. D. 'Miss Harrison's *Greek Religion'. Classical Review*, XVIII (December, 1904), 465–70.
Saussure, Ferdinand de. *Course in General Linguistics.* Edited by Charles Bally and Albert Sechehaye in collaboration with Albert Riedlinger. Translated by Wade Baskin. New York, 1966.
Schmid, W. 'Erwin Rohde'. *Jahresbericht über die Fortschritte der klassischen Altertumswissenschaft. Bibliotheca Philogica Classica.* Index, XXVI (1899), 87–114.

Schmidt, Wilhelm. *The Origin and Growth of Religion. Fact and Theories.* Translated by H. J. Rose. London, 1931.

Schopenhauer, Arthur. *The World as Will and Idea.* Translated by R. B. Haldane and J. Kemp. 2 vols. London, 1883.

——, *Essays of Arthur Schopenhauer.* Translated by T. Bailey Saunders. New York, n.d.

Sellière, Ernest, A. A. L. *Nietzsches Waffenbruder, Erwin Rohde.* Berlin, 1911.

Smith, Alfred. 'The Dionysian Innovation'. *American Anthropologist.* 66 (1964), 251–65.

Streng, Frederick J. *Understanding Religious Man.* Belmont, California, 1969.

Tylor, E. B. *Primitive Culture.* Part II *Religion in Primitive Culture.* New York, 1958.

Verdenius, W. J. 'Review. *Epilegomena and Themis'. Mnemosyne,* 4th Series, XVI, Fasc. 4 (1963), 434–35.

Vogel, Martin. *Apollinisch und Dionysisch. Geschichte eines genialen Irrtum.* Regensburg, 1966.

Waal Malefijt, Annemarie de. *Religion and Culture: An Introduction to Anthropology of Religion.* New York, 1968.

Waardenburg, Jean Jacques. *L'Islam dans le miroir de l'Occident; Comment quelques orientalistes occidentaux se sont penchés sur l'Islam et se sont formés une image de cette religion.* Paris, 1963.

Widengren, George. 'Evolutionism and the Problem of the Origin of Religions'. *Ethnos,* X (April–September, 1945), 57–96.

Wilamowitz-Moellendorff, Ulrich von. *Der Glaube der Hellenen.* 2 vols. 3rd ed., rev. Darmstadt, 1959.

——, *My Recollections: 1848–1914.* Translated by G. C. Richards. London, 1930.

Index of Modern Authors

Index of Subjects